STRUGGLING FOR THE UMMA

CHANGING LEADERSHIP ROLES OF KIAI IN JOMBANG, EAST JAVA

STRUGGLING FOR THE UMMA

CHANGING LEADERSHIP ROLES OF KIAI IN JOMBANG, EAST JAVA

Endang Turmudi

Department of Sociology
Faculty of the Arts

February 1996

Published by ANU E Press
The Australian National University
Canberra ACT 0200, Australia
Email: anuepress@anu.edu.au
Web: http://epress.anu.edu.au

National Library of Australia
Cataloguing-in-Publication entry

Endang, Turmudi.
Struggling for the Umma : changing leadership roles of kiai in Jombang, East Java.

ISBN 1 920942 42 4 (pbk.)
ISBN 1 920942 43 2 (online)

1. N. U. (Organization) - Publishing. 2. Community leadership - Indonesia - Java. 3. Ulama - Indonesia - Java. 4. Islam and politics - Indonesia - Java. 5. Java (Indonesia) - Politics and government. I. Title.

303.34095982

All rights reserved. No part of this publication may be reproduced, stored in a retrieval system or transmitted in any form or by any means, electronic, mechanical, photocopying or otherwise, without the prior permission of the publisher.

Cover design by ANU E Press

This edition © 2006 ANU E Press

Islam in Southeast Asia Series

Theses at The Australian National University are assessed by external examiners and students are expected to take into account the advice of their examiners before they submit to the University Library the final versions of their theses. For this series, this final version of the thesis has been used as the basic for publication, taking into account other changes that the author may have decided to undertake. In some cases, a few minor editorial revisions have made to the work. The acknowledgements in each of these publications provides information on the supervisors of the thesis and those who contributed to its development. For many of the authors in this series, English is a second language and their texts reflect an appropriate fluency.

Table of Contents

Foreword	ix
Preface	xi
Abbreviations and Glossary	xiii
Abstract	xvii
Acknowledgements	xix
Chapter 1. Introduction	1
1.1. Background of the Study	1
1.2. Review of the Literature	4
1.3. The Fieldwork	8
1.4. Source of Data	14
1.5. The Survey	17
1.6. The Importance of the Study	18
1.7. Organisation of the Thesis	19
Chapter 2. Kiai and the Pesantren	21
2.1. Concept and Variation of Kiaiship	21
2.2. The Pesantren Tradition	25
2.3. Nahdlatul Ulama (NU)	29
2.4. Modernisation of the Pesantren	31
2.5. The Main Pesantren Observed	33
Chapter 3. Kiaiship Through the Tarekat Movement	43
3.1. The Nature of the Tarekat Movement	43
3.2. The Tarekat Qadiriyah Wa Naqsyabandiyah	50
3.3. The Jam'iyah Ahli Thoriqoh Al-Mu'tabaroh An-Nahdliyah: Tarekat Cukir	56
3.4. Other Tarekat Movements	60
Chapter 4. The Social Reality of Kiaiship	67
4.1. The Kiai's Role in the Society	67
4.2. The Underlying Principle of Relationship: Baraka	71
4.3. The Fragmented Organisation of Islam	78
4.4. The Modern Kiai and Santri	84
Chapter 5. The Kiai and the Dynamics of Politics at the Local Level	89
5.1. The Kiai's Politics in the Tarekat	89
5.2. The Followers' Perspective	96
5.3. NU at National Politics	102
5.4. Local Political Conflict	104
Chapter 6. Islam and Politics: Implications in Electoral Behaviour	111
6.1. The Islamic Political Party	112
6.2. The Politics of Javanese Muslims	117
6.3. The Penggembosan and Changing Muslims Political Support	128
6.4. New Social Groupings	133
6.5. Islam and Electoral Behaviour	143

Chapter 7. The Kiai in the Context of Socio-Political Change   149
    7.1. Changing Kiai's Islamic Politics   149
    7.2. Kiai's Political Influence: Post-'Back to Khittah'   155
    7.3. The Charisma factor   163
    7.4. The Kiai's New Relationship with Authority   166
Chapter 8. The Kiai's Effort in Remoulding Relationships with Other Muslim Groups   175
    8.1. Differences and Locality   176
    8.2. The Conflict Reduced   182
    8.3. Reformulation of Ukhuwa Islamiya   190
    8.4. Expanding Da'wa   196
Chapter 9. Conclusion   201
Bibliography   207

List of Tables

2.1. The Number of Santri Attending Schools within the Pesantren Darul Ulum, 1990–1991	36
2.2. The Number of Santri with their Place of Origin	41
6.1. Percentage of Votes Shared by Political Parties in Jombang in General Elections	121
6.2. Number of Votes of the Major Parties in the 1971 General Election in Jombang	122
6.3. Percentage of Islamic Parties' and PPP's Share of Votes in Various Kecamatan in Jombang	125
6.4. Percentage of the Decline in PPP's Vote Share in Various Kecamatan in the 1987 General Election	127
6.5. Muslim Respondents' Standpoint on Political Manoeuvres of *Penggembosan*	131
6.6. Percentage of Muslim Respondents' Reasons for their Support for PPP	144
6.7. Percentage of Voting Pattern of Muslim Respondents in the 1977, 1982, 1987 and 1992 General Elections	144
6.7a. Changing Voting Pattern of PPP Respondents	145
6.8. Percentage of the Muslim Respondents' Perspective on the Difference in PPP after 1985, and the Area in which such a Difference Occurs	147
7.1. Number of Respondents in the Four Villages of Three Districts of Jombang to whom Jombang Kiai are Known (The Kiai are Listed in Alphabetical Order)	164
7.2. The Respondents' Views on the Idealised Person to Lead an Islamic Organisation	166
8.1. Percentage of Respondents' Attitude to the Availability of Many Islamic Organisations	192
8.2. Percentage of Respondents' Perspective of the Ideal Society	193
8.3. Perception of Intermarriage Between Members of Various Muslim Groups	194
8.4. Reasons to Accept and Refuse Intermarriage	195
8.5. Percentage of Respondents' Preference as Marriage Partner for their Children	195

List of Figures

1.1. Map of East Java	9
1.2. Jombang: Kecematan	10
6.1. Results of the General Election in Jombang	121
6.2. Muslim Support for Political Parties in Various Kecamatan in Jombang in the 1971 General Election	124
6.3. A Tendency of Social Grouping and Support for a Certain Political Organisation among NU Members (Former PPP Supporters) in Jombang	135
6.4. Muslim Political Orientation in Jombang	139

Foreword

Endang Turmudi's *Struggling for the Umma* is an appropriate volume with which to initiate this new series of publications on Islam in Southeast Asia. This is a study that focuses on the heartland of the *Nahdlatul Ulama* (NU), the largest Islamic organization in Indonesia, and on the role of *ulama*, or *kiai* as they are known in Java, within NU. Based on substantial fieldwork, this study provides an informed glimpse into the intimate relationships among *kiai*, their role in local and national politics and their leadership of the Islamic community.

In this study, Dr Turmudi considers the critical role that Javanese *kiai* play both in organization of Islamic education through local boarding schools, *pesantren*, and in the guidance of particular Sufi orders, *tarekat*. Thus, throughout Java, certain key boarding schools function both as centres of learning and as centres of wider religious practice in accordance with adherence to a specific Sufi order.

Dr Turmudi examines the position of various pesantren and their associated *kiai* in Jombang, a regency noted as a centre of Islamic learning in East Java. He uses a particular event – the transfer of the allegiance in 1977 of *Kiai* Musta'in from the Islamic United Development Party (PPP) to the government party Golkar – as the basis for an extended case study that is particularly revealing. The setting for this case study is one of the oldest and most renowned schools in Jombang, *Pesantren Darul Ulum* located in the village of Rejoso and involves the largest Sufi order in Indonesia, the combined order, *Qadiriyah wa Naqsyabandiyah*. For a succession of five generations, the spiritual leader, *murshid*, of *Qadiriyah wa Naqsyabandiyah* for all of East Java, was based at Darul Ulum. So when *Kiai* Musta'in, as the head of *Pesantren Darul Ulum* and *murshid* of *Qadiriyah wa Naqsyabandiyah*, made his decision to join Golkar, this precipitated a profound reconsideration of political relations in Javanese Islamic circles. It is the implications and consequences of this reconsideration that Dr Turmudi analyses effectively, thus providing an exceptional portrait of the politics of NU.

As a contribution to ongoing Islamic discussions in Indonesia, this study has already made its impact. The thesis was translated into Indonesian and was published under the title, *Perselingkuhan Kiai dan Kekuasasan* by the Yogyakarta publisher, Lembaga Kajian Islam dan Sosial (LKiS) in 2003 and has since been the subject of seminars from Jakarta to Jombang. Given the fact that the book in its Indonesian translation continues to contribute to a lively national discussion, it is all the more important that the original English version be made available.

When Endang Turmudi returned to Indonesia after completing his doctoral work at the Australian National University, he took up a position as a researcher in the Research Center for the Society and Culture (*Pusat Penelitian Kemasyarakatan dan Kebudayaan*) in the Indonesian Institute of Sciences

(PMB-LIPI). However, in 2004, he was chosen as the Secretary General of *Nahdlatul Ulama*. His research background as well as his background as a santri educated at Pesantren Cipasung in Tasikmalaya under the former Rais Aam of NU, K. H. Ilyas Ruhiyat and his further education at the State Institute for Islamic Studies (IAIN) Sunan Kalijaga in Yogkakarta combined with his M.A. from Flinders University and PhD from The Australian National University were all qualifications for the position of importance that he now holds in NU.

It is fortunate for the ANU that it is able to initiate this series of publications with a volume by one of the University's notable graduates.

James J. Fox

Preface

The transliteration of Arabic words in this thesis follows a general English standard. But in regard to the names of persons or institutions I leave them written as the Indonesian write them. The name of 'Usman or Usman, for example, will not be written with 'Uthman as the general English standard does. This includes other non-Indonesian Arabic names. Also the name of Indonesian institutions, such as madrasah aliyah will not be written as madrasa aliya.

In addition, certain concepts of Indonesianised Arabic which are important in relation to the topic of this thesis, like tarekat or mu'tabarah, will not be transliterated into the general English standard. It is best that these concepts be more contextual to the Indonesian situation as Indonesian Muslims use them.

Although I follow a general English standard in regard to transliteration, I do not transliterate the Arabic words precisely as the standard requires. For example, I do not use any punctuation symbol to differentiate a long vowel from a short vowel. Also certain Arabic harf (characters) would be written in the same character. This is because my computer does not have the punctuation symbol required for Arabic transliteration. These harf are:

1. ت and ط = t
2. ز and ظ = z
3. د and ض = d
4. ح and ه = h
5. س and ص = s

The general transliterations I use therefore in this thesis are as follow:

أ	'	د	d	ض	d	ك	k
ب	b	ذ	dh	ط	t	ل	l
ت	t	ر	r	ظ	z	م	m
ث	th	ز	z	ع	'	ن	n
ج	j	س	s	غ	gh	و	w
ح	h	ش	sh	ف	f	ه	h
خ	kh	ص	s	ق	q	ى	y
ة	a						
ة.	at						

Another area I need to mention here is my usage of Indonesian names. In almost all cases I call the Indonesians by their first name. This is not only because I want to be more contextual in accordance with my discussion but also because there are differences between Indonesian and Westerners in regard with name usage. Firstly, the Indonesian do not acknowledge surname or family name as the Westerners do. It is common that a person has a very short name, such as Soekarno. Secondly, those Indonesian who have family name do not relate their name to larger family but strictly to their father; and many who use a family name take the first name of their father. For example, a member of the Hasyim Asy'ary family will not use Asy'ary as his family name. Only Hasyim's children would use 'Hasyim' as their family name, such as Wahid Hasyim. But Abdurrahman as Wahid Hasyim's son does not use Hasyim but Wahid as his family name. So his full name is Abdurrahman Wahid, not Abdurrahman Hasyim. Finally those who have a multi word name do not necessarily included a family name. The name of my son, Fikri Zaki Muhammadi, for example, does not incorporate our family name. Therefore I would call Musta'in Romly Musta'in. However, because Indonesian Muslims commonly attache informal titles, such as *kiai*, to those deserve them, I will call Musta'in, Kiai Musta'in as all Muslims in Jombang did it.

Abbreviations and Glossary

Abangan	nominal Muslim
Aliran	stream or faction of ideologically oriented groups.
Bai'a	to take an oath for allegiance (in tarekat, sufi orders, to practise the ritual)
Baraka	blessing
Bathin	spiritual world
Bid'a	a type of heresy
Da'wa	preaching
Dhikr	recollection of God
Fatwa	religious advice
Fiqh	Islamic jurisprudence
Golkar	Golongan Karya (political organisation)
GUPPI	Gabungan Usaha Perbaikan Pendidikan Islam (Joint Effort for the Development of Islamic Education)
Hadith	the second source of Islam after the Qur'an
Hajj	pilgrimage to Mecca
Haram	religiously prohibited
Ijaza irshad	an authority to lead the tarekat
Ijma'	consensus
Ijtihad	the exercise of independent judgement
Imam	prayer leader. In the tarekat, the person who leads the ritual.
Istighatha	dhikr activities in the tarekat
Kabupaten	regency
Kafir	infidel
Karama	a quality possessed by a holy man which can bestow baraka
Kecamatan	district
Khalifa	deputy or assistant of the murshid in the tarekat
Kiai	religious leader, higher 'ulama
Kualat	being cursed

Khurafat	a type of heresy
LDII	Lembaga Dakwah Islam Indonesia (Indonesian Council for Islamic Preaching)
Madhhab	school of law in Islam
Madrasa	Islamic school
Masjumi	Majlis Sjuro Muslimin Indonesia (the Consultative Council for Indonesian Muslims)
MIAI	Majlis Islam A'la Indonesia (the High Indonesian Islamic Council)
MUI	Majlis Ulama Indonesia (Indonesian Council of Ulama)
Mu'tabarah	legitimate
Mujahada	tarekat ritual
Muhammadiyah	a more modern Islamic Organisation
Murshid	lit, a person who guides (spiritual teacher)
NU	Nahdlatul Ulama (Islamic organisation)
Nyai	a title for the wife of a kiai
Pesantren	Islamic educational institution
PDI	Partai Demokrasi Indonesia (Indonesian Democratic Party)
PKI	Partai Komunis Indonesia (Indonesian Communist Party)
Pondok	dormitory, pesantren
PPP	Partai Persatuan Pembangunan (United Development Party)
Qur'an	Muslim holy book
Santri	lit. means a pupil of the pesantren
Slametan	Javanese traditional ritual
Shari'a	the Law of Islam
Silsila	lit. means a chain
Shahada	the profession of faith
Shirk	idolatry, polytheism
Sholawat	a prayer for the Prophet Muhammad
Tarekat	sufi order, tariqa
Tasawwuf	the mysticism of Islam

TPA	Taman Pendidikan Al-Qur'an (Qur'anic Education for Kindergarten)
'Ulama	lit. scholar, erudite (religious leader)
Ustadh	lit. teacher
Umma	Islamic society
Wajb	religiously obligatory
Waqf	endowment
Wird	litany
Ziyara	visit, pilgrimage to a holy place

Abstract

This thesis focuses on the relationship between Indonesian *kiai* ('*ulama*: religious leaders) in Jombang to their wider social and political situation. There are three kinds of *kiai* discussed in the thesis, that is the *pesantren kiai*, the *tarekat kiai*, and the *kiai* involved in politics. Two important aspects of *kiai* leadership are highlighted. The first is the strong attachment of the *kiai* to Islam. As a religious leader, this attachment to Islam has resulted in his leadership being generally seen as charismatic. One might therefore pose the question as to whether a change in society's political and social attitudes has an effect on the pattern of *kiai* leadership. The second is the independence of each *kiai* and hence the specific following he maintains. This independence from other *kiai* indicates that Muslims in Jombang are socially fragmented along the lines of allegiance to various local *kiaiship*. This means that the authority of the *kiai* is dispersed. This structural situation creates the possibility of conflict. The unity of Muslim society as a whole can be threatened when conflicts occur between *kiai* especially in the field of politics. The persistent attachment of the *kiai* to Islam, moreover, imbues any political conflict with religious justification.

I argue in this thesis that the charismatic authority exerted through the leadership of the *kiai* in Java has limitations in terms of its legitimacy. At the very least it has boundaries that determine areas or circumstances for its legitimate expression. These boundaries are normative and are loosely expressed by the concept of 'to struggle for Islam'. This concept can be used by any *kiai* follower or by groups within society tacitly to evaluate a *kiai*. As holders of charismatic authority, the *kiai* can often induce action or emotional responses from their followers since they are held in the high regard. However, in certain situations such authority may be rendered useless when the *kiai's* entrenched lines of authority are perceived to deviate from a socially accepted religious base. At this point followers have a possible basis to challenge the legitimacy of the *kiai's* pronouncements particularly on social and political issues. Voting in a general election is a good example. The *kiai's* encouragement to support a party other than the Islamic party, for example, has incurred negative responses from followers. A few *kiai* have even been deserted by a large number of their followers because of their political stand.

This thesis further argues that the *kiai's* influence in politics is not as strong as in other domains. Despite his being a charismatic figure, only a minority of followers feel compelled to follow the *kiai's* political example. Differences between the *kiai* and his followers in relation to political behaviour are common, especially after the transformation of the Islamic political party. Nevertheless, the role of the *kiai* in general remains important in the eyes of Muslim society, since the *kiai* is in the forefront guarding the morality and the religious orthodoxy of Muslim society.

Acknowledgements

I realise that I would not have finished this thesis without the support and encouragement of so many people both as individuals or members of an agency. I would like first to thank AusAID, which provided me with a four year scholarship, and its staff in Jakarta and Canberra who have been very helpful and cooperative since the inception of my study at the Australian National University. Also my thanks are due to the Indonesian Institute of Sciences (LIPI), especially Dr. Hilman Adil of the Centre for Social and Cultural Studies, who encouraged me to pursue the program at the Australian National University. In addition, I would like to thank 'Yayasan Supersemar' which provided me with a grant to cover my survey costs during my fieldwork in Jombang.

I also would like to express my gratitude to my supervisor, Dr. Frank Lewins of the Department of Sociology. Since the beginning of my program he has kindly spent his time discussing with me the problems of my research. He has been very supportive of the subject I was researching. His continuous contact with me during my research in Jombang was very helpful in solving the problems I encountered in the field. His advice and his comments on my thesis drafts have been valuable. My gratitude is also due to Professor James J. Fox of the Department of Anthropology, RSPAS, who not only supervised me during my study but also provided me with facilities without which I would have needed additional time to finish this thesis. It was in some seminars led by him that I was able to enrich my theoretical knowledge and broaden my perspective in understanding the subject I was studying. As an Indonesian specialist, his advice and suggestions have very much helped me to clarify the focus of my study and to sharpen my analysis. Also his support and encouragement has widened my interest in Islamic studies generally. I would like also to thank Dr. Rachel Bloul, my adviser, who gave some comments on the drafts of my thesis. Another scholar whom I have to thank is Dr. Martin van Bruinessen of Utrecht University. He read the drafts of some chapters of the thesis and gave me some valuable comments. Dr. Margot Lyon of the Department of Anthropology, who gave of her time to discuss my work, also deserves my thanks for her support and encouragement.

I would also like to thank Dr. Owen Dent, the head of the Department of Sociology, who provided me with facilities; also his staff, Helen Felton and Rose-Mary Swan, who provided me with assistance in relation to bureaucratic matters during my study at ANU. Some friends studying Indonesia in the Department of Anthropology, especially Kim Hyung Jun, provided encouragement during my study at ANU, and gave me a chance to discuss with them my proposal and my findings. Two Ph.D students who had the same interests as me, Muhamad Hisyam and Greg Fealy from Leiden and Monash University respectively also took the time to discuss my research with me and provided me with needed information. I need also to thank Mandy Scott and Barbara Knackstedt for their assistance in helping me to express myself in better English.

My thanks also go to two intellectuals from Jombang, Dr. Nurcholis Madjid and Abdurrahman Wahid, who gave me valuable insights about Muslims in Jombang before I went into the field. Their introduction to Jombang helped me gain a general understanding of how Islam was embedded in the lives of its population. My great thanks are also due to a number of *kiai* in Jombang who sincerely provided me with information. Without their cooperation this study would not have been possible. As my informants, they were also my subject of study. Special thanks are due to Kiai Aziz Masyhuri, Kiai Makki Ma'shum and Kiai Arwani. I also would like to thank Mas Hafidh Ma'shum and Mbak Fauziyah who were always ready to give me the information which I needed and to clarify the socio-political problems surrounding Muslim life in Jombang.

I have to mention two people who assisted me during my study in Jombang, that is Mustofa and Mas Sukamto, a student and a lecturer at the *Universitas Darul Ulum* respectively. Both helped me in managing the survey I conducted. They are also friends with whom I enjoyed my stay in Jombang. Another person who should receive my thanks is Ibu Hindun, my landlord during my stay in Jombang, and her family. Her readiness to lease some parts of her house during my research was very helpful, and allowed me to settle very quickly in Jombang. My father, Aan Sukandi, and my father-in-law, H. Hamdani Hambali, in Karawang West Java, were very helpful and provided me with facilities which made my movement in Jombang easier. My thanks are also due to the people of Jombang, whom I cannot mention individually here, especially those Muslims who took the time to answer my questionnaire.

Finally I would like to express my thanks to my beloved wife, Wini, who has offered moral support, encouragement and patient companionship during my study. My thanks are also due to Fikri Zaki Muhammadi and Reza Aulia Ahmadi, my children, whose presence during my stay in Jombang and Canberra was the spirit which always encouraged me to continue with my study. I dedicate this thesis to these people whom I love very much.

Chapter 1: Introduction

1.1 Background of the Study

Studies on Islamic religious leaders or *kiai* in Indonesia (Geertz, 1959a and Horikoshi, 1976) reveal that they have a strategic and central position in their society. The centrality of their position is related to their being educated and wealthy people in their community. As an educated elite, the *kiai* provide knowledge of Islam to villagers. The *pesantren* as a traditional Islamic educational institution is an important means through which the transfer of knowledge to each *kiai's* local society takes place. Through their wealth, on the other hand, the *kiai* become patrons on whom many villagers depend. The centrality of the *kiai's* position can be seen in the pattern of patronage, especially as it relates and ties the *kiai* to his *santri* or students (see Fox and Dirjosanjoto, 1989).

As an informal Islamic leader, the *kiai* is a man perceived by villagers to have great worth and charismatic authority. This is because he is a holy man endowed with *baraka* or blessing. As this type of authority is "outside the realm of the everyday routine and profane sphere" (Weber, 1973:53), the *kiai* is seen to have exceptional qualities which make his leadership popularly acknowledged. Furthermore, in addition to his personal qualities, the *kiai's* authority in the eyes of his community and his involvement in a pattern of tight relationships with its members, are shaped by his concern for, and orientation toward, the interests of the *umma* or Islamic community.

The *kiai*, because of his position, plays a brokerage role for Muslims to give them an understanding of what is going on at the national level (Geertz, 1959a). Villagers who usually call themselves *wong cilik* or ordinary people, realise that they are not well equipped with knowledge to understand events at a national level. Their close relationship with the *kiai* makes him a translator who provides illumination in a religious context and clarifies Indonesian problems in general. The *kiai's* prominent position has been particularly evident when party politics have been intense, penetrating rural Javanese communities. This is because the *kiai* is also part of a political elite, a position related to the religious significance of having legitimate power to unify the *umma* in the face of real and imagined threats from other groups.

Recent studies, however, suggest that changes in regard to the *kiai's* position in society (Usman, 1991) and their socio-political perspective (Abdullah, 1988 and Bruinessen, forthcoming) require a new approach. The role of the *kiai* in rural Java, which was previously decisive and charismatic and long encompassed all aspects of village life, is beginning to erode. Usman (1991) in his study of villages in Jombang has illustrated this point by showing that most religious leaders[1] he studied were less popular in their villages compared to other village elites, such as the village headman or wealthy villagers. The religious leaders were less involved in local government projects to improve village standards. This study also reveals that the *kiai* have a smaller network, either within their own midst or in relation to other village elites. In many cases, according to Usman, people did not go to religious leaders to discuss matters relating to their worldly lives but, rather, went to bureaucratic officials at the village level.

Although Usman's focus is more general and outside the field in which the *kiai* traditionally and culturally has been involved, his findings reveal that the leadership of the *kiai* is in general undergoing change. The inevitable processes of *pembangunan* or development taking place throughout villages in Java have resulted in a change in the Muslims' broad socio-political situation and perspectives. This has affected Muslim perception in relation to the leadership role of *kiai* as well.

As a result of the introduction of development programs or modernisation in general, there are three factors which give rise to challenging the leadership role of the *kiai*. The first is the emergence of a younger *santri* generation in the *pesantren* who are modern in character. By modern[2] I mean they have a greater capacity and a greater freedom to think about and evaluate the *kiai's* attitude, at least in the domain of politics. Such a change raises a legitimacy problem for the leadership role of the *kiai*. This is a result of the modernisation program in the *pesantren* system of education, which is marked by an increase in the number of the schools in its environment. As will be discussed, some modern *pesantren* in Jombang provide a modern schooling system from primary to tertiary level. The second factor is the increase in the number of educated middle class Muslims in Javanese society. The emergence of younger scholars, both secular and religious among Nahdlatul Ulama[3] (NU) members has not only made the *kiai's* position as legitimator competitive, but has also led to his credibility and authority being examined. This situation indicates that in Javanese villages and within NU, people can now go to a variety of agents who provide them with knowledge of Islam and leadership in a more general sense. The third factor is the enlargement of the sphere of operation of the state under the guise of

---

[1] What Usman means by 'religious leader' is a *kiai* in my terminology. Usman's term 'religious leader' is more general in meaning, and does not follow local terminology. This is so since Usman's focus of study was not on religious leaders per se, but rather on village elites, like the wealthy or the village officers. So, 'religious leader' in Usman's study is a general category to contrast with these other elite groups.

[2] My definition of modernisation here is concerned with attitudes and behaviour. I am affected by what is conceptualised by Inkeles (1966) and Tamney (1980). Modernisation, however, does not occur only at the level of attitude but also at the level of structure as well (see Weiner, 1966).

[3] Nahdlatul Ulama is an Islamic organisation established in 1926. The *kiai* of this organisation are usually considered traditionalist orthodox Muslims. They are different from those commonly called Modernist Muslims, who belong to such organisations as Muhammadiyah.

enhancing the quality of Muslim life. The state, among others, became concerned with inequality and involved in matters previously under the *kiai's* concern. The introduction of birth control has involved the state in the definition of social knowledge about birth, which was traditionally subsumed under the religious domain in which the *kiai* play an important role.

These factors have not only produced younger Muslims who are critical to the *kiai* leadership but have also provided an alternative in the existence of other forms of leaderships. The *kiai's* position and his charismatic leadership is therefore inevitably challenged. It is no accident, for example, that a *kiai* whom I knew well was accused of being corrupt for taking money from a *waqf* property (endowment) which he had managed. In this particular case, the *kiai's* respected position was shaken, not only because he committed a religiously prohibited act, but also simply because of the changes in social norms which dominate social relationships among villagers. This type of accusation had never occurred before because villagers would not have considered it appropriate to criticise a *kiai*. The same holds true for the case of some *santri* of the *Pesantren Darul Ulum* in Jombang who held a demonstration, protesting against their *kiai's* policy on education in the formal schools of his *pesantren*. Such instances confirm Usman's findings that the *kiai* are becoming less influential compared to the government's officers.

Even though the problem faced by the *kiai* is not new, its intensity and capacity to shake their position are relatively recent. The problem faced by the *kiai* in Javanese villages is similar to that experienced by religious leaders in other Islamic countries. It has become a general problem encountered by religious leaders throughout the Islamic world. It is also a problem faced by leaders of other religions, since the problem of acceptability, in the sense of how the religion's values and norms are internalised and applied by people in their daily lives, is a problem faced by many religious leaders.

Seen from a more popular perspective, these changes in the *kiai's* social position and in the Muslim perception of the *kiai* leadership seem to be taken for granted in the sense that it is a logical result of the intense changes in social structure which have been occurring in Java lately. These changes in social structure have also changed the pattern of *kiai* leadership since they need to adapt to the changing situation if they want their leadership to be continually accepted by Muslim society.

Despite being influenced by the development of society in general, the leadership of *kiai* continues to influence the development of Muslim society itself. There are two reasons which sustain this. Firstly, the *kiai* is traditionally an influential elite in Muslim society. Secondly, the *kiai* is also a political elite with great influence on the political attitudes of Muslim society. As some *kiai* from Jombang, where my study took place, also held political leadership at provincial and national levels, the changes brought about through their leadership have a national character. In other words, changes which occurred at the local level are often the result of changes which occurred in the wider society. In the political domain, this matter was more obvious. The acceptance of Pancasila[4] by the *kiai* through NU as their ideological base has not only altered political views among *kiai* at all levels but also Muslim society at its grassroots. Thus, in the political field the change at the grassroots is a reflection of a change in the wider society.

This study tries to look at the leadership of *kiai* generally by focusing on the cultural and political aspects of their leadership. As the relationship between the *kiai* and society is governed by norms derived from their understanding of Islam, the changes in their relationship are not only affected by changes at the wider social level, but also by changes in these existing norms. The shift in the latter is very much related to the process of Islamic reinterpretation. As the Javanese attachment to Islam is "the dominant force of their religious belief and rite and by which the character of their social interactions in daily life are shaped" (Woodward, 1989:3), changes in the wider social realm are closely related to the new Javanese understanding of Islam. These changes in the norms and in the wider social structure are crucial. They raise questions about the emergence of a new order, which regulates a new pattern of relationships between the *kiai* and society or between various segments of Javanese society. This, in turn, involves the recognition by these different groups of their new "social location."

A general question pertaining to this study is to what extent social change influences the change in Muslim religious belief and understanding, and to what extent this change contributes to change in the wider social and cultural domains. A more specific question relates to the leadership of the *kiai* in general. How far do these changes influence the pattern of relationships between the *kiai* and Muslim society? As these changes are assumed to impinge on the norms and values underlying the *kiai's* relationship with society, a second important question is directed to understanding the political influence of the *kiai*: to what extent can the *kiai* influence socio-political action within Muslim society? The study also tries to clarify the problem of the relationship between the *kiai* and his own colleagues and the *kiai* with other Muslim groups.

1.2 Review of the Literature

In this section, I will review the literature that examines the changes and development of Islam in Java, especially studies concerned with the *pesantren* and the role of the *kiai*. These sources examine (1) the system of *pesantren*

---

[4] Pancasila is a national ideology, which consists of five principles: believe in one God, humanitarianism, nationalism, representative government and social justice.

education and its role in the formation of the pattern of Islamic belief and culture in Indonesia; and (2) the *kiai's* efforts in maintaining the *pesantren* and their social and political role in spreading and maintaining Islam in general. All of these studies were conducted in Javanese villages. The researchers used anthropological and sociological approaches, with participant observation and interviews as their main methods of collecting data.

An interesting study on Islam, especially on the Javanese *kiai*, was conducted by Geertz in the 1960s. The study has drawn the attention of both Indonesian and Western scholars interested in Islamic development in Indonesia. This study is of great significance since it laid a framework for understanding Javanese Islam. Geertz's study also illuminated the political problems of modern Indonesia in general. Nevertheless, this study has been criticised by some scholars (see Pranowo, 1991). Woodward (1989), for example, contends that Geertz failed in understanding the nature of the development of Islam in Java. Hodgson (1974) sees this failure as derived from his being too influenced by modernist Muslim perspectives. Notwithstanding this criticism, Geertz has pioneered modern Javanese Islamic studies. Later studies on Islam in Java always refer to Geertz's study.

These later studies differ from Geertz's approach in many respects, although they use his framework in a loose way. Horikoshi (1976) conducted research on the role of the *kiai* of West Java in maintaining the social order, while Dhofier (1980) focused on the *kiai* and *pesantren*, or what he calls "the pesantren tradition". Dhofier presented the pattern of *kiai-santri* relationships and of traditional Islamic education. He also discussed the network of relationships between *kiai* in a wider geographical territory, and their reliance on close family relations. Other studies were conducted by Mansurnoor (1990), Usman (1991) and Pranowo (1991). These studies respectively analysed the *kiai* and the *'ulama*[5] of Madura either as agents of change, the *'ulama* as religious elites, and the role of *kiai* and *pesantren* in creating the Islamic tradition. From these analyses, it is evident that the same cultural patterns exist for the *'ulama* in Javanese, Sundanese and Madurese society. The *'ulama* in these areas constitute an elite who have a strong influence in establishing a religious community. The pattern of value transmission which is institutionalised through the education system is also based on similar processes. *Pondok* (dormitories for *santri*) or *madrasa* (Islamic schools) in these areas are the main educational institutions and are seen by these researchers to be an important means of socialisation. Informal institutions of religious instruction are also a significant means in transmitting values, norms and religious symbols to the society.

---

[5] The term *kiai* and *'ulama* have much the same meaning. The term *'ulama* derives from Arabic, while the term *kiai* derives from Javanese. I will discuss this in Chapter II.

In addition, *'ulamaship* in various regions in Java is hierarchical. Although the hierarchy is not formally created, there is a general recognition from Muslim society which influences the position of the *'ulama*. A higher *'ulama* will receive different treatment from those within society compared to a lower *'ulama*. According to these three latter studies, the hierarchical pattern of *'ulamaship* is sustained and institutionalised by the fact that *'ulamaship* or *kiaiship* is ascriptive in nature. This pattern is more evident in Madura, as observed by Mansurnoor, where the *'ulamaship* is inherited geneologically. An educated or erudite Muslim who would like to run a *pesantren* but does not come from a *kiai* family will have difficulty gaining the recognition of society since he does not have the proper social status (Mansurnoor, 1990:217). However, it should be realised that in areas other than Madura, there is a distinction between *'ulamaship* at a lower level and a higher level in relation to this question of ascription. At the higher level, as in Madura, *'ulamaship* in Java is mostly inherited, especially among those who run *pesantren*. This is because at a lower level, *'ulamaship* can be obtained by any Muslim in so far as he receives social recognition, while at a higher level *'ulamaship* requires considerable wealth. Almost all *pesantren* which complement a higher *'ulamaship*, for example, were built with the *'ulama's* own money. Also, because at a higher level *'ulamaship* needs a more extensive background of Islamic knowledge (most of the earlier great Javanese *'ulama*, for example, studied in Mecca for years before they reached their *'ulamaship*), it was only the *'ulama* with rich family backgrounds who could acquire that.

Nahdlatul Ulama (NU), an organisation established by the *kiai*, provides a forum for the discussion of all important issues facing the Muslim community in Indonesia. It has also produced a wide ranging network among *kiai* and has become a symbol of solidarity between them (Mansurnoor, 1990:319). It is through NU that the brotherhood and friendship between *kiai* are institutionalised; and it is also through NU that one's *kiaiship* is legitimised. A *kiai* who establishes a new *pesantren*, for example, needs recognition from his senior *kiai* for society to recognise his *kiaiship*. These networks of *kiai* relationships are not confined to the regency level; rather they constitute a national network, through which the *kiai* receives a variety of information which illuminates problems ranging from the religious to the political.

From these studies, it is evident that the critical role of the *kiai* lies in their position as religious leaders and teachers. The *kiai* are members of the village elite, who try to bring their community into an idealised situation as conceptualised by Islam. Each *kiai* also tries to interpret developments and changes in the socio-cultural and political fields in order that the people in villages can understand them.

While an *'ulama* in the past had quite a comprehensive role in his community, this role now seems to be eroding in contemporary Javanese society. The *'ulama* is another functionary, whose position is in competition with other social leaders. Usman (1991) in his research in Jombang, for example, found that some religious leaders are now less influential than some other functionaries, such as village heads. People do not ask the *'ulama* for advice about worldly matters as they did before. This change in the *'ulama* position may be caused by modernisation[6] through which traditional values are threatened and lose their meaning being replaced by modern values. In addition, the change may also be caused by the fact that many *'ulama* cannot meet all the needs of people because of their limited secular knowledge — most of their knowledge is religious. Therefore people now turn to other functionaries, such as village heads, when they face problems relating to developments in their villages and their worldly lives.

In brief, it is evident that the studies under review explored the nature of the *'ulama's* world and described the general pattern of relationships between the *'ulama* and their followers. Although some of the *'ulama's* traditional relationship with their followers continues to the present, Usman's research shows that there are some changes occurring in the *'ulama's* position in the wider society. Thus the pattern of relationship between the *'ulama* and society in general is in the process of change.

It should be stressed that Usman's findings are worth noting since they contradict the views of other scholars. Compared to other studies, Usman's findings indicate changes in relation to the *'ulama's* role in general, which give rise to a change in their position in the wider society. Nevertheless, there are many questions which remain unanswered, since Usman only focused on the role of the religious leader in relation to that of other functionaries in development projects conducted in three villages. Usman's study does not consider how the *kiai* exercises his power in Javanese society in general. This study will attempt to address this question by focusing on the *kiai's* role in politics. This issue is important because, at the formal level of organisation, Muslim society conceptualises no separation between politics and religion, and maintains that political decisions and attitudes should be religiously legitimate. One aspect I will consider in detail in this thesis is the extent to which the *kiai's* political actions influence their followers.

I chose Jombang as the place of research because it is often regarded as a 'microcosm' of Indonesian Islam. Firstly, Jombang has a large number of *pesantren* located in certain districts. Secondly, it has three active *tarekat* (sufi orders) organisations which involve thousands of Muslims. Finally, *kiai* in Jombang have long been involved in politics. Because of their close relations with the *kiai*, a situation which made them imitate the *kiai's* political example, the majority of Muslims in Jombang are affected by politics, and in general are 'active' in

---

[6] Included in what I have mentioned as the modernisation process (see footnote 2) is the transformation of Indonesian politics. This transformation, as will be discussed in this thesis, is influential in changing the *kiai* leadership.

politics. The long existence of *pesantren* has enabled them to perform what is called 'Islamic politics'. In addition, some *kiai* in Jombang were, or are still active politically in NU's national leadership. This means that very often political change among Muslims in Jombang is a result of political change at a national level.

1.3 The Fieldwork

I had not been to Jombang before I began my PhD research, starting in October 1992 and continuing until September 1993 (see Figure 1.1 and 1.2). My knowledge of Jombang came from reading scientific reports, especially those by Dhofier (1982), and newspapers and magazines. This knowledge stemmed from my work in the Indonesian Institute of Sciences (LIPI), the government institution conducting research in various disciplines.

Actually I had a roomate, a *santri* from Jombang, when I studied in IAIN (State Institute for Islamic Studies) in Yogyakarta from 1974 to 1980. However, I was not interested in Jombang at that time, having no desire to do research. Jombang later came to my attention when my interest in Islamic studies was aroused at my work place. This was because Jombang is a medium size city which has a large number of *pesantren*. In addition, some famous Islamic leaders and intellectuals were and are natives of Jombang.

Based on such general knowledge, Jombang offered the impression of a Muslim city in which Islamic life flourishes. It is a place where Islamic studies are well developed in the *pesantren*, and where some highly regarded *kiai* provide religious leadership for their communities. This impression was borne out by my discovery, while taking a walk on my first day in Jombang, of a sign on the bank in the main street of Jombang city on which was written "Jombang Kota Santri" (Jombang is the City of Santri). Labelling a city with a certain characteristic is a common pattern that holds throughout Java. Every regency in Java characterises its capital city with a metaphor that marks the nature of the life of its people. In West Java, for example, there is a city called, or at least its people gave it the name of, "The City of Rice", because it produces huge amounts of rice compared to other places in Indonesia. The same holds true for the methapor "The City of Civilization" given to Yogyakarta because in this city, local culture and civilization are well developed and maintained. For me, the sign I found in the heart of Jombang city, describing Jombang as "the City of Santri" is not merely a facet of the Javanese trend to label cities, but also indicates something of the social reality of the people of Jombang.

Figure 1.1. Map of East Java

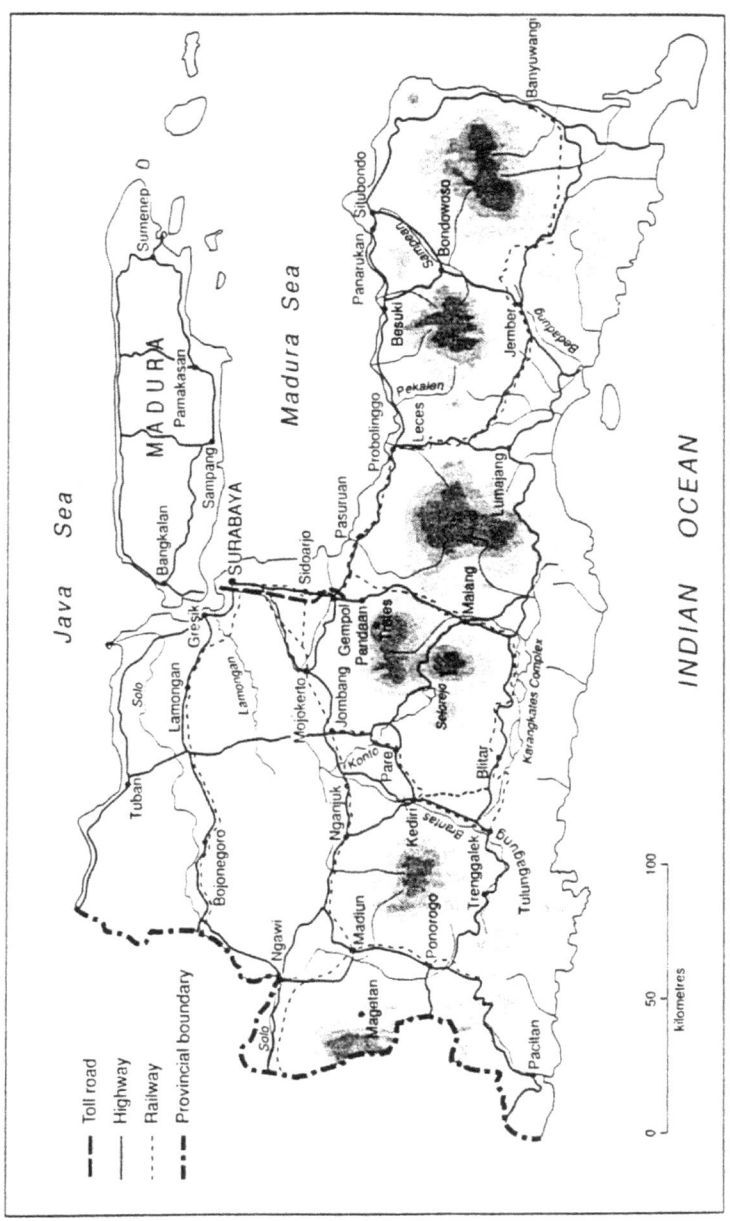

Figure 1.2. Jombang: Kecematan

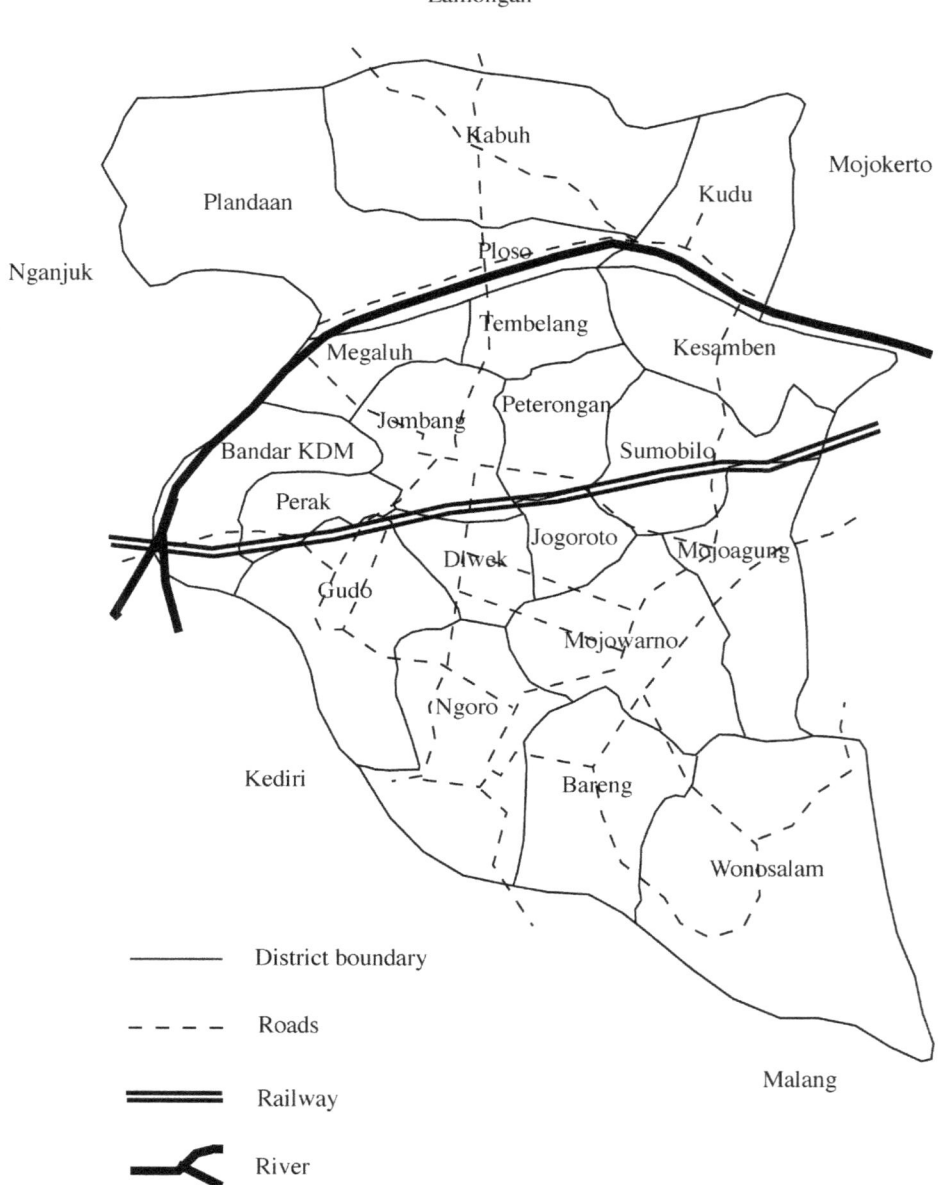

Nevertheless, my assumptions about the *santri*-ness (piousness) of Jombang was disturbed and threatened by another fact I encountered in the first week of my stay. On the same main street in Jombang I saw a large poster hanging on a cinema. The poster, which depicted a pair of naked humans was, in my judgement, most disturbing in the moral sense. The sociological question that arose was: what sort of *santri*-ness is it that actually surrounds the people of Jombang?

Such a question seemed to be partially answered when I began to talk with a public figure from Jombang. This person used to be an activist in NU, the biggest religious organisation in Jombang and Indonesia in general, which is currently embroiled in a *tarekat*-like movement. When I talked with him in his hotel, he suggested that it is not actually appropriate to call Jombang "the City of the Santri". In his opinion, Malang[7] would be more a suitable candidate for this title.

Syifa, the person I talked to, seemed to be right in his judgement about Jombang, for after two months I found that Jombang is similar to other cities in East Java. It does not seem to have any specific character associated with the piousness of its inhabitants. It is not a city dominated by devout members of society as the metaphor describing it, but rather it can be called a mixed city, since neither it nor the life of its people are characterised by the life of the *santri* and devout Muslims in general. Under the cloak of *santri*-ness attributed to Jombang society live a substantial number of Javanese whose practice of Islam is minimal. This population could be higher in number than the devout Muslims in Jombang. While not all devout Muslims in Jombang studied Islam in *pesantren*, it should be noted that the metaphor "the City of Santri" is related to the fact that Jombang has so many *pesantren* which attract a large number of students from outside Jombang.

The difference between Jombang and other cities in East Java and, at the same time, what leads it to be known as "the City of the Santri" is the existence of four large *pesantren* which have been run by well known *kiai*. When NU was established, its early top leader was a *kiai* from Jombang. It is little wonder that Jombang impresses other Indonesians as "the City of Santri".

I need to comment on my impressions to explain why I came to change the direction and scope of my study. When I wrote my research proposal, I planned to conduct the research in a *kecamatan* (district) of Jombang characterised by pluralism in relation to the nature of the people's attachment to their religion or their orthodoxy. In other words, I was concerned with Javanese piousness

---

[7] Malang is a neighbouring city to the southeast of Jombang. In Malang, according to Syifa, people are more *santri* because the tradition of *santri* in the life of people generally is more obvious. It is common, for example, for people to go to the city wearing *sarong* (traditional Muslim dress). This situation does not happen in Jombang.

concerning their Islam. Here one needs to differentiate Muslims into two categories related to their attachment to Islam. The first category consists of devout Muslims. Devout Muslims consistently carry out what is prescribed by Islam, such as performing prayer five times a day and fasting during *ramadan*. This category comprises both Javanese Muslims in general and the *santri* in the *pesantren*. The second category are those whose attachment to Islam is loose and their practice of Islam is minimal. Some people in Jombang call the latter *abangan*.

Concerning the variation in Muslim orthodoxy, I refer to the different religious orientations among what is called the devout community. Such variation is commonly characterised by patterns of affiliation with various Islamic organisations. I thus intended to focus on the members of these organisations, for example Muhammadiyah and NU, to see how they interacted with and perceived each other. For this purpose I chose Ngoro as a suitable *kecamatan* for my research. This choice was supported by an Indonesian Muslim scholar, Dr Nurkholis Madjid, who is from Jombang and knew much about Ngoro, since he grew up in a village in the neighbouring *kecamatan*. Ngoro has a long established *kauman*[8] area in which a large mosque was established. The mosque is an important characteristics of a Muslim community anywhere.

In addition, Ngoro has a number of *pesantren* run by *kiai*. These *pesantren*, however, are not located in the areas around the *kauman*, since it is more common for *pesantren* to be erected in less Islamic environments. Ngoro has a fanatical Muslim community which inhabits the centre of its town and spreads throughout its villages. By fanatical I mean that their concern about Islam, its importance and its role on everyday behaviour, assumes immense priority in their lives. It is important to note that it is this community which has given rise to Ngoro's being regarded as a pious district in Jombang. The piousness of the Ngoro community in general is evidenced by their long affiliation with the Islamic political party, another indication of their concern about Islam.

When I was told about the piousness of Javanese Muslims in Ngoro, I questioned what maintains this state of affairs and the process of socialisation there. I received my answer when I tried to examine the *tarekat* (sufi order) which has a huge number of followers throughout Jombang and the nearby regency. After I had been in Ngoro for three months, I found that people's piousness was connected to several factors, such as their submission to a *kiai's* leadership, their membership in a *tarekat* or their view of Islam. These factors were interrelated and affected people's attitudes and behaviour. Muslims in Ngoro are affiliated with various *tarekat* and their allegiance to a *kiai* is not always related to the

---

[8] *Kauman* is a Javanese word referring to a place in which a big mosque is established, so that it becomes a centre of Islamic activity. Due to its centrality to Islamic religious activity, people who live around it are commonly devout Muslims. *Kauman* is derived from Arabic, *qaum*, which means people or group of people.

Introduction

local *murshid* [9] (a common word referring to the spiritual leader of a *tarekat*), but could be connected to a *murshid* (or *kiai*) in another area in Jombang. I was therefore determined at that time to look at the role of the *murshid* in the *tarekat* itself. This meant that I had to observe the religious practice of certain *tarekat* and the relationship between the *murshid* and his followers.

The *tarekat* is a widespread religious movement in Jombang. I was told by an informant that the *tarekat* is embraced widely both in Jombang and the neighbouring regency, Kediri. After being in Jombang for three months, it became apparent that around one third of the devout population in Jombang were involved in or were members of one of the *tarekat* there. There are three different centres of *tarekat* which happen to be on three different sides of the Jombang regency. The first is the *Tarekat Qadiriyah Wa Naqsyabandiyah*, which is located on the eastern side of Jombang. This *tarekat* is affiliated with the *Jam'iyah Ahli Thoriqoh Al-Mu'tabaroh Indonesia*. The second is the *Tarekat Qadiriyah Wa Naqsyabandiyah* coordinated by *Jam'iyah Ahli Thoriqoh Al-Mu'tabaroh An-Nahdliyah*, which is centred in south Jombang. The third is the *Tarekat Shiddiqiyah*, which established its central activity in the northern area of Jombang. In addition, there is also a *tarekat*-like movement, *Penyiar Sholawat Wahidiyah*, which is located around ten kilometres to the south of the second *tarekat*.

In brief, the *kiai* leadership in Jombang in general is an important and longlasting religious leadership. People's affiliation to certain *kiai* is apparent when it is related to politics, and the term "Kiai Saya" (my *kiai*) is a common metaphor that indicates people's connectedness to certain *kiai*. If *kiaiship* in other areas of Java (see Horikoshi, 1976; and Mansoornur, 1990) has produced a pattern of patronage in relation to followers in general, it is important to note that in Jombang a stronger patronage is more likely to be established through *murshidship* [10]. Although such patronage could be built through *kiaiship*, as far as I found in Jombang, it seems to be looser than that related to *murshidship*. In other words, the relationship between a *murshid* and his followers is stronger than that between another type of *kiai* and his followers.

These insights gained after spending three months in Ngoro prompted me to change my research scope and focus. As Jombang is often regarded as a microcosm of Indonesian Islam, everything that transpires in Jombang could be seen as a reflection of what is happening in the wider Javanese or Indonesian context. Relocating my case study to Jombang would help to understand changes among all Indonesian Muslims. But I realise that to have limited this study of

---

[9] In North Africa, the common term with a similar meaning is *sheikh*.
[10] As I will discuss in Chapter II, there are various types of *kiai* in term of their leadership in society, that is the *pesantren kiai, tarekat kiai, political kiai* and *stage kiai*. The *murshid* as the *tarekat kiai* is thus only one category among others.

Indonesian Islam to Ngoro would not have represented Jombang as a whole due to the various intertwined socio-religious phenomena described above. Therefore I broadened the locations of my study to include Diwek, Peterongan and Ploso, the three *kecamatan* which are centres of *tarekat* movements and *pesantren*. I realised that I could not help studying the development of *pesantren* and *tarekat* in Jombang, since these two institutions are closely related to the people's lives. In addition, studying *kiai* leadership would be inadequate without taking these institutions into consideration, since they are led by *kiai*. Also, I was reminded by an Islamic intellectual, who comes from Jombang and is the leader of the biggest socio-religious organisation in Indonesia, Abdurrahman Wahid, that studying a Muslim community in Java would be inadequate without taking into consideration the political situation. I therefore tried to focus my study not simply on the transformation of people's beliefs and how they are applied in their behaviour but on the Muslims' changing attitudes and behaviours related to *kiai* socio-political leadership in general.

In general I did not encounter any serious problems in the course of my fieldwork. The people I interviewed or surveyed by questionnaires understood what I was doing and cooperated with the study. I was able to attend *tarekat* activities, and the *murshid* welcomed my research on their *tarekat*. The same held true for the *pesantren*. In general, no *kiai* hesitated to answer my questions about his *pesantren*. The *kiai* seemed to be happy that their *pesantren* or *tarekat* was being examined. They even told me that they welcomed some input from outsiders in order to develop their *pesantren* or *tarekat*. In their opinion, research could provide information about what is lacking or what should be done in relation to their *pesantren* or *tarekat*. The one exception to the above was the *Pesantren Shiddiqiyah* in Ploso whose *kiai*, Kiai Muchtar Mu'thi, who also leads the *Tarekat Shiddiqiyah*, did not allow me to research his *tarekat* and *pesantren*. I therefore have little information about this *tarekat*, as described in Chapter II.

1.4 Source of Data

My research in Jombang was largely taken up with indepth interviews and observation. The data I gathered therefore were mostly qualitative in nature. The data in this thesis mostly derives from interviewing *kiai* and other NU members. Also I have some notes from field observations of religious rituals of the *Tarekat Qadiriyah Wa Naqsyabandiyah* affiliated with the *Jam'iyah Ahli Thoriqoh Al-Mu'tabaroh Indonesia*, the *Tarekat Qadiriyah Wa Naqsyabandiyah* coordinated by the *Jam'iyah Ahli Thoriqoh Al-Mu'tabaroh An-Nahdliyah* and the *Penyiar Sholawat Wahidiyah*. In addition, I interviewed people who were not *kiai* but were involved in politics. They were activists in NU Since a variety of formal lines or attitudes related to the political situation were launched by various NU leaders, the different perceptions, attitudes or steps taken by some NU activists came to the surface. Such a phenomenon was of great importance since it helped to illuminate frictions which had arisen among NU members as well as the network among *kiai*.

In addition to qualitative data, I also collected quantitative data through a questionnaire. The questionnaire was concerned especially with politics, that is the politics of Islam as understood by Muslims, and the politics of the *kiai*. Questions related to the latter tried to identify the effect of the politics of *kiai* on Muslims in general in Jombang. In other words, they focused on the relationship between charismatic *kiai* and Muslims' general political and social behaviour. As political activities at the village level in Java are evident only during general elections, and the period of my fieldwork did not include such an election, I was not able to collect direct data about these activities during my stay in Jombang. Using the questionnaire, however, I was able to ask people about their voting attitudes and behaviour during the last four general elections (1977, 1982, 1987 and 1992), their perceptions of Islamic politics and the motivation for their political behaviour.

The scope of my research covered a variety of *kiai* leaders in Jombang. I focused my analysis on *kiai* leadership in particular in two *tarekat* movements, that is two *Tarekat Qadiriyah Wa Naqsyabandiyah* coordinated by the *Jam'iyah Ahli Thoriqoh Al-Mu'tabaroh Indonesia* and the *Jam'iyah Ahli Thoriqoh Al-Mu'tabaroh An-Nahdliyah*. Data from the questionnaire were confined to those Muslim respondents living in three *kecamatan*, that is Diwek, Peterongan and Ploso, especially those who lived in the towns of these *kecamatan*. The data I collected from the *pesantren* and the *kiai*, however, were not confined to those located and living in these three *kecamatan*. The data were mainly derived from the *Pesantren Tebuireng* (Diwek), *Pesantren Cukir* (Diwek), the *Pesantren Darul Ulum* (Peterongan), the *Pesantren Bahrul Ulum* (Jombang district), and the *Pesantren Attahdhib* (Ngoro). In addition, I interviewed *kiai* who had no *pesantren* and were not involved in a *tarekat*.

The categories of informants from whom I collected the data through in-depth interview are as follows:

 A. *Pesantren Kiai*:
   1. Kiai As'ad Umar
   2. Kiai Aziz Masyhuri
   3. Kiai Shohib Bisri
   4. Kiai Faruq
   5. Kiai Hamdan Adlan
   6. Kiai Hasib Wahab
   7. Nyai Musta'in Romly
   8. Kiai Mahfuz Anwar
   9. Kiai Sulthon
   10. Kiai Mochammad Dawam Anwar

B. *Kiai* with no *pesantren*:
    1. Kiai Abdurrahman
    2. Kiai Ismail
    3. Kiai Mahalli

C. *Tarekat Kiai*:
    1. Kiai Makki Ma'shum
    2. Kiai Abdullah Sajad
    3. Kiai Khoerul Anwar
    4. Kiai Rifai Romly
    5. Kiai Arwani
    6. Kiai Ihsan Mahin
    7. Kiai Arifin Khon

D. Political *Kiai* and Politicians:
    1. Kiai Abdurrahman 'Usman
    2. Hajj Yusuf Hasyim
    3. Muhammad Baidlowi
    4. Hafidh Ma'shum
    5. Kiai Abdurrahman Wahid
    6. Thoyyib

E. NU Activists:
    1. Fauziah
    2. Masykuri
    3. Hanafi
    4. Ibu Masrurah
    5. Cak Mat
    6. Ibu Sholihah

F. Intellectuals:
    1. Sukamto, SH., MA.
    2. Drs. Nachrowi, MA.
    3. Drs. Mahfudh Karim
    4. Adil Amrullah
    5. Dr. Nurkholis Madjid
    6. Ali Yahya, Msc.
    7. Drs. Musin

G. NU members:
    1. Lurah Ihsan

2. Mahfudh Effendi
3. H. Syifa
4. Ibu Hindun
5. Abdul Hamid
6. Kusnan

H. *Muhammadiyah* Members:
1. Shiddiq Abbas
2. Azhar
3. Cak Arifin

1.5 The Survey

The quantitative data used in this thesis derives from the survey I conducted in four villages of the three *kecamatan*. The four villages were deliberately chosen. As the survey aimed to collect data on the political affiliation of Muslims and the role of *kiai* in influencing Muslim politics, it was conducted in villages in which the influence of *kiai* and Islam in general is perceived to be great. I chose four villages which are very close to a *pesantren* but which also represent the two categories of Muslims, that is, devout and less devout Muslims. This choice was made to obtain a variety of Muslim perceptions and viewpoints on *kiai* leadership and Islamic politics. Three of the villages, that is Cukir, Puton and Peterongan, were under the influence of the *Pesantren Tebuireng, Pesantren Cukir* and the *Pesantren Darul Ulum* respectively; and the fourth, Rejoagung, was near the *Pesantren Shiddiqiyah*. The four villages are under the jurisdiction of the Kecamatan Diwek, Peterongan and Ploso.

Devout villages (or *kecamatan*) are those in which the Islamic influence on people's life was perceived to be great, while the less devout are those in which Islamic influence was less perceptable. In addition, a devout village (or *kecamatan*) can be defined as one in which the number of devout Muslims is greater than the less devout, so that Islamic life flourished. How I categorised a village was based on my interview with Islamic figures who gave me a general description of various villages in the three *kecamatan*. They pointed out that a village, like Cukir in Diwek, was devout because the Muslim practice of Islam is maximal. On the other hand, they called a village as less devout, such as Puton in Diwek, because Muslim's attachment to Islam is minimal. I tried to relate the explanation I received from these Islamic figures to the 1971 general election results in Jombang. I assumed that because of their greater concern with Islam, devout Muslims were more likely to affiliate with the Islamic party than other parties[11]. The 1971 general election results in Jombang revealed that the average share of

---

[11] A close relationship between religious attachment and politics has been widely discuss by scholars (see Geertz's, 1959a; Feith, 1974).

votes for the Islamic parties in Jombang as a whole was 43 percent. In the *kecamatan* which are commonly known[12] as devout *kecamatan* more than 50 percent of the share of votes was cast for the Islamic parties, while the share of votes for these parties in less devout districts was less than 30 percent. On this basis, two *kecamatan*, Diwek and Peterongan, were chosen to represent devout *kecamatan* and Ploso was chosen to represent a less devout *kecamatan*. However, this is only a general categorisation. Each district, in fact, contains a variety of villages in terms of religious attachment. For example, Diwek, a devout *kecamatan*, can contain a village classified as less devout. Of the four villages chosen as my survey sample, I considered two, Cukir in Kecamatan Diwek and Peterongan in Kecamatan Peterongan to represent devout villages. Two other villages, Puton in Kecamatan Diwek and Rejoagung in Kecamatan Ploso, represented the less devout villages.

I tried to survey around 200 respondents spread throughout these four villages. Unfortunately, data from only 182 respondents could be collected: 45 respondents from Cukir, 42 respondents from Puton, 45 respondents from Peterongan and 50 respondents from Rejoagung. These respondents were chosen from sub-village areas which were close to *pesantren* or to *kiai* in order to understand the extent of people's attachment to Islam. The respondents were chosen randomly from the list provided by local 'Ketua RT' (sub-village heads).

1.6 The Importance of the Study

It has been some time since Geertz conducted his monumental research in Java. Changes have since taken place as indicated by more recent studies and by my own observation. New studies are therefore worth conducting to delineate religious influence on Javanese life and its ability to govern social relations. The same holds true of the role of the *'ulama* or *kiai*, as informal Muslim religious leaders. Changes in Muslim life will impinge on *kiai* leadership in general and their relationship with society.

My study describes the general pattern of *kiai* leadership. It delineates the limitations of the *kiai's* influence on society. Although, in general, the *kiai's* position remains unchallenged, their influence in politics shows a change. The influence of *kiai* in politics is confined to those having strong emotional attachments with their followers. The finding of this study may not only illuminate the difference between the *'ulama* leadership in Indonesia and other Islamic countries but should also shed light on the extent to which Muslims use Islam to guide their worldly lives.

---

[12] Muslims in Jombang commonly referred to certain *kecamatan* as *abangan*, meaning less devout, and *santri*, meaning more devout *kecamatan*. Sometimes, as Professor Fox informed me, local villagers also referred to *kecamatan* as either *hijau* (green), meaning 'more devout' or *merah* (red), meaning 'less devout'. *Abangan* in Javanese means 'red'. *Hijau* and *merah* also indicate the degree of people's affiliation with the Islamic and other parties.

1.7 Organisation of the Thesis

This thesis has nine chapters, including an introduction (Chapter I) and conclusion (Chapter IX). Chapters II and III describe the nature of the *pesantren* and the *tarekat*. These institutions are attached to *kiaiship* and are managed informally by NU Almost all the great *kiai* have a *pesantren*, and some of them are also members of *tarekat*. These chapters are generally descriptive and focus on *pesantren* and two *tarekat* organisations.

The nature of *kiaiship* and how the *kiai* leadership is accepted by society are discussed in Chapter IV. The chapter also describes how Muslims in Jombang are socially fragmented under a variety of *kiai* leadership. Although their affiliation with certain *tarekat* has reduced this fragmentation, since the *tarekat* can accommodate a large number of Muslims from various districts of Jombang, the fragmentation still exists. This is not only because there are various *tarekat* movements, but also because the affiliation of Muslims with a *tarekat* is affected by politics. The politics of the *tarekat* are discussed in Chapter V and clearly show this fragmentation. The chapter also describes the involvement of NU in the conflict between the *kiai* managing the *tarekat* and the strict affiliation of NU with one political party which has resulted in widespread conflict among *kiai* in Jombang.

Chapter VI discusses the influence of Islam on electoral behaviour, and Chapter VII analyses the influence of the *kiai's* politics. If the *kiai* is a charismatic figure, to what extent can he influence Muslims' political behaviour? This chapter also discusses the change in the *kiai's* perception of the government. Chapter VIII discusses the effort of the *kiai* to remould their relationship with other Muslim groups. They are in the process of reformulating the essence of *ukhuwa Islamiya* (Muslim brotherhood). The chapter also describes Muslim efforts to expand *da'wa* (preaching) activities. These efforts, for NU members, are a manifestation of their determination to use NU as a socio-religious organisation as it was originally conceptualised when NU was established. For Muslims in general, this is a religious duty.

Chapter 2: Kiai and the Pesantren

This chapter is mainly descriptive. In it I will describe the nature of *pesantren* life, and briefly trace the history of three *pesantren* in Jombang. The *pesantren* has been the main institution through which a large number of Islamic society in Jombang have been educated. The significance of the *pesantren* lies not only in the fact that they have implanted a system of Islamic values which has created at least the appearance of a more religious society in Jombang, but also that the *kiai* who lead the *pesantren* are often involved in politics. The *kiai* thus represent a means through which Muslim society can pursue its political interests. Some *pesantren kiai* are political leaders with a national reputation. The fact that the fragmentation of the Islamic society in Jombang is related to the presence of so many *kiai* running *pesantren*, each having his own independence, authority and power in relation to the others (this matter will be discussed in Chapter IV), shows that the role of the *pesantren* in shaping the society is evident.

The description of the *pesantren* in this chapter shows how they have directly contributed to the development of Muslim society in Jombang. All of these *pesantren* are modernised, and their *kiai* are heavily involved in politics. The *Pesantren Tebuireng*, which is located in the district of Diwek in southern Jombang is led by Hajj Yusuf Hasyim, a national Islamic figure and politician. The two other *pesantren* are the *Pesantren Darul Ulum* and the *Pesantren Bahrul Ulum*. The *Pesantren Darul Ulum* is centred in the village of Rejoso in the district of Peterongan, which is situated in the eastern part of Jombang, while the *Pesantren Bahrul Ulum* is located in a region to the north of Jombang, though still administratively in the district of Jombang city. The *Pesantren Darul Ulum* has been used as the centre of one order of *Qadiriyah Wa Naqsyabandiyah* and is led by Kiai As'ad Umar, a member of parliament at the provincial level. The *Pesantren Bahrul Ulum* was formerly led by Kiai Wahab Chasbullah, a national politician and a co-founder of the largest Islamic organisation in Indonesia, NU.

The necessity to describe these *pesantren* became apparent from a survey that I conducted in four nearby villages. As the people's attachment to the *kiai* is great, the influence of the *pesantren* on the society I was surveying was evident. Hence, the change in the attitude of the Islamic society in Jombang in regard to politics or leadership in general, which I will discuss in the following chapters, is related to the change in the *pesantren* world.

2.1 Concept and Variation of Kiaiship

It is a common practice (throughout the Islamic world) for a well known *'ulama* to run a religious educational institution. In Saudi Arabia, as well as in Iran, the *madrasa* (lit. school) constitutes such an institution. In Indonesia, this institution is traditionally called a *pesantren*. The *pesantren* is a system of learning in which the students, called *santri*, gain Islamic knowledge from a single *kiai*, who usually has some specialist knowledge which he teaches. Before describing the *pesantren*, I need first to present the concept of *kiaiship* in general, since the main focus of this thesis is on the *kiai*. The *pesantren* need to be discussed because they represent an influential Islamic institution in regard to Muslim social development and also because they are important institutions through which the *kiai* exercise their power. Not all *kiai* operate *pesantren*, however, so those who do are more influential.

In various regions of Indonesia the use of the term *kiai* differs from that of *'ulama*. Horikoshi (1976) and Mansurnoor (1990) distinguish the *kiai* from *'ulama* in terms of their role and influence in society. *'Ulama* is a more general term that refers to a knowledgable Muslim. The *'ulama* as a group "had clearly defined functions and social roles as the literate guardian of the tradition which was held to be the very ground of individuals' and whole societies' primordial identities" (Gilsenen, 1973). In other words, "the most significant function of the *'ulama* has been their orthodox and traditional roles as upholders of the faith itself, by teaching religious doctrines, and ensuring orthodox religious practices among Muslim followers" (Horikoshi, 1976:232). The term 'ulama is widely used in the Islamic world. In Indonesia, some local terms are nonetheless applied to denote various levels of 'ulamaship. The term kiai, on the other hand, is used only in certain regions like Central and East Java. But it is common practice that at the national level the kiai is also used to refer to a higher 'ulama.

In Jombang such variation in usage does not exist as explicitly as in Madura (cf. Mansoornur, 1990). An *'ulama* from the highest to the lowest level are called *kiai*. So the term *kiai* in Jombang does not necessarily refer to those running *pesantren*; it can also be applied to the *guru ngaji* (religious instruction teacher) or to the *imam* (leader) of a mosque who has more Islamic knowledge than other citizens. Moreover, the hierarchy of the *'ulamaship* in Jombang is different from that, say, in Madura. It is not attached to any formal structure but is located more in social recognition, with the result that it is fairly difficult to recognise the level of an individual's *kiaiship*. Only those *kiai* running *pesantren* are easily recognised. They are recognised as higher *kiai*.

The pattern of hierarchical *'ulamaship* in general is sustained and institutionalised by the fact that *'ulamaship*, especially *kiaiship*, is ascriptive in nature. This pattern is more prominent in Madura, since at the highest level, that is that of *kiai*, the *'ulamaship* is inherited geneologically. However, although the basis underpinning one's *'ulamaship* is in fact geneological, it is the recognition of the society which determines it. An educated or erudite Muslim who would like to run a *pesantren* but does not come from a *kiai* family will have a problem obtaining the recognition of society, though it is not unusual for many prominent *kiai* not to come from a *kiai* family. So, the problem of ascription of *kiaiship* might need to be distinguished at various levels. At the higher level, *kiaiship* in Jombang is mostly inherited, especially among those who run a *pesantren*. The inherited pattern of *kiaiship* seems to be due to the larger role and wider responsibility of this *kiai* level and also to the extensive background in Islamic knowledge required. Most well known Javanese *kiai* in the past, for example, have studied in Mecca for a couple of years before they reached their *kiaiship*. In addition, as a *kiaiship* is almost always provided with the centre of learning represented by the *pesantren*, which is built with the *kiai*'s own money, it requires considerable capital.

Compared to that in Madura, the *'ulamaship* in Java, including West Java, seems to be more open, in the sense that it is established in a more achievement oriented pattern. Although some well known *kiai* in these areas come from a *kiai* family, the *'ulamaship* is not inherent in the existing social structure. The promotion of a *kiai* in these areas is based on social recognition. As long as a candidate is equipped with higher Islamic knowledge, social members will easily recognise him as an *'ulama*. So, a *santri* who does not have kin relations of *kiaiship*, also can obtain *kiaiship*. It is not rare to find that a well-educated *santri* is married to a daughter of a *kiai* just to continue the latter's leadership of his *pesantren* when it is thought that there is no member of his family to succeed him. In addition, it can happen that a *santri* married to a daughter of a wealthy farmer is asked to establish a *pesantren*. Another difference between *'ulamaship* in Madura and Java is evidenced by the fact that in the latter the existing structures of *'ulamaship* are in no sense hierarchical. An *imam* (a person who leads a mosque) for example, is not always higher than an *ustadh* (lit. teacher). Moreover, a member of MUI (Indonesian Ulama Council) at the regency level is not automatically paid higher respect than an *ustadh* in a village if the latter is more knowledgable of the content of Islam than the former.

Of the various levels of *'ulamaship* in Java, only a higher *'ulama*, that is a *kiai*, has a supra-village influence. An *ustadh* usually has limited local influence, not only because his Islamic knowledge is not as great as a *kiai* but also because he does not have a *pesantren* as a training centre. A *pesantren* is an important institution attached to one's *kiaiship*[1]. It is through *pesantren* that a *kiai* builds a pattern of patronage which relates him to his *santri*, and to the society outside his own village or town. This pattern of patronage can easily be established, since most, if not all, *pesantren* are privately owned by the *kiai*. This can tie the parents of the *santri* to the *kiai* because the former psychologically feel indebted as their children's education in the *pesantren* is free. Furthermore, the wider influence and supra-village pattern of leadership of the *kiai* enables him access

---

[1] As I mentioned, not all *kiai* run *pesantren*. But a great *kiai* usually operates a *pesantren*. Kiai Syamsuri Badawi, one of Jombang's most respected *kiai*, has no *pesantren*. He used to teach at the *Pesantren Tebuireng*. Now he is a member of national parliament.

to private and government agencies. The *kiai* sometimes play a brokerage role in transmitting the government messages of development to the society, and the society can more easily accept any government's program when they are presented by the *kiai*.[2]

The *kiai* in Jombang can be categorised into *pesantren kiai, tarekat kiai, political kiai and stage kiai (kiai panggung)* according to their special activities in regard to Islamic development. Nevertheless, a *kiai* in practice can be subsumed under more than one category. Kiai Khoerul Anwar, for example, is a famous *stage kiai*. But he is also a *tarekat kiai*, since involvement in the *tarekat* (sufi orders) is also a major concern of his. In addition, he is a *political kiai*, since he has represented NU in the local parliament. From these four categories, we can divide the *kiaiship* into two broader categories in terms of their followers. The first is the *kiai* who have larger followings and a wider influence than the second category. The influence of the former is spread throughout regions other than Jombang because some of their followers come from other cities or even other provinces. This first category comprises the *pesantren kiai* and the *tarekat kiai*.

The *pesantren kiai* focuses his attention on teaching at his *pesantren*, improving society through education. The relationship between the *santri* and the *kiai* in the *pesantren* has resulted in the family of the *santri* indirectly following their *kiai*. As the parents send their children to this *kiai*, they indirectly acknowledge that the *kiai* is the right person to follow and an appropriate teacher to develop knowledge of Islam. The *santri* are another source of support for the *pesantren kiai*. The *santri* are not only important for the existence of the *pesantren* but could also be the source that guarantees its very future. In addition, the *santri* are the source of the network that relates one *pesantren* to another. Those who finish their studies in the same *pesantren* and become *kiai* establish a network which connects them to their former *kiai* (their teacher) or his successor who continues the leadership of the *pesantren*.

The *tarekat kiai* focus their activities on building the *batin* (inner world) of Muslim society. As the *tarekat* is a formal institution, the followers of the *tarekat kiai* are formal members of the *tarekat*. The number of these followers could be higher than that of the *pesantren kiai*, since through its branches in various cities in Indonesia members of the *tarekat* would automatically be followers of the *tarekat kiai*. It so happens that the *murshid* (spiritual teacher) of two large *tarekat* movements, that is the *Tarekat Qadiriyah Wa Naqsyabandiyah* coordinated by the *Jam'iyah Ahli Thoriqoh Al-Mu'tabaroh Indonesia* and another *Qadiriyah Wa Naqsyabandiyah* order coordinated by the *Jam'iyah Ahli Thoriqoh Al-Mu'tabaroh An-Nahdliyah*, live in Jombang. It should be stressed, however, that what I have

---

[2] In Madura, for example, where people's submission to *kiai* is greater, the government, through a *kiai*, has succeeded in sending "spontaneous transmigrants" from Madura, whereas without his involvement such a program was faced with difficulty (see Mansurnoor, 1990).

mentioned here concerns the *tarekat kiai* who are *murshid*. Other *tarekat kiai*, such as the *khalifa* (*murshid* assistants), have fewer followers, since their authority in leading *tarekat* rituals is limited to a certain region. Followers from other regions might not know them. In accordance with the influence of the *murshid* himself, we should consider the extent of his influence in relation to his formal leadership. There exists a variation in the degree of a *murshid's* influence among those followers directly led by the *murshid*, such as those who live in the same city as the *murshid* or in neighbouring cities, and those who live far away from the *murshid*. So, the network laid down by the *tarekat kiai* is formal in the sense that communication between them is chanelled through a formal network (*tarekat* organisation).

The second category of *kiai* consists of the *stage kiai* and the *political kiai*. The *stage kiai* are preachers. They spread and develop Islam through *da'wa* (preaching) activities. The followers of the *stage kiai* may spread throughout the regency. A *stage kiai* can also have followers from other regencies. Such a case, however, is very rare, since only a very popular *stage kiai* is usually invited to give a sermon in another regency. Most of the *stage kiai* are very local, in the sense of being known by Muslims in their own regency only. The *political kiai* is a more mixed category. It refers to those *kiai* whose concern is to develop NU politically. The development of NU has for a long time been administered by this category of *kiai*, who do not have followers as other types of *kiai* do.

As there are a great number of *pesantren* in Jombang, there are more *pesantren kiai* than other types of *kiai*. According to the report of the Jombang regency office, there are around 46 *pesantren* in Jombang. As a *pesantren* is not always managed by a single *kiai*, the number of *pesantren kiai* would exceed the number of *pesantren* which they manage. It is, however, hard to count other types of *kiai*. The *tarekat kiai* usually occupy a rather formal position in the institutional structure of the *tarekat* itself. They constitute the *khalifa*, whose duty is to assist the *murshid* in performing the religious rituals of the *tarekat*. The number of *tarekat kiai* in Jombang is less than the *pesantren kiai*. On the other hand, the number of *stage kiai* could be less than *tarekat kiai*. There might be many *stage kiai* in Jombang, since the duty of *da'wa* is the obligation of all Muslim, not only *kiai*. But there are only a few *stage kiai* who become popular at the level of the regency.

2.2 The Pesantren Tradition

A *pesantren* is usually run by a *kiai* assisted by a number of his senior *santri* or other family members. The *pesantren* is an important part of the *kiai's* life, since it is a medium through which he expands his preaching and influence through teaching. In the *pesantren* system, there are several interconnected elements. The first is the *kiai*, the main factor through whom the *pesantren* system is established. He is the person who underpins the system. Secondly, there are the *santri*, that is the students who learn Islamic knowledge from the *kiai*. This element is also of great importance, since without the *santri* the *kiai* would be like a king without subjects. The *santri* are human resources, who not only support the existence of the *pesantren* but also sustain *kiai* influence in society. It is nonetheless common that some *kiai* have neither *santri* nor *pesantren*. The third element is the *pondok* [3], a dormitory system provided by the *kiai* to accommodate his students. *Pondok* is usually a simple form of accommodation and has fewer facilities than halls or colleges in Western universities. While a college or hall provides a student with a room, the *pondok* usually consists of shared rooms, each of which may be occupied by five to ten *santri*. The *pesantren*, therefore, comprises a complex of housing, which includes the houses of the *kiai* and his family, some *pondok*, and teaching buildings, including a mosque.

As discussed by Dhofier (1982), the *pesantren* usually uses a traditional system of learning. There are various techniques of teaching, but the most commonly used are *bandongan* and *sorogan*. *Bandongan* is a kind of religious instruction conducted by either the *kiai* or his senior *santri*. It is like a lecture attended by a large number of *santri*. In a big *pesantren*, such as the *Pesantren Tebuireng*, attendance at *bandongan* can vary from about 5 to 200 *santri* (Dhofier, 1982). *Santri* attendance does not depend on either their level of knowledge or their age. The system in this sense is just to provide the *santri* with regular daily learning, in which the *kiai* or senior *santri* read certain works written (in Arabic) by previous *'ulama*, translating it into local languages, and giving some explanation about it.

In a *pesantren* there should be some *bandongan* sessions which teach *kitab* [4] at various levels, from the lowest to the highest. Such sessions reflect the standard of teaching in any single *pesantren*. As each session just discusses one section of the *kitab*, learning the entire *kitab* will take a couple of weeks or even months. The *bandongan* system differs from the *sorogan* system. If in the *bandongan*, *santri* knowledge of grammar and Arabic language is assumed, the sessions are held for those who have already attained a basic understanding of the Arabic language and the Qur'an. In contrast, *sorogan* is provided either for beginner *santri* or those who want to have more explanation of the problems discussed in the *kitab*. The *sorogan* session is usually attended by only two to five *santri*, and is provided

---

[3] The term *pondok* and *pesantren* are commonly used to refer to the same thing. The term *pondok pesantren* is also often used. The term *pondok* is derived from the Arabic, *funduq*, which means a dormitory; whereas the term *pesantren*, according to Dhofier (1982:18), stems from the word *santri*, student. The Javanese commonly add a prefix *pe* and suffix *an* to denote the place where a subject resides. So, *pesantren* is a place where the *santri* reside.

[4] *Kitab* means book. But in the *pesantren* tradition, *kitab* refers to the traditional writings of *'ulama* in Arabic which are different in style and format from a modern book. Learning *kitab* in a *pesantren* is different from studying, say, a sociology textbook in a university. Learning *kitab* means learning a single *kitab*. In a *bandongan*, the *kiai* read only part of a section of a single *kitab*, translate it into Indonesian and give necessary explanation. In one session, the *kiai* may read only a half to one page. Usually no question is posed during the session.

by any senior *santri* who has knowledge and ability in certain subjects. This system aims to give special training to *santri* to assist them to develop certain knowledge and skills.

The *pesantren* in Indonesia has become a centre of learning and *da'wa*. It has played an important role in Indonesia because it is the oldest system of learning and education. Before the modern education system was introduced by the Dutch, the *pesantren* was the only educational institution available in Indonesia. It should be noted of course that the *pesantren* in Indonesia still plays its role as an education centre, but it has also to compete with modern secular educational institutions[5].

Socially, the *pesantren* has played an important role in the spread of Islam in Indonesia. It has become a means of formal socialisation through which Islamic belief, norms and values are transmitted and inculcated through teaching. It also constitutes a medium for developing Islamic precepts and maintaining orthodoxy. The *pesantren* is but one example of the scholarly tradition and the traditional schools of Islam in Indonesia today. But it should be noted that the *pesantren* maintains the oldest scholarly tradition that has ever existed in Indonesia and other Malay regions.

Madrasa is another system of Islamic learning. It literally means school. However, the *madrasa* system in Indonesia is rather different from that in other Islamic countries. It also differs from the *pesantren* system. The student of a *madrasa*[6] needs to pass in one grade to ascend to a higher grade in the same way as in a public school. The students at *madrasa* usually learn Islamic subjects, but the modernised *madrasa* system provides the student with a variety of material on Islam and secular subjects which should be mastered within a certain number of years. The *pesantren* system, on the other hand, specialises in Islamic teaching and has no time limitation. Due to its wider coverage of the subjects under study, the *madrasa* system does not produce or push the student to become an *'ulama* in the way the *pesantren* does. It is recognised that the contemporary *madrasa* system is a product of efforts to modernise the traditional system of learning and teaching. However, it should also be realised that the present *madrasa* system is not designed to produce *'ulama*. It is a medium to provide Muslims with basic Islamic teaching, which can be formally established at every district level. Also at a tertiary level, the *madrasa* system, like IAIN (State Insitutes of Islamic Studies), cannot produce knowledgable *'ulama*. Those students who want to get a higher educational attainment in Islam must go to the *pesantren*.

---

[5] Generally, Muslims in Indonesia prefer to send their children to public school. Although many *pesantren* are provided with a modern schooling system, the government shooling system is better. However, devout Muslims, especially in East Java, prefer to send their children to the modern *pesantren* since the children still receive Islamic knowledge in addition to secular knowledge.

[6] To have a detail description about *madrasa*, see Steenbrink's (1974) *Pesantren, Madrasah, Sekolah*.

In the *pesantren* and *madrasa* training system "though ritual accuracy and rote learning may be important, understanding and scholarship are never incidental; they are the most valued goal to be attained" (Fisher, 1980:33). The practical importance of this is that the *pesantren* and *madrasa* system of the Islamic world are "not merely a place of preparation for a ritual leader" (Fisher, 1980:33), but also a place that provides the *umma* (Muslim society) with more general leadership. Since the *pesantren* develops Islamic scriptural thoughts, it should be seen as a means of production of religious scholars, who may develop Islam or withstand all outside negative effects. However, as evidenced throughout Indonesian history, the *pesantren* has not only created village religious elites, who guard the Islamic tradition and its orthodox theology, but also national political elites who aggregate and articulate Muslim interests in their pursuit of an ideal world by accommodating or making reality compatible with the ideals of Islam.

Despite their similarities, there are some differences between the *pesantren* system in Indonesia and the *madrasa* system in other Islamic countries, especially Iran. The *madrasa* system in Iran has really been the source of Islamic strength. It has become a source of authority which competed with the authority of the royal court. The *madrasa* system in Iran could thus be considered a kind of legislature and judiciary (Fisher, 1980:33). The *pesantren* system, on the other hand, does not have such strong authority and position. It is just a medium by which Islamic learning is developed and Islamic belief and norms are maintained. Moreover, the *pesantren* does not show itself in a fashionable manner as a center for the development of Islamic thought in Indonesia in the way the *madrasa* in Iran does[7]. Nevertheless, we should not ignore the fact that the *kiai* as individuals often have some concerns in regard to the problems of Muslim society in general; and a few of them have expressed their thoughts on Islam by writing books or papers.

Another aspect of *pesantren* life which needs to be mentioned is the practice of *tarekat* (sufi orders). It should be noted that only a few *pesantren* formally practice the *tarekat*. As its character is to emphasise the exercise of *batin*, the *tarekat* movement in the *pesantren* has become part of their objective to maintain Islam. Of the four large *pesantren* in Jombang, only *kiai* of the Pesantren Darul Ulum formally practice the *tarekat*. As I will discuss in the next chapter, *tarekat* is a practice of approaching Allah by performing a certain ritual, and reciting certain *wird* (formulae, mostly derived from the Qur'an). It is different from *tasawwuf* (sufism) which is taught in almost all *pesantren*.

---

[7] Among *kiai* in Indonesia in general, there is a common view which suggests that the gate of *ijtihad* (lit. independent reasoning) is closed. This view resulted in the fact that the *pesantren* did not develop and offer new thoughts on Islam in its various aspects.

2.3 Nahdlatul Ulama (NU)

I would like here to give a brief description of NU as a socio-religious organisation through which most *kiai* in Jombang are organised. NU stands for *Nahdlatul Ulama* (lit. the awakening of the *'ulama*). This Islamic organisation was established in 1926 by the *kiai* of the *pesantren*, and was led nationally at that time by Kiai Hasyim Asy'ari from Jombang. The NU national leadership has since been held by *kiai* from Jombang on several occasions. As the relationship between the *kiai* and their society has always been extremely close, the society's affiliation with NU is taken for granted. It is therefore not surprising that the majority of Jombang's population are members of or affiliated with NU. Only a few are members of other Islamic organisations, such as Muhammadiyah.

NU was a socio-religious organisation when it was formed in 1926. Its aim was to develop and maintain the Islamic orthodoxy held by most Indonesian *'ulama*. The orthodoxy was the *ahl al-sunna wa'l-jama'a* [8]. Muslims who follow this orthodoxy are called *sunni*. The *sunni*, as mentioned by the hadith, are those who practise what was practised by the Prophet Muhammad and his companions. The *ahl al-sunna wa'l-jama'a* is hence a sect within Islam which, according to NU's *kiai*, bases its understanding on the four *madhhab* (schools of law)[9]. In their Islamic practices, the followers of the *ahl al-sunna wa'l-jama'a* continually refer to Syafi'i, Hanafi, Maliki or Hambali (the founders of the *madhhab*). However, the religious practices of NU are mostly derived from Syafi'i. The practices I mention here are related to those things subsumed under the domain of *fiqh* (lit. Islamic jurisprudence). In the domain of theology, NU refers for its practice and beliefs to Abu'l-Hasan Al-Ash'ari and Abu Manshur Al-Maturidi. In addition, NU refers to the basics or guidelines laid down by Abu'l-Qasim Al-Junaid in its practice of sufism (Dhofier, 1990:149).

Although the aim of NU was to develop the existing orthodoxy, its formation was also related to the development of modern Islam in Indonesia. Islam in Indonesia which had been exposed to Dutch colonialism for a long time was affected by the development of Islam in Saudi Arabia at the beginning of the 20th century. The emergence of the *Wahhabis* movement inspired some Muslims in Indonesia to form a similar movement to lift Muslims out of their backwardness. As the *Wahhabis* movement was based on the purification of Islam, its influence on Indonesian Islam was marked by the emergence of an Islamic reformation movement. One of the movements which became involved in the Islamic reformation was Muhammadiyah, a religious movement whose

---

[8] A saying of the Prophet Muhammad suggests that his *umma* will be divided into 73 groups. All would go to hell except one, that is the *ahl al-sunna wa'l-jama'a*. This saying is interpreted differently by various Muslim groups.

[9] They are different from what are commonly called modernist Muslims, who have, to a large extent, freed themselves from any attachment to the *madhhab*. I will discuss this matter in more detail when I discuss the relationship between NU and Muhammadiyah in Chapter VIII.

objective was to revive the spirit of Islam by returning to the Qur'an and the hadith in all its practices and thoughts of Islam.

Muhammadiyah was established in 1912 and seemed to have a similar concern to *Wahhabis* thought in regard to Muslim stagnation. They considered that Muslims were preoccupied with such things as superstition and conducting heretical practices. Such presumptions were regarded as sources contributing to stagnation. In the view of Muhammadiyah, however, Islam was essentially dynamic, and that was why it should always be stimulated in order to provoke development. The efforts of this movement confronted or even undermined the existing religious orthodoxy, which was more accommodating to the local practice of Islam. The basic principle underlying this orthodoxy was to nurture the existing understandings and practices which had for a long time been performed by Muslims, unless they were un-Islamic. The emergence of Muhammadiyah was hence considered as a menace to the religious authority of the *'ulama*, the guardians of the orthodoxy. The formation of NU was, among other things, a response to the purification efforts set in motion by Muhammadiyah. Thus, while Muhammadiyah encouraged independent reasoning (*ijtihad*)[10] as one of the steps in developing Islamic thoughts, NU's *kiai* persisted in their reference to the four *madhhab*, whose authority on Islam was reinforced and remoulded. This led to inevitable conflict between Muslims affiliated with NU and those affiliated with Muhammadiyah. Such conflict was endemic, especially in Java, during the 1950s and the 1960s[11].

Since NU was an embodiment of the *'ulama's* response toward the purification efforts set in motion by Muhammadiyah, it was in essence a socio-religious organisation in which the *'ulama* played an important role. In its organisational structure, NU has two institutions, the *suriyah* (similar to a legislative body) and the *tanfidhiyah* (the executive). The *'ulama* constitute the *suriyah* which controls the organisation. On the other hand, the *tanfidhiyah*, which is responsible for the policy launched by the *suriyah*, can be composed of non-*'ulama*. In other words, the function of the leadership of the *tanfidhiyah* is to implement what is formulated by the *'ulama* of the *suriyah*. It should be noted, however, that although NU gives a chance for the non-*'ulama* to become members of the *tanfidhiyah*, in most cases the chairman of the *tanfidhiyah* is always a younger *'ulama*, especially at the national level. Since NU is an Islamic organisation concerned with preserving the existing orthodoxy, most of its members and supporters come from rural areas.

---

[10] NU *kiai* basically are not anti-*ijtihad*. What is shared by them is the notion that to be a *mujtahid* (a person does an *ijtihad*) certain prerequisites are needed, since to understand the Qur'an requires specialised knowledge. The Qur'an cannot be understood literally. Because it is hard to find a well equipped *'ulama* to conduct an *ijtihad*, NU's *'ulama* share the same opinion as earlier *'ulama* that the 'gate of *ijtihad*' has been closed.
[11] I will discuss this conflict at length in a later chapter.

2.4 Modernisation of the Pesantren

During the 1960s, I often heard a common humiliating phrase directed towards groups of young educated Muslims who spent their time learning in the *pesantren*. The phrase, *santri budug*, sounded humiliating even to those educated religiously, but such an insult was an expression of the reality surrounding *santri* life at that time. *Santri budug* in Sundanese referred to the unhealthy situation surrounding life in the *pesantren* which made the *santri* vulnerable to certain diseases. This referred to the life of the *pesantren* in the past in Java, which was mostly very humble in comparison to that of modern students studying in a more secular university. The *santri* in the *pesantren* did not think about worldly matters, such as health, since such matters were deemed unimportant in comparison to their Islamic study with their *kiai*.

The *santri* were usually housed in a dormitory of the *pesantren*. Until the 1960s, most of the *pesantren* in Java did not have electricity, being located in villages. The humbleness of the *pesantren* life was also expressed by the life style of its *santri*. There were some *santri*, for example, who came to the *pesantren* without sufficient money. Their families could not actually afford their education in the *pesantren*. Their attendance was determined by their eagerness to obtain Islamic knowledge. To support their living costs during their studies in the *pesantren* these *santri* worked on the *kiai's* land (cf. Fox and Dirjosanjoto, 1989)[12] or were employed by the *kiai* and his family as a *khaddam* (servant).

Although humbleness dominated the life of traditional *pesantren*, the education of the *santri* has not been simple. The lessons taught ranged from basic Arabic and its grammar to Islamic law, sufism, Qur'anic exegesis and theology, which needed much time to understand. In minor *pesantren*, the *kiai* would be the single teacher offering such lessons, but in a larger *pesantren*, such as the *Pesantren Attahdhib* in the southern part of Jombang, the *kiai* was assisted by some senior *santri*. Although the *pesantren* tradition does not acknowledge payments in regard to teaching activity, the senior *santri* recruited by their *kiai* do their best in such teaching. These senior *santri* also conduct tutorials, which are separate from formal lessons, or offer private tutorials for those who want expertise in a certain field. They therefore have particular students.

---

[12] Most *kiai* came from rich families, so their *pesantren* were built with their own money. The *kiai* did not and do not receive any payment from the *santri*. On the contrary, the *kiai* could help *santri* to afford their education in the *pesantren* by employing them. The youngest poor *santri* were usually asked to help the *kiai* family by performing duties such as cooking or attending to the *kiai's* guests. In so doing, the *santri* not only obtained knowledge from the *kiai* but also economic benefit. This pattern of the relationship has laid the foundation for a long lasting client-patron pattern which marks the *kiai* relationship with his *santri*. The attachment of a former *santri* to his *kiai* did not cease even after the former *santri* returned to his own village, which in many cases was far from the *kiai's*. A feeling of 'hutang budi' (morally indebted) would be a reminder which pushed the former *santri* to get in touch with his former *kiai*.

This is a picture of *salaf* (traditional) *pesantren*. I need to emphasise here that in such a *pesantren* only Islamic knowledge is taught. Apart from the fact that they changed their system of teaching by classifying it hierarchically so that the *santri* had to follow certain lessons at certain levels from the lower to the higher, the subjects taught in *salaf pesantren* are the same. They focus on teaching Islamic subjects. A good example of this is the *Pesantren Attahdhib* [13] in southern Jombang. Here, the *santri* learn the subjects enthusiastically. I stress this enthusiasm since in the development of the *pesantren* it is becoming quite rare and is found among fewer and fewer *santri*.

Modern *pesantren* are different from traditional ones in many respects. The difference lies especially in their system of education. Not only are secular subjects taught in modern *pesantren*, due to the adoption of a modern system of education, but the aim of education itself also seems to have changed slightly. This change in the pattern of schooling among traditional *santri* seems to be widespread. It is easy to find examples of *pesantren* everywhere with this dualistic system. Only a few *pesantren* still persist in running their traditional system of learning. By traditional I mean those *pesantren* where only Islamic subjects are taught.

In Jombang almost all large *pesantren* have a semi-secular system of learning in addition to their traditional system. The *Pesantren Tebuireng* and *the Pesantren Darul Ulum* seem to be good examples of how traditional Islamic schooling has changed. Besides the *pengajian* system (religious instruction or teaching), where the *santri* learn Islamic topics, most of which are the works of traditional scholars such as Shafi'i or Ghazali, these *pesantren* provide modern schooling, '*Aliyah* and *SMA* [14]. Such schooling is held during the day, while the *pengajian* is conducted at night.

This tendency has implications not only in terms of the objective of the *pesantren* as the centre of Islamic learning but also in terms of the motivation of the students coming to the *pesantren*. The idea of *nyantri* or *mesantren*, that is learning at the *pesantren*, has changed. People used to come to the *pesantren* to be educated in Islamic subjects. They did not consider whether or not their knowledge would be competitive in the job market. Their principal aim was to obtain the

---

[13] This *pesantren* is managed by a very sufistic *kiai*, who stresses the building of the *akhlaq* (lit. ethics or conduct). This tendency is sustained by the fact that this *kiai* is a prominent leader of the *tarekat*-like movement called *wahidiyah*. This *pesantren* is attended by 400 *santri* who come from various regions of Indonesia. The classical system has been introduced into its teaching system without changing the subjects studied. This *pesantren* is commonly called the *pesantren karya* (lit. means working) due to the fact that a significant number of its *santri* work in order to afford their living costs during their study. Some of the poor *santri* work on the *kiai's* land, and some of them work outside the *pesantren* during the day. I was told that the *kiai* supports around 40 *santri* who help him with various work.

[14] '*Aliyah* is a *madasa* at the level of high school. The '*aliyah* provides students with Islamic subjects which range from 50% to 75%, while the *SMA* is a secular high school. However, as this school is owned by the *pesantren*, it also provides Islamic subjects which range from 10% to 15%.

knowledge needed to uphold Islam. Such a motivation is rarely found among contemporary *santri*. Parents send their children to the *pesantren* for more pragmatic considerations. Students study at the *pesantren* because of the wishes of their parents, who hope their children can obtain some Islamic knowledge in addition to secular knowledge, their main objective. The parents prefer their children to be well versed in more secular disciplines, rather than to be knowledgable in Islam. At the same time, they hope the children will be socialised in Islamic norms and values[15] so that they are not too secularised.

This tendency is related to the general process of modernisation occurring in Indonesia. The introduction of modern values into Muslim life has brought about changes in regard to the importance of Islamic knowledge itself. In present day Jombang, people generally give more respect to those who graduate from a secular university and have expertise in a secular field rather than those who graduate from the *pesantren*, even those who become *kiai*. This situation has both affected the change in motivation of parents towards sending their children to the *pesantren* and influenced the internal condition of the *pesantren* itself. But what is more important in regard to the internal change of the *pesantren* is the change in motivation of the *kiai's* own family towards obtaining Islamic knowledge. Few sons of *kiai* now follow their father's foot steps in terms of their education. Instead, sons go to secular university, mastering secular knowledge. It is not uncommon for the *kiai* of a *pesantren* to cry because none of his sons will follow his foot steps in developing Islam through teaching in the *pesantren*. This situation has, in effect, made it difficult to maintain the continuity of leadership in some modern *pesantren*. Such a situation does not necessarily mean that there is a shortage of leaders. The possible stock for *kiaiship* is sufficient. There are a number of *kiai* candidates in any *pesantren* who are ready to assume its leadership. The problem is that very often the candidates do not come from the *kiai's* family. In addition, they are not educated in the *pesantren*, but in a more modern Islamic institution. I mean by this that the candidates have graduated from an Islamic tertiary education like an IAIN. Such graduates are commonly deemed to have insufficient knowledge of Islam. These different sources of Islamic knowledge also undermine the general *kiai* leadership.

2.5 The Main Pesantren Observed
2.5.1. The Pesantren Darul Ulum

The *Pesantren Darul Ulum* is located in the eastern part of Jombang. It is around three kilometres from the centre of the city of Jombang. This *pesantren* is classified as modern. It has around 3,600 *santri* living in its dormitories. The

---

[15] The trend throughout Indonesia is to send children to public schools, even if the *pesantren* offer secular courses. However, in Jombang the number of students attending *pesantren* schools exeeded those at public schools at the beginning of the 1990s (interview with Adil Amrullah, 12 October 1992).

Pesantren Darul Ulum runs a modern school system from primary school to university. It has a rather large university, that is the *Universitas Darul Ulum*, one of the three tertiary educational institutions available in Jombang. In addition to its modern system of education, it also runs its traditional system. The *santri* in this *pesantren* go to school or university during the day and attend the *pengajian* (religious teaching) in the evening.

The *Pesantren Darul Ulum* was established in 1885. This is the formal date acknowledged by the *kiai* currently leading this *pesantren*. The *pesantren* was established by a young *kiai*, Tamim, who came from Madura island. Since Tamim started teaching Islam (*pengajian*) among his neighbours soon after he arrived in Rejoso village, the exact date of the establishment of his *pesantren* could be earlier than the formal date. His kindness and knowledge of Islam had already made him a public figure in his society.

Following Tamim was Muhammad Djuremi, a young Muslim who came from Demak, the northern region of Central Java. Muhammad Djuremi, who by that time had followed his father to live in Pare (around 30 kilometres from Jombang), was interested in Tamim's activities because Tamim was widely known as an expert on Islam and on *ilmu kanuragan* (lit. supernatural power). Muhammad Djuremi became Tamim's close *santri* and helped him to teach other junior *santri* in Tamim's *pesantren*. Kiai Tamim, as people called him a few years later, married Muhammad Djuremi to his daughter. Muhammad Djuremi later changed his name to Muhammad Kholil after he returned from the hajj. According to Sukamto (1992) the number of *santri* studying in Kiai Tamim's *pesantren* after Muhammad Djuremi involved himself in its teaching was around 200. Kiai Kholil, as people called Muhammad Djuremi later, succeeded Kiai Tamim as leader of the *Pesantren Darul Ulum* after the latter died in 1930.

In contrast to his father-in-law, Kiai Kholil involved himself in *tarekat* activities. He took *bai'a* (lit. allegiance) and followed the *Qadiriyah Wa Naqsyabandiyah* order (*tarekat*). He was then regarded as one link in the chain of the *murshidship* of the *Qadiriyah Wa Naqsyabandiyah* order (see discussion on this sufi order in Chapter III). His formal leadership of the *pesantren* lasted for about seven years. After his death, the leadership of the *Pesantren Darul Ulum* was assumed by (Muhammad) Romly Tamim, one of the four children of Kiai Tamim. Two years later, Kiai Kholil's son (Kiai Dahlan Kholil) returned from Mecca, and helped Romly Tamim in managing the *Pesantren Darul Ulum*.

The period during which Kiai Romly Tamim and Kiai Dahlan Kholil led the *Pesantren Darul Ulum* was a period of development. Both of these *kiai*, assisted by Kiai Ma'shum Kholil, contributed significantly to this development. The three *kiai* introduced *madrasah ibtidaiyah* (Islamic primary school) and *mu'allimin* (teacher school) in 1952 and 1958. The *mu'allimin* is similar to a high school. It then changed to SMP (junior high school) and SMA (senior high school) in 1964.

The formation of these schools aimed to introduce a new system of learning in the *pesantren*. It can be suggested that the leadership of these three *kiai* created a favourable situation for the development of the *pesantren* they were managing. All three *kiai* spent some of their time in Mecca studying Islam. The impression they gained from the pattern of teaching in the *Darul Ulum Addiniyyah* in Mecca, an Islamic school in which they took Islamic studies, inspired them to make a breakthrough in regard to the system of education in their own *pesantren*. Kiai Dahlan Kholil, who spent around thirteen years studying in this Islamic school, proposed naming the *pesantren* they led *Darul Ulum* (literally, the house of knowledge).

In 1958, the *Pesantren Darul Ulum* was shocked by the death of Kiai Dahlan Kholil on the 16th of March, followed by that of Kiai Romly a month later. The same held true when Kiai Ma'shum Kholil died in 1961. The *Pesantren Darul Ulum* lost its three well educated *kiai* within three years. The new leadership under Kiai Musta'in Romly, who succeeded his father, Kiai Romly Tamim, was successful in continuing the development of the *pesantren*. Kiai Musta'in, assisted by other *kiai* from his family, not only introduced a more modern system of education in his *pesantren* but was also successful in establishing a modern higher educational institution. Impressed by what he saw in Germany, Kiai Musta'in was keen to create modern Muslim intellectuals through the *pesantren* he led. He established the *Universitas Darul Ulum* in 1965. Like his predecessor, Kiai Musta'in was also deeply involved in the *tarekat* movement.

After Kiai Musta'in died in 1984, the leadership of the *pesantren* passed to Kiai As'ad Umar. In contrast to the *kiai* in larger *pesantren* in Jombang, the *kiai* in the *Pesantren Darul Ulum* try to introduce *tarekat* practice to the *santri*. Although the *santri* are not obliged to perform *tarekat* practices or to become members, the introduction of the *tarekat* has become a part of their *pesantren* programs. In the *Universitas Darul Ulum, tarekat* is also introduced to the students, the majority of whom are *santri* of the *Pesantren Darul Ulum*. This introduction is quite limited, since it is confined to providing students with a brief knowledge of *tarekat* and how it is practised.

2.5.1.1. Schools of the Pesantren

Almost one in every fifty members of the devout Islamic community in Jombang attended a *pesantren* in Jombang. Nevertheless, those studying in the *Pesantren Darul Ulum* come mostly from other regions, either Java or the outer islands. Some students come from big cities such as Surabaya or Jakarta. Although this pattern of enrolment might be different from that of the 1950s or 1960s, it indicates that the *santri* of the current *pesantren* derive from various segments of society. The *pesantren* in this sense does not interest only those with a strong Islamic background but also those with a fairly secular background. This situation further indicates that Muslim society, in general, still trusts the *pesantren* as a good medium for educating their children and building them morally.

The *Pesantren Darul Ulum* provides students with both traditional and modern systems of education. The traditional system of teachings (*pengajian*) is held in the evening. Its aim is to learn traditional works on Islam by previous Islamic scholars. The work of these scholars varies from *fiqh* (Islamic jurisprudence), theology, and sufism to Arabic grammar. During the day, the *santri* attend the formal school at the *pesantren*. In this *pesantren*, the *santri* are not allowed to study only in the traditional system. They are obliged to attend the school as well. On the other hand, *santri* whose main purpose is to attend formal school are strongly recommended also to attend the session of *pengajian*. The number of *santri* living in this *pesantren* is around 3,600. They live in 29 dormitories with 202 rooms (see Sukamto, 1992). The total number of *santri* attending the school and the university managed by the *Pesantren Darul Ulum*, however, would be greater than the number staying in this *pesantren*. This is so not only because the institutions are attended by local people who do not need to stay in the *pesantren*, but also because many older students, especially at the university, prefer to live outside the *pesantren* environment (see Table 2.1).

Table 2.1. The Number of Santri Attending Schools within the Pesantren Darul Ulum, 1990–1991

	Male	Female	Total
1. Madrasah Ibtidaiyah Negeri	187	181	368
2. Madrasah Tsanawiyah Negeri	250	374	624
3. Madrasah 'Aliyah Negeri	294	463	757
4. SMP Darul Ulum I	243	165	408
5. SMP Darul Ulum II	75	55	130
6. SMA Darul Ulum I	527	466	993
7. SMA Darul Ulum II	217	121	338
Total	1793	1825	3618

(Source: Sukamto, 1992).

2.5.2. The Pesantren Tebuireng

The centre of this *pesantren* is located in Cukir village in the district of Diwek, in the southern part of Jombang. It is around seven kilometres from Jombang city. The *pesantren* was founded in 1899 by Kiai Hasyim Asy'ari, the co-founder of NU. It is one of the four largest and most modern *pesantren* in Jombang. It has had a classical system since 1916 when its founder introduced two levels of classes in which the *santri* were prepared to take five years *madrasa*. In the *Pesantren Tebuireng* there are now some modern educational programs, providing either Islamic or more secular studies. The *pesantren* also includes a tertiary educational institution, the *Institut Keislaman Hasyim Asy'ari* (Hasyim Asy'ari Institute for Islamic Studies).

The *pesantren* began when young Hasyim Asy'ari erected a ten square metre building to teach Islam in a hamlet of Tebuireng. He started his teaching with only eight *santri*. This was a very difficult task since the surrounding community was only nominal Muslims. The religious services held by Hasyim Asy'ari were uncomfortable challenge to them. His determination to revitalise Islam, however, resulted in a great success. According to Dhofier (1982) this *pesantren* only needed ten years to establish its reputation. The number of *santri* increased to about 200 by 1910. Kiai Hasyim Asy'ari was then acknowledged as a great Muslim scholar (Hadhro Al-Syeikh) not only because he had successfully developed his *pesantren*, but also because of his knowledge of Islam. His intellectual genealogy included a number of well known Muslim scholars and many great *kiai* in Jombang, such as Kiai Wahab Chasbullah of the *Pesantren Bahrul Ulum* and Kiai Romly Tamim of the *Pesantren Darul Ulum*. Other *kiai* in other areas also learned Islam from Kiai Hasyim Asy'ari.

Kiai Hasyim Asy'ari initially learned Islam from his father and other local *kiai*. He also learned from Kiai Kholil of Bangkalan (Madura), an *'ulama* well known throughout Java and Madura in the 19th century. He also spent nine years in Mecca learning Islam from a great Islamic scholar, Syeikh Mahfuz Al-Tarmisi. His studies with this scholar also introduced him to a *tarekat*. According to some sources (see Arifin, 1993:72), in addition to the Islamic instruction which Kiai Hasyim Asy'ari received from Syeikh Mahfuz Al-Tarmisi, he also received *ijaza irshad* which enabled him to perform the practice of the *Qadiriyah Wa Naqsyabandiyah* order. Nevertheless he never passed on this *ijaza irshad* to another *kiai*, with the result that he did not have followers as other *murshid* do. Moreover, he did not allow his *pesantren* to be used as a place for *tarekat* activities[16].

Kiai Hasyim Asy'ari was not alone in managing his *pesantren*. He was assisted by other *kiai* close to him, such as Kiai Alwy or Kiai Ma'shum. Kiai Ma'shum was the first *kiai* to introduce the classical system in *Pesantren Tebuireng*. Secular subjects such as mathematics, geography or Dutch language were taught from 1919. Another *kiai* who was extremely helpful in managing and modernising his *pesantren* was his son, Kiai Wahid Hasyim. Kiai Wahid Hasyim recommended that the *Pesantren Tebuireng* introduce a tutorial system, as a substitute for the traditional teaching system of *bandongan*. Although not all Kiai Wahid Hasyim's recommendations were accepted by Kiai Hasyim Asy'ari, *madrasah nizomiyah* was then established in his *pesantren* in 1934. This offered secular subjects, which accounted for about seventy percent of the teaching program (Dhofier, 1982:106).

---

[16] It is important to note that individual *santri* of Kiai Hasyim Asy'ari, however, did practise a *tarekat*. Kiai Adlan, for example, was one of Kiai Hasyim Asy'ari's *santri* who later became a *murshid* of the *Qadiriyah Wa Naqsyabandiyah* order coordinated by *Jam 'iyah Ahli Thoriqoh Al-Mu 'tabaroh An-Nahdliyah*.

After Kiai Hasyim Asy'ari died on the 27th of July 1947, his older son, Kiai Wahid Hasyim, succeeded him in leading the *Pesantren Tebuireng*. The promotion of Kiai Wahid was agreed to by *Bani Hasyim* (the Hasyim Family), not only because he had a good reputation but also because he was a knowledgable younger *kiai*. He was a very active *kiai*, involving himself in the political arena before and after Indonesia gained independence from the Dutch. When Kiai Wahid Hasyim was appointed as the Minister of Religion from 1949 to 1952, he paid much greater attention to national politics than to his *pesantren*. The *Bani Hasyim* therefore appointed Kiai Karim Hasyim to lead the *Pesantren Tebuireng*, as a substitute for his brother, Kiai Wahid Hasyim.

Kiai Karim Hasyim led the *Pesantren Tebuireng* for only about one year. He was then succeeded by his brother-in-law, Kiai Baidlowi. Kiai Baidlowi was a very knowledgable *'ulama* and the oldest *kiai* of the *Bani* Hasyim teaching at the *Pesantren Tebuireng* at that time. As Kiai Hasyim Asy'ari had allowed *kiai* outside his family to lead his *pesantren* if there was no appropriate member of the family to occupy such a position, the promotion of Kiai Baidlowi presented no problem. It was decided to replace Kiai Karim Hasyim because the *Bani Hasyim* did not agree with his politics, which leaned towards the Islamic political party of Masjumi. As NU had left Masjumi and transformed itself into another Islamic political party in 1952, the proper political affiliation of the leader of the *Pesantren Tebuireng*, in the view of *Bani Hasyim*, was with the NU political party.

The Kiai Baidlowi leadership of the *pesantren* did not last long. After one year, he was replaced by Kiai Kholik Hasyim, another son of Kiai Hasyim Asy'ari, in 1952. This substitution was based on the right of inheritance to the leadership of the *pesantren*. Despite the unwritten rule suggested by Kiai Hasyim Asy'ari, which allowed a *kiai* outside his descendants to lead his *pesantren*, the promotion of Kiai Baidlowi seemed to be regarded as deviating from tradition, according to which the leadership of a *pesantren* usually passed from the former leader to his son. There was no conflict in regard to this decision about the succession. Kiai Baidlowi was not ambitious and was content to let Kiai Kholik Hasyim lead the *pesantren*. Kiai Kholik Hasyim then ran his *pesantren* for about thirteen years (1952– 1965). He was then succeeded by his brother, Hajj Yusuf Hasyim. Hajj Yusuf Hasyim, despite his busy activities in politics, has led *Pesantren Tebuireng* since that time. To allow more practical management, the *Pesantren Tebuireng* is now run by his sons.

2.5.2.1. Modern Schooling System

The *Pesantren Tebuireng* has played a large role in moulding the unity of Muslim society especially in Jombang. Together with Kiai Wahab Chasbullah of the *Pesantren Bahrul Ulum*, Kiai Hasyim Asy'ari initiated the formation of an Islamic movement in 1926. This idea received great support from other *kiai* in Java. His involvement in this organisation (NU) involved him in politics at the national level. He was then appointed to the presidential position in the first Islamic political party in Indonesia, Masjumi. He was followed by his son, Kiai Wahid Hasyim, who was appointed as the Minister of Religious Affairs during the Soekarno government. The current leader of this *pesantren*, Hajj Yusuf Hasyim, another son of Kiai Hasyim Asy'ari, has also been involved in national political activities.

There are some differences in terms of the policy laid down by each top leader of the *Pesantren Tebuireng*. The essence is nonetheless the same. The *pesantren* has developed into a more modern institution. However, this does not mean that it has abandoned its former traditional system entirely. Although its schooling system operates a modern system of teaching, it still has *pengajian* activities which are held in the evenings. All schooling is carried out in the morning and afternoon; and as in other modern *pesantren*, attending formal school is compulsory for all *santri*. The *santri* are also strongly recommended to attend *pengajian*.

The *Pesantren Tebuireng* now encompasses various levels of learning. The schooling system which was started during the leadership of Kiai Karim Hasyim has been further developed. It not only has the *pesantren* modern schools which provide both religious and secular subjects but also schools which provide only secular subjects. The development of this modern system of schooling seems to have changed the main objective of the *pesantren*. Most of the modern *pesantren* in Jombang have decreased their traditional Islamic teaching sessions. In other words, the objective of the *pesantren* now is not to produce the *'ulama* (many people doubt that the *pesantren* graduates have sufficient Islamic knowledge to become *'ulama*), but to provide pupils (the *santri*) with general knowledge. Nevertheless, the foundation for an ideal type of *pesantren*, that is the *pesantren* which creates the modern *'ulama* or intellectual *'ulama*, has been laid down by some *kiai*. To this end, the *Pesantren Tebuireng* provides ten kinds of teaching activities:

1. Teaching *Kitab Kuning* (older Islamic books)
2. Madrasah (preparatory level)
3. Madrasah Tsanawiyah (Islamic school at the level of secondary school)
4. Madrasah 'Aliyah (Islamic school at the level of high school)
5. SMP (secondary school)
6. SMA (high school)
7. Madrasah Al-Huffaz (Islamic school to memorise Qur'an)
8. Jam'iyah[17]
9. The Islamic Institute of Hasyim Asy'ari
10. Arabic Language

---

[17] *Jam'iyah* is a session in which the *santri* are given practical knowledge about organisation. The *santri* learn how to establish an organisation, etc. (see Dhofier, 1982:120).

The *santri* attending the *Pesantren Tebuireng* come from various backgrounds. Most of them come from cities other than Jombang. As in other modern *pesantren*, the *santri* do not only come from rural areas but also from urban areas, like Jakarta or Surabaya. The *santri* live in dormitories provided by the *pesantren*. According to the data provided by the *pesantren*, there are around 1,526 *santri* living in the *Pesantren Tebuireng* in 138 rooms among 15 dormitories. As in other *pesantren*, the number of *santri* attending the schools of the *Pesantren Tebuireng* would be greater than those staying at it, since there are some local *santri* from Jombang who come to school daily from their homes.

2.5.3. The Pesantren Bahrul Ulum

The *Pesantren Bahrul Ulum* is another of the four largest and most modern *pesantren* in Jombang. It is the oldest *pesantren*, since it was established in 1825 by Kiai 'Abdussalam, also known as Kiai Shoichah. It was initially called *Pesantren Nyelawe* (a Javanese term for *selawe*, literally 25) or *Telu* (literally three) because the *pesantren* had around 25 *santri* with three buildings. According to an information book written at this *pesantren*, Kiai Shoichah had royal blood. He was a descendant of the King of Mojopahit, Brawijaya VI. People called this *pesantren*, *Tambak Beras* after Kiai Chasbullah assumed leadership. Kiai Chasbullah was a rich man who often stored huge amounts of rice in his storehouse. The village and his *pesantren* were thus known as *Tambak Beras* (lit. rice-barn). The name *Bahrul Ulum* was given in 1967 by Kiai Wahab Chasbullah, who led this *pesantren* from 1926 to 1971.

At the early stage of the development of his *pesantren*, Kiai Shoichah was assisted by two *santri*. These *santri* were 'Usman and Sa'id who were later married to his daughters. 'Usman married Layyinah, while Sa'id married Fatimah. After they assumed *kiaiship*, Kiai 'Usman then married his daughter, Winih, to his student, Asy'ari (the father of Kiai Hasyim, the founder of the *Pesantren Tebuireng*). But, the continuation of the *Pesantren Nyelawe* was passed on through Kiai Sa'id. Kiai Sa'id had four children, one of which was Chasbullah. Chasbullah then became a famous *kiai*, and was regarded as the founder of the *Pesantren Tambak Beras*.

Table 2.2. The Number of Santri with their Place of Origin

Place of Origin	Number	Place of Origin	Number
1. Sidoarjo, East Java (EJ)	455	14. Kediri (EJ)	270
2. Tulungagung (EJ)	96	15. Surabaya/Gresik (EJ)	700
3. Pacitan (EJ)	145	16. Malang, East Java	113
4. Madiun (EJ)	105	17. Pasuruan (EJ)	160
5. Lamongan (EJ)	400	18. Bojonegoro (EJ)	215
6. Mojokerto (EJ)	192	19. Banyumas, C. Java (CJ)	108
7. Jember (EJ)	63	20. Probolinggo (CJ)	37
8. Banyuwangi (EJ)	40	21. Bumiayu (CJ)	112
9. Pati (EJ)	40	22. Brebes (CJ)	97
10. Tuban (EJ)	143	23. Magelang (CJ)	87
11. Banyuwangi (EJ)	25	24. Cirebon, West Java	162
12. Blitar (EJ)	63	25. Jakarta	127
13. Jombang (EJ)	476	26. Sumatra Island	135

(Source: Pengurus Pondok Pesantren Bahrul Ulum, 1994:37)

The increase in number of Kiai Shoichah's *santri* forced Kiai 'Usman and Kiai Sa'id, his sons-in-law, to assist him either in managing the *pesantren* or teaching the *santri*. Both of these younger *kiai* were advised to establish other *pesantren* nearby. Since the *pesantren* of Kiai 'Usman and of Kiai Sa'id were part of the *Pesantren Nyelawe*, some of the *santri* of Kiai Shoichah either lived in these *pesantren* or learned Islam from these *kiai*. After Kiai Shoichah died, the management of the *Pesantren Nyelawe* was centred on the *pesantren* of Kiai Sa'id and Kiai 'Usman. Kiai Sai'id was assisted by his son, Kiai Chasbullah, in managing and developing his *pesantren*. Kiai Chasbullah then united the two *pesantren* after his father and Kiai 'Usman died.

The most well known *kiai* of this *pesantren* was Kiai Wahab Chasbullah. He continued the leadership of the *pesantren* after his father, Kiai Chasbullah, died. He introduced a classical system while his father still led the *pesantren*. He established a three year *madrasa* in 1915, one year after he returned from Mecca; and in 1932 he provided the *madrasa* with a five year learning system. What made Kiai Wahab Chasbullah well known was his involvement in national politics, representing the NU. He was deemed to be a co-founder of NU[18]. After Kiai Wahab Chasbullah died in 1971, the *pesantren* came under the leadership of Kiai 'Abdul Fatah. Kiai Najib Wahab continued to lead the *pesantren* after Kiai 'Abdul Fatah died in 1977. Since 1987 the leadership of the *pesantren* has been held by a *Dewan Majlis* (a joint leadership council) which relies on modern management practices with several *kiai* as advisers.

---

[18] For more detail of Kiai Wahab Chasbullah, see Greg Fealy (forthcoming) "Wahab Hasbullah, Traditionalism and the Political Development of Nahdlatul Ulama". In Barton, Greg and Greg Fealy eds (Forthcoming) *Nahdlatul Ulama, Traditional Islam and Modernity in Indonesia*. Centre of Southeast Asian Studies, Monash University.

Like other modern *pesantren*, the *Pesantren Bahrul Ulum* has always been attended by *santri* of various backgrounds. It had around 2,503 *santri* in 1994. According to the data collected by this *pesantren*, around 90 percent of the *santri* come from places other than Jombang. The *pesantren* runs both a modern and a traditional system of schooling. The modern schooling is funded by the *pesantren* with little support from the government. In 1984, the *pesantren* established a tertiary educational institution.

Chapter 3: Kiaiship Through the Tarekat Movement

This chapter will provide a basic picture of various sufi orders or *tarekat* which exist in Jombang. *Tarekat* is one of the two institutions attached to *kiaiship*. In Jombang, its role is significant, not only because a significant number of Muslims here join a *terakat* movement, but also certain *tarekat kiai* are involved in politics. As will be discussed in Chapter V, *tarekat* in Jombang plays an important political role, contributing to the formation of what is known as 'Islamic politics'.

Whereas the primary activity of the *pesantren* lies in educating the *santri*, the *tarekat's* activity focuses on building *batin* (the inner life of a person). As the *tarekat's* role is to mould the society's religiosity by practising special *wird* (litany comprising Qur'anic excerpts recited many times), it contributes to the development of Islam in the society. The *tarekat* is an important institution attached to certain individual *kiai*. They are coordinated indirectly by NU. However, not all *tarekat* are accepted by this Islamic organisation. NU *kiai* only recognises and allows Muslims to practise *tarekat* which are *mu'tabarah* (religiously legitimate). These *tarekat* must have certain characteristics to be classified as *mu'tabarah*.

The discussion of the nature of the *tarekat* in Jombang will be a starting point to understand both the political conflict between various groups in Muslim society in Jombang and their political standpoint. In addition it will also shed light on the *kiai* leadership generally. As some *kiai* are leaders of certain *tarekat* which are affiliated with certain political parties, the conflict among *kiai* is reflected by clear political divisions in society.

3.1 The Nature of the Tarekat Movement

Tarekat practices are derived from the Muslim interpretation of the Qur'an. According to *tarekat* followers, there are verses in the Qur'an which encourage Muslims to practise *tarekat*. These verses are very important since there are other Muslim groups who do not agree with and are very cynical about *tarekat* practices. Of the most frequently quoted verse is : *Wa an law istaqamu 'ala al-tariqati la'asqainakum ma'an ghadaqa*, which states "Moreover, if they, the Meccan, keep straight on in that way, we will surely give them to drink of abundant water" (Sura, 72:16). The word *al-tariqati* (*tarekat*, Indonesian) mentioned in the verse, in the perspective of *tarekat* followers, indicates that approaching Allah necessitates a certain method, that is the *tarekat*. By using such verses, *tarekat* members not only legitimise their involvement in this religious movement but also express their religious satisfaction with it.

Tarekat are sufi orders through which Muslims practise religious rituals by performing special *wird*. The term *tarekat* derives from the Arabic *tariqa*, which literally means the mystical path to approach Allah. The members of the *tarekat* perform a ritual, known as *dhikr*, with the aim of placing themselves close to Allah. *Dhikr*, a distinctive form of worship of the sufi, is only one form of *wird* practice. It is the remembrance or recollection of God. The difference between *dhikr* in general and that conducted by *tarekat* members is that *dhikr* in general is done in more profane situations, while in a *tarekat* it is practised in a more sacred situation. In the *tarekat*, such *dhikr* are aimed at gaining a depth of religious feeling. The practice of *dhikr* is founded upon the Qur'anic order, "and recollect God often" (Sura, 33:40), since, "the recollection of God makes the heart calm" (Sura, 13:28).

Practising *tarekat* needs to be guided by a *murshid*, a carrier of the order (lit. spiritual teacher). The *murshid* not only provides his followers with certain *wird* but also helps them in practising the *wird*. *Murshid* literally means the person who 'shows the way'. This term is used in the *tarekat* to indicate that the *murshid* is to lead the members to approach Allah, using a certain way. Initiation into a *tarekat*, moreover, follows the receipt of *bai'a*. *Bai'a* is an important element of the *tarekat*. A *kiai*[1] told me that in Jombang there was a Muslim who practised *tarekat* without having a *bai'a* from any *murshid*. As a result he suffered from mental illness. There are seven *bai'a* given by the *murshid* for each followers. *Bai'a* in the *tarekat* is not an oath of allegiance as the term suggests, but an event in which followers receive certain *wird* and a determination to practise them continuously.

According to Kiai Makki[2], one of the leaders of the *tarekat* in Jombang, there are three stages through which Muslims develop their religion. The first is the *shari'a*, Muslim law. At the *shari'a* level, Muslims perform their Islam as it is ordered in the Qur'an and the hadith (the two sources of Islam). Like the physiological functions of human beings, Makki further explained, Islam cannot survive without people practising its *shari'a*. Secondly, as human life, from a certain perspective, does not make sense without *batin* (spiritual world), Islam would be nothing if Muslims could not reach the inner aspect of their practice of Islam. It is hence emphasised that the significance of Muslim life, in the *tarekat* perspective, lies not in the performance of what is ordered but rather in the acknowledgement of the necessity of such performance (not simply because it is ordered). This is the *haqiqa* (the essence or the Truth). Thirdly, when a Muslim is accustomed to this situation, he will move to another level of *ma'rifa* (gnosis). At this level, what is alive in the Muslim's practice of Islam is not his physical

---

[1] Interview with Kiai Arwani, 13 December 1994.
[2] Interview with Kiai Makki, a *murshid* of the *Tarekat Qadiriyah Wa Naqsyabandiyah* (*Tarekat Cukir*), 13 March 1993.

movement but his heart. It is his heart that continuously connects him to Allah. However, it is not easy to come to this level. According to Makki[3], it is necessary to perform religious exercises continuously and be guided by an expert who has reached such a level of religious attainment. The *tarekat* functions at this stage. It provides a Muslim with methods and exercises, so that he or she can reach the highest stage in religious performance. Practising *dhikr*, from the perspective of *tarekat* followers, leads to complete spiritualisation, for Allah has promised "I am the companion of him who recollects Me" or "I am with those whose hearts are broken for My sake" (*hadith qudsi*[4]). The basic goal of practising *tarekat* is hence "a purification on different levels, first from the lower qualities and the turpitude of the soul, then from the bondage of human qualities, and eventually a purification and election on the level of attributes" (see Schimmel, 1975:16). So, in the sufi world, the process of *dhikr* or *mujahada* constitutes a stage in the achievement of a higher religious level of *ma'rifa* (gnosis).

The main ritual of the *tarekat* is reciting the *dhikr* of *la 'ilaha 'illa Allah* (there is no God but Allah). In contrast to a common *dhikr* performed after daily prayer by Muslims, where *la 'ilaha 'illa Allah* is recited out loud, the *dhikr* in the *tarekat*, according to Kiai Makki[5], is spoken silently. Although the practice of *dhikr* may differ from one *tarekat* to another, the essence is the same. The *dhikr* is of great importance in the *tarekat* world, since reciting it can lead to safety in this world and the hereafter.

Although the essence of all *tarekat* is to approach Allah, each of its *aliran* (lit. streams, fractions) has its own character. In addition, there exist variations and nuances which differentiate one *tarekat* from another. In the *tarekat*, variation is marked by the numbers of *aliran*, each of which has different ritual practices. By practice I refer to the *wird* they usually use. Each *aliran* also has different *murshid*. The aim of practising *wirid* in the *tarekat* seems to be similar between groups, that is to attain a closeness to Allah; but because the *wird* practised by each group is not the same, the *silsila of murshidship* (the chain of the carrier) of the *tarekat* is also different. In the *tarekat* world, the appropriateness of *silsila of murshidship* is very important, since it is through such *silsilah* that the *wird* can be regarded as *mu'tabarah* (legitimate).

There are two criteria for a *tarekat* to be *mu'tabarah*[6]. Firstly, the teachings of the *tarekat* must conform with the *shari'a*. Secondly, the *wirid* practised by the

---

[3] Interview with Kiai Makki, 13 March 1993.
[4] The *hadith* is the sayings of the Prophet Muhammad. The *hadith qudsi* is the saying of Allah spoken through Muhammad. What differentiates the *hadith qudsi* from the Qur'an is that the Qur'an represents the actual words of Allah, while the *hadith qudsi* contains Allah's message out in the words of the Prophet.
[5] Interview with Kiai Makki, 13 March 1993.
[6] see *Kitab Pembina Moral dalam Rangka Membentuk Manusia Seutuhnya*, published by the *Tarekat Qadiriyah Wa Naqsyabandiyah* (1992).

tarekat must be traced through the unbroken line of links between the *murshid* and the Prophet Muhammad. That means that the *wird* was practised by the Prophet and has passed to the current *murshid*. The *wird* of the *Tarekat Qadiriyah Wa Naqsyabandiyah* are traced from the current *murshid* to the Prophet Muhammad through the great sufi, Sheikh 'Abdul Qadir Al-Jailani. In other words, the *silsila* must connect the current *murshid*, as the carrier of the *tarekat*, to the Prophet Muhammad. This requirement is meant to ensure that the *wird* is not invented, but rather was practised by the Prophet himself. If there is any missing link in the chain, the *tarekat* would be regarded as religiously not *mu'tabarah*.

The promotion of a person to *murshid* usually follows receipt of *ijaza irshad* (authority, special *bai'a*) from a previous *murshid*. *Ijaza irshad* (in the *tarekat*) is an important event through which the leadership of a *murshid* candidate is legitimised and accepted by his followers. It is through the *ijaza irshad* that the link of *murshidship* in the *tarekat* is continually passed down, so that the legitimacy of a certain *wird* is also acknowledged. The centrality of the *murshid* in the *tarekat* in Indonesia is evidenced by the fact that not everyone has a chance to be promoted to *murshid*, since it constitutes a link which determines the validity of a *tarekat*. While the *murshidship* can potentially be acquired by any individual *tarekat* member, only a highly qualified member can achieve such *murshidship*. In addition to *murshid*, there are the *khalifa* who assist in conducting the rituals of the order. The *khalifa*, sometimes called the *badal* (lit. substitute), not only assist the *murshid* in performing the *wird*, but also, sometimes, conduct *bai'a*[7] for the followers.

The 44 Tarekat Aliran Acknowledged as Mu'tabarah by NU's Kiai[8]:

1. Rumaniyah
2. Rifa'iyah
3. Sa'diyah
4. Bakriyah
5. Juztiyah
6. 'Umariyah
7. 'Alawiyah
8. 'Abasiyah
9. Zainiyah

---

[7] The term *bai'a* in practice is often understood improperly. Lay followers and some *khalifa* applied the term *bai'a* for *ijaza irshad* as well. The difference between these terms is apparent. *Bai'a* is a session in which followers are given certain *wird* by the *murshid* (and takes an allegiance to practise the *tarekat* rituals), while *ijaza irshad* is an authority given by the *murshid* to senior *khalifa* to become *murshid*. In some *tarekat*, conducting the *bai'a* for followers can be carried out by the *khalifa*. But in any *tarekat* only a *murshid* passes an *ijaza irshad* to a *murshid* candidate.

[8] Kiai Abdullah Sajad, a *khalifa* of Tarekat Cukir told me about these *tarekat*. However, he did not tell me the source in regard to these *tarekat* (Interview with Abdullah Sajad, 25 November 1994).

10. Dasuqiyah
11. Akbariyah
12. Bayumiyah
13. Malamiyah
14. Ghoibiyah
15. Tijaniyah
16. 'Uwaesiyah
17. Idrisiyah
18. Samaniyah
19. Buhuriyah
20. Usaqiyah
21. Kubrowiyah
22. Maulawiyah
23. Jalwatiyah
24. Barumiyah
25. Ghozaliyah
26. Hamzawiyah
27. Haddadiyah
28. Mathuliyah
29. Sumbuliyah
30. Idrusiyah
31. 'Usmaniyah
32. Syadziliyah
33. Sya'baniyah
34. Kalhaniyah
35. Khodziriyah
36. Syattariyah
37. Khalwathiyah
38. Ba'dasiyah
39. Sukhrowardiyah
40. Ahmadiyah
41. 'Isawiyah Ghorbiyah
42. Thuruqu Akbaril Auliya
43. Qadiriyah Wa Naqsyabandiyah
44. Thoriqotul Muslimin

Of the great number of sufi orders in the Muslim world, NU's *'ulama* examined 44 *aliran* and acknowledged them as *mu'tabarah*. Of these 44 *aliran*, according to Kiai Arwani[9], only seven exist in Indonesia. They are the *Qadiriyah, Naqsyabandiyah, Tijaniyah, Syadziliyah, Khalidiyah, Syattariyah,* and *Khalwatiyah*

---

[9] Interview with Kiai Arwani, 16 December 1994.

[10]. The *Qadiriyah Wa Naqsyabandiyah* is the best known sufi order in Indonesia, due to its large number of followers. This *tarekat* comprises two different *aliran*, that is *Qadiriyah* and *Naqsyabandiyah*. In Jombang, the majority of *tarekat* followers are affiliated with this combined *aliran*.

It is important to note that the *tarekat* world in Indonesia is associated with NU society[11]. Among modernist Muslims, the practice of *tarekat* is not found due to their orientation, which tends to be anti-*bid'a* (not heretical)[12]. In Jombang, in spite of the affiliation of the majority of NU members to the *Tarekat Qadiriyah Wa Naqsyabandiyah*, there are some who practise *tarekat* which, from the NU's point of view, are not *mu'tabarah*. For example, some belong to the sufi order, *Tarekat Shiddiqiyah*, headed by an NU *kiai*. This *tarekat* is regarded not *mu'tabarah* because it does not have an acceptable *silisila* of *murshidship*. According to Dhofier (1982) it is really a new *tarekat* established in 1958 by Kiai Muchtar Mu'thi in Jombang. Also, in Jombang there is a *tarekat* like movement called *Wahidiyah* or *Penyiar Sholawat Wahidiyah*, which focuses its *wird* practice on reciting *shalawat* (prayer for the Prophet). These religious movements are assessed slightly negatively by some *kiai* due to their novelty.

In brief, we can say that *kiaiship* in Jombang is related to leadership either in the *pesantren* or in the *tarekat*. These two institutions are of significance in relation to NU (as a socio-religious organisation). Both the *pesantren* and the *tarekat* are led by *kiai*. The difference is that the *pesantren* is an educational institution controlled by the *kiai* himself, while the *tarekat* is a religious movement, with a large number of followers, led by a number of *kiai* with a *murshid* as their central leader. Unlike the situation among non-*santri* followers of a *pesantren*, membership in the *tarekat* is formal, and emotional attachment between members and especially between them and their *murshid* is particularly strong.

Of the existing three sufi or quasi-sufi orders in Jombang, that is the *Qadiriyah Wa Naqsyabandiyah*, the *Shiddiqiyah* and the *Wahidiyah*, the first has the large number of followers. However, there are no exact figures concerning the

---

[10] Bruinessen told me, however, that actually more than seven *tarekat* exist in Indonesia. Among those not mentioned by Arwani are *Rifa'iyah*, *'Alawiyah*, *Idrisiyah*, *Samaniyah* and *Haddadiyah* (personal communication with Dr. Martin van Bruinessen). It needs to be noted that the *Khalidiyah* is not included in the 44 *tarekat mu'tabarah*. This could be because *Khalidiyah* is a branch of the *Naqsyabandiyah*.

[11] NU is generally considered traditionalist, while Muhammadiyah is regarded as modernist. NU, due to its principle of *al-Muhafada bi'l-qadim al-salih wa'l-akhdhu bi'l-jadid al-'aslah*, i.e. "nurturing the existing culture as long as it is good or can be coloured by Islam, and adopting the new better one", tends to be syncretic; while Muhammadiyah, on the other hand, is more puritan because it is *anti-bid'a* (not heretical). Such conceptualisation, however, seems to be inadequate. Currently NU society seems to be just as dynamic as Muhammadiyah. There is an emerging younger generation in NU society who have modern thoughts and attitudes.

[12] The criticism of the *tarekat* made by the modernist wing of Indonesian Muslims occured particularly in West Sumatra where the echo of Islamic modernisation sounded strongly (see Bruinessen, 1992:109–117).

membership in this sufi order, although efforts were made by asking the members to renew their membership. From my interviews with some *khalifa* of this order, it can be assumed that the followers of *Qadiriyah Wa Naqsyabandiyah* in Jombang may number around thirty to forty thousand. This sufi order consists of two groups derived from the same *aliran*[13] (lit. stream), that is the *Qadiriyah Wa Naqsyabandiyah* coordinated by the *Jam'iyah Ahli Thoriqoh Al-Mu'tabaroh Indonesia* and the *Qadiriyah Wa Naqsyabandiyah* coordinated by the *Jam'iyah Ahli Thoriqoh Al-Mu'tabaroh An-Nahdliyah*. The *tarekat* coordinated by the *Jam'iyah Ahli Thoriqoh Al-Mu'tabaroh Indonesia* is centred in the eastern side of Jombang and is commonly called the *Tarekat Rejoso* because its centre is located in Rejoso village. The *tarekat* coordinated by the *Jam'iyah Ahli Thoriqoh Al-Mu'tabaroh An-Nahdliyah* is commonly known as the *Tarekat Cukir* or *Tarekat An-Nahdliyah* because its centre is located in Cukir, a village in southern Jombang[14].

Both of these *aliran* derive from the same source. During the first half of the 1970s, their members were followers of Kiai Musta'in, the *murshid* of the *Qadiriyah Wa Naqsyabandiyah*. This *tarekat* split after Kiai Musta'in joined the government political party, Golkar. A significant number of followers of Kiai Musta'in left his *tarekat* and organised another *Qadiriyah Wa Naqsyabandiyah* affiliated with the *Jam'iyah Ahli Thoriqoh Al-Mu'tabaroh An-Nahdliyah*[15]. The rest persisted in giving their allegiance to Kiai Musta'in, who continued to lead the *Tarekat Qadiriyah Wa Naqsyabandiyah*. After Kiai Musta'in died in 1984, the *tarekat* was led by his brother, Kiai Rifai who died in a car accident in December 1994. The *tarekat* has since been led by a new *murshid*, Kiai Dimyati, who succeeded his brother.

Similar to *tarekat* in other Islamic countries, members of *tarekat* in Java mostly come from villages. In addition, the majority of the members are mature and older Muslims. This is not only because younger Muslims are not interested in joining the *tarekat*, but also the NU's *kiai* in the past did not allow them to join this spiritual movement. This prohibition seems to have been discarded, so that the *tarekat* can be attended by younger Muslims as well. It is not surprising now to find Muslims as young as seventeen attending ritual activities of the *tarekat*.

---

[13] I have to make clear the difference between the *tarekat* as a practice and the *tarekat* as an organisation which coordinates and manages such a practice. The *Qadiriyah Wa Naqsyabandiyah* is a *tarekat*, but both the *Jam'iyah Ahli Thoriqoh Al-Mu'tabaroh An-Nahdliyah* and the *Jam'iyah Ahli Thoriqoh Al-Mu'tabaroh Indonesia* are organisations which practise the *tarekat*. These two tarekat organisations managed some *aliran*. However, there is no exact number of how many *aliran* they comprise. No *kiai* of these *tarekat* organisations know about the number (Kiai Arwani of the *Jam'iyah Ahli Thoriqoh Al-Mu'tabaroh Indonesia* mentioned that this *tarekat* consists of seven *aliran*. See my discussion further in this chapter).
[14] The names *Tarekat Rejoso* and *Tarekat Cukir*, hold only in the context of Jombang.
[15] This conflict between *kiai* in the *Tarekat Qadiriyah Wa Naqsyabandiyah*, after Kiai Musta'in joined Golkar, is discussed at length in Chapter V of the thesis.

Like the *pesantren*, the *tarekat* does not have a formal organisational relationship to NU. It is acknowledged as an NU institution because those performing the ritual practices of the *tarekat* are NU members, and some of the *kiai* managing the *tarekat* are also involved in the NU leadership. Any problem concerned with the *tarekat* is discussed in NU. NU has thus been involved in many respects in (indirectly) managing the *tarekat*. The formation of the *Jam'iyah Ahli Thoriqoh Al-Mu'tabaroh An-Nahdliyah*[16], for example, was decided on at an NU congress in Semarang in 1979. It was done because Kiai Musta'in (the *murshid* of the *Qadiriyah Wa Naqsyabandiyah* and the leader of the *Jam'iyah Ahli Thoriqoh Al-Mu'tabaroh*[17] deviated from the NU's political policy by joining Golkar (at that time NU was a main component of the United Development Party, PPP).

3.2 The Tarekat Qadiriyah Wa Naqsyabandiyah

Muslims in Indonesia were introduced to *tarekat* practices in the 17th century. Bruinessen (1992), for example, mentioned Sheikh Yusuf Makasar as an *'ulama* who learned and then spread the *tarekat* among Indonesian Muslims. Sheikh Yusuf's introduction to the *tarekat* happened when he set out to study Islam and make his pilgrimage to Mecca. "In Aceh, a town which constituted a centre for Islamic education in Nusantara, he did a *bai'a* to join a *tarekat*, that is the Qadiriyah order" (Bruinessen, 1992:34)[18]. Sheikh Yusuf Makassar was not the only Indonesian *'ulama* who performed and spread the *tarekat*, since there was another *'ulama*, 'Abd Al-Rauf Singkil, who by that time had introduced the *Syattariyah* order. In addition, the *tarekat*, as Bruinessen noted, had already developed in some other regions of Indonesia. Sheikh Yusuf could nonetheless be regarded as an important *tarekat 'ulama*, since through his efforts the *tarekat* then developed in Nusantara[19]. He wrote some *risala* (short papers) about the ritual practices of the *tarekat*. Returning from Saudi Arabia, he then lived in Banten, Western Java, though he actually originated from the Gowa kingdom in South Sulawesi. According to Bruinessen (1992:35), Syeikh Yusuf became an influential *'ulama* and assumed a powerful position after the Sultan of Banten married him to his daughter and appointed him as his most trusted assistant. Although Sheikh Yusuf learned the *Qadiriyah, Naqsyabandiyah, Syattariyah and*

---

[16] This organisation of *tarekat* is similar to that led by Kiai Musta'in in the sense that it did not make any change in regard to its *wird*. It followed the *Qadiriyah Wa Naqsyabandiyah* tradition. Its formation as a *jam'iya* (organisation) was very political. NU was involved very much in this matter.

[17] The *Jam'iyah Ahli Thoriqoh Al-Mu'tabaroh* was established by NU's *kiai* in 1957. It aimed to coordinate all *aliran* classified as *mu'tabarah*. After NU established another *tarekat* organisation, the *Jam'iyah Ahli Thoriqoh Al-Mu'tabaroh* was formally not acknowledged by NU. This organisation changed its name to the *Jam'iyah Ahli Thoriqoh Al-Mu'tabaroh Indonesia* in 1991.

[18] The original wordings of quotation is in Indonesian.

[19] Nusantara is another term to indicate Indonesia. Nusantara literally means a variety of islands. What we call Indonesia now has hundreds of islands in which its people live. The concept of Indonesia seems to be recent. It has been acknowledged since the 20th century when modern organisations were formed by native Indonesians. People usually referred to various groups of people in Nusantara, such as the Javanese or Sumatranese, by their place of origin.

Khalwatiyah orders, his teaching was mostly on *Khalwatiyah*. Among his followers to date, according to Bruinessen, are nobles of Bugis and Makassar in South Sulawesi.

The early perception of *tarekat* by the colonial government was negative. The *tarekat* was regarded as a threat to the existing authority since some messianistic revolts were conducted by *tarekat* followers. The colonial government's perception of Islam in Nusantara changed when Snouck Hurgronje, a colonial government adviser, differentiated Islam from the political aspirations of Muslim society. Hurgronje's observations of Islam during his stay in Mecca in 1885 and his close relationship with a *sheikh* of the *Naqsyabandiyah* order, Muhammad Salih Al-Zawawi, not only changed the colonial government's political perception of Islam, but also prompted the government to allow *tarekat* followers to practise and develop their *tarekat*. What is interesting from Bruinessen's notes is that the *tarekat* was also practised by native government officers. The regent of Cianjur, for example, was a loyal follower of the *Naqsyabandiyah* order (Bruinessen, 1992:24– 25 and 107).

The increase in the number of Muslims from Nusantara who went to Saudi Arabia had a significant impact on Islamic development in Nusantara. It also favoured the development of the *tarekat* there. While the *Qadiriyah* or the *Naqsyabandiyah* order had come to Nusantara during the 17th century, the *Qadiriyah Wa Naqsyabandiyah* was introduced to Muslims in Nusantara at the end of the 19th century. This *tarekat* is basically a fusion of the two sufi orders, that is the *Qadiriyah* and the *Naqsyabandiyah*. The difference between one sufi order and another is not simply based on differences in regard to the *silsila* of their *murshid*, but also on their different ritual practices. The merging of one sufi order with another is common in the *tarekat* world. However, the *Qadiriyah Wa Naqsyabandiyah* that exists in Indonesia, according to Bruinessen (1992), is more than a merger of two streams of sufi order, but constitutes a new *tarekat*, in which chosen aspects from *Qadiriyah* and *Naqsyabandiyah* are combined and emerge as something new. This *tarekat*, Bruinessen (1992:90) suggested further, was possibly established by an Indonesian *'ulama*, Ahmad Khatib Al-Sambasi, who lived and taught in Mecca in the mid 19th century.

The *Qadiriyah Wa Naqsyabandiyah* order has developed well in various regions of Indonesia. The *Pesantren Darul Ulum* in Rejoso has been its centre for the East Java region. The five latest *murshid* of this *tarekat* derived from this *pesantren*. Kiai Khalil was the first *murshid* from this *pesantren*. Kiai Khalil received his *ijaza irshad* to lead the *tarekat* from Ahmad Hasbullah in Mecca. He passed on his *ijaza irshad* to his brother-in-law, Kiai Romly Tamim, who passed it to his son, Kiai Musta'in Romly. The leadership of the *tarekat* remains in the *Pesantren Darul Ulum*, with Kiai Dimyati Romly as the current *murshid*. Kiai Dimyati Romly succeeded to the leadership after the former *murshid*, Kiai Rifai Romly, died in a car accident in December 1994. It is important to note that the current *murshid*, Kiai Dimyati Romly, did not receive *ijaza irshad* from the former *murshid*, but from Kiai Ma'shum Ja'far, who received his *ijaza irshad* from Kiai Romly Tamim and Kiai Musta'in Romly (see the *silsila* below).

The Silsila of the Murshid of the Tarekat Qadiriyah Wa Naqsyabandiyah:

1. The Prophet Muhammad
2. 'Ali Ibn Abi Thalib
3. Husein Ibn Ali
4. Zainal-Abidin
5. Muhammad Al-Baqir
6. Ja'far Al-Sadiq
7. Musa al-Kazim
8. Abu Hasan 'Ali Ibn Musa Al-Riza
9. Ma'ruf Al-Karkhi
10. Sari A-Saqati
11. Abu Qasim Al-Junaid Al-Baghdadi
12. Abu Bakr Al-Shibli
13. 'Abdul Wahid Al-Tamimi
14. 'Abdul Faraj Al-Tartusi
15. Abu Hasan 'Ali Al-Hakkari
16. Abu Sa'id Al-Makhzumi
17. 'Abdul Qadir Al-Jailani
18. 'Abdul Aziz
19. Muhammad Al-Hattak
20. Syams Al-Din
21. Syarif Al-Din
22. Zain Al-Din
23. Nur Al-Din
24. Wali Al-Din
25. Husam Al-Din
26. Yahya
27. Abi Bakr
28. 'Abd Rahim
29. 'Usman
30. Kamal Al-Din
31. 'Abdul Fattah
32. Muhammad Murad
33. Syams Al-Din
34. Ahmad Khatib Al-Sambasi
35. 'Abdul Karim
36. Ahmad Hasbullah ibn Muhammad Madura

37. (Muhammad) Khalil
38. (Muhammad) Romly Tamim
39. 'Usman Al-Ishaq
40. (Muhammad) Musta'in Romly
41. Rifai Romly Romly   41. Ma'shum Ja'far
                          42. Dimyati Romly (current *murshid*)

There is an important note that should be presented here in accordance with this *silsila*. Sukamto (1992) notes that when Kiai Musta'in led this *tarekat*, there were two versions of the *silsila*. After 1977, according to Sukamto (1992)[20], one of the chains of the *murshid*, Kiai 'Usman Al-Ishaq (No. 39), disappeared from the *silsila*. This version of the *silsila* means that Kiai Musta'in received *ijaza irshad* directly from his father, Kiai Romly Tamim[21]. However, this version became a matter of dispute between *kiai* who were concerned about the *tarekat*. According to some, Kiai Romly had not yet finished giving all *bai'a* to Kiai Musta'in (*bai'a* should be done seven times), as Kiai Musta'in was still young. This means that it was unlikely that Kiai Romly Tamim gave *ijaza irshad* to Kiai Musta'in. Kiai Musta'in, according to some *kiai*, therefore went to Kiai 'Usman, who had received *ijaza irshad* from Kiai Romly Tamim, to complete the necessary *bai'a*. It was from Kiai 'Usman that Kiai Musta'in received his *ijaza irshad*, enabling him to be eligible for *murshidship*, succeeding his father. Kiai 'Usman was hence included as one of the links in the chain of the *silsila* of *murshidship* of the *Tarekat Qadiriyah Wa Naqsyabandiyah* (see Dhofier, 1982). For some *kiai* the deletion of Kiai 'Usman in the *silsila* has become a big problem for the *tarekat* followers in general since it means that Kiai Musta'in has cut out one person in the chain of *murshidship*. For other *kiai*, however, there is no problem with regard to Kiai Musta'in's *murshidship*, even though he cut out one person in the chain. According to a reliable source[22], Kiai Musta'in received his *ijaza irshad* directly from the former *murshid*, his father, Kiai Romly Tamim. Kiai Musta'in was asked by his father to continue leading the *Tarekat Qadiriyah Wa Naqsyabandiyah*.

Beside being a *murshid* of the *Tarekat Qadiriyah Wa Naqsyabandiyah*, in 1975 Kiai Musta'in was a leader of the *Jam'iyah Ahli Thoriqoh Al-Mu'tabaroh*. This organisation was established by NU in 1957. It coordinated all *tarekat*

---

[20] Sukamto (1992) in his thesis mentions two versions of the *silsila* of the *tarekat* previously led by Kiai Musta'in. The first one puts Kiai 'Usman (no.39) as a member of the chain of the *murshid* of the *Qadiriyah Wa Naqsyabandiyah* order, bridging Kiai Romly Tamim and Kiai Musta'in. The other does not include Kiai 'Usman. Dhofier (1982) uses the first version.
[21] I also received this information from Kiai Makki who showed me a printed version of the *silsilah* when I interview him.
[22] Kiai Ma'shum Ja'far made a clear statement about the *ijaza irshad* passed from Kiai Romly Tamim to Kiai Musta'in. Kiai Ma'shum Ja'far indicated that he himself heard when Kiai Romly Tamim passed his *ijaza irshad* to Kiai Musta'in. He is a very close *khalifa* to Kiai Romly (see Sukamto, 1992).

acknowledged *mu'tabarah* by NU. The *Tarekat Qadiriyah Wa Naqsyabandiyah* and its umbrella, the *Jam'iyah Ahli Thoriqoh Al-Mu'tabaroh* split after Kiai Musta'in became affiliated to the government political organisation of Golkar, preceding the 1977 general election. NU, as the socio-religious organisation which organises *tarekat*, then established another *tarekat* group when it held its *mu'tamar* (congress) in Semarang in 1979. This new *tarekat* organisation was the *Jam'iyah Ahli Thoriqoh Al-Mu'tabaroh An-Nahdliyah*. As I will discuss at length in Chapter V, the followers of Kiai Musta'in were bewildered when he joined Golkar, and some *khalifa* felt obliged to establish another organisation of *Tarekat Qadiriyah Wa Naqsyabandiyah* with another leader. The initial underlying reason for the separation of some *kiai* and *khalifa* from Kiai Musta'in was thus political. Later, however, some *kiai* used the deletion of a person in the chain of *murshidship*, that is Kiai 'Usman, as justification for their separation. As the *tarekat* should be passed on through a continuous chain of *murshidship*, this deletion, in the view of some *kiai*[23], makes the *tarekat* of Kiai Musta'in doubtful in terms of its legitimacy.

The change in leadership from Kiai Musta'in to Kiai Rifai in 1984 was deemed by some *kiai* from another *tarekat* as a further problem for the *Tarekat Qadiriyah Wa Naqsyabandiyah* centred in Rejoso, since Kiai Musta'in never passed his *ijaza irshad* to Kiai Rifai. In other words, Kiai Rifai had an ever bigger problem than Kiai Musta'in in terms of his leadership in the *tarekat*. Nevertheless, the *murshidship* of Kiai Rifai was regarded as legitimate by his followers because Kiai Musta'in himself indirectly hinted that he approved of Kiai Rifai's succession. Kiai Musta'in symbolically showed his trust for Kiai Rifai several times. He asked Kiai Rifai, for example, to substitute for him to lead the prayer when Kiai Musta'in could not do it. The acceptance of *ijaza irshad* by Kiai Rifai was thus symbolised through *ishara* (a sign).

However, Kiai Rifai's name, according to Kiai Arwani[24], would not have appeared in the *silsila* of the *murshid* of the *Tarekat Qadiriyah Wa Naqsyabandiyah* (Rejoso Version). Kiai Rifai died in a car crash before he could give *ijaza irshad* to his brother, Kiai Dimyati, the current *murshid*. Kiai Dimyati received his *ijaza irshad* from Kiai Ma'shum, who had received his *ijaza irshad* from Kiai Romly Tamim and Kiai Musta'in Romly.

---

[23] Only relatively few *kiai* held this perspective. They nonetheless stated their judgement clearly. One *kiai*, for example, suggested that "dengan begitu, umat menjadi kasihan" (with this situation I feel sorry for the *umma*). But this does not necessarily mean that no lay followers of the *tarekat* have the same perspective as the above *kiai*. A lay follower of the *Tarekat Cukir* suggested that "Tarekat Rejoso itu silsilahnya pedot" (the *tarekat* formerly led by Kiai Musta'in has its *silsila* disconnected).
[24] Interview with Kiai Arwani, 13 December 1994. I interviewed this *kiai* a few days after Kiai Rifai died. The question of "who is going to succeed Kiai Rifai" spread among followers. Arwani is one of the senior *khalifa* of the *Tarekat Rejoso*. He knew that Kiai Dimyati received *ijaza irshad* from Kiai Ma'shum.

Despite the split of the *Tarekat Qadiriyah Wa Naqsyabandiyah* previously led by Kiai Musta'in, the leadership of Kiai Rifai and (now) Kiai Dimyati has been strongly accepted. The necessity for loyalty and obedience to the leaders of the *tarekat*, especially the *murshid*, are factors that bind the followers and their *murshid* together. There is no problem at all for followers to give their allegiance to the new *murshid* and their respect to the family of previous *murshid*. That is why the *Pesantren Darul Ulum* has been continuously attended by loyal followers of the *Tarekat Qadiriyah Wa Naqsyabandiyah* (Rejoso).

It is estimated that around ten to fifteen thousand[25] Muslims in Jombang are members of this *tarekat*. This sufi order has around fifty six *khususiya* (location for *dhikr* ritual), and according to its administrative staff, each place of *khususiya* is attended by 200 followers. *Khususiya* or *istighosa* are *tarekat* rituals usually performed by an *imam* (a senior *tarekat* member) on a weekly basis. The biggest session of *khususiya* is usually held once a week in the *Pesantren Darul Ulum*. This *khususiya* is more crowded since it is attended not only by followers from Jombang but also from other regencies of East Java. Attending *khususiya* at the *Pesantren Darul Ulum* gives the followers the chance to perform *dhikr* held by the *murshid*, and they can also visit to the graves[26] of previous *murshid* who are buried at the backyard of the *pesantren*. In addition, the current *murshid* in this session can do *bai'a* for his new followers or followers who have not completed their *bai'a*[27].

---

[25] It is hard to obtain exact data about the number of *tarekat* followers in Jombang because the *tarekat* is administratively weak. The above data may be an underestimation, since it is far lower than the number of followers of the *Tarekat Cukir*. According to one of its *khalifa*, Kiai Abdullah Sajad (interview, 25 November 1994), the *Tarekat Cukir* has around 40,000 followers in Jombang. I do not know whether this *kiai* exaggerated the number of his *tarekat* followers, but from my observation during a big ritual such as 'sewelasan', which commemorates the death of a great sufi, Sheikh 'Abd 'Abdul Qadir Al-Jailani, the number of followers of the *Tarekat Rejoso* was larger than that attending the same ritual held by the *Tarekat Cukir*. Nevertheless, this number does not indicate how big both *tarekat* are in Jombang itself, since followers coming to such rituals are not simply derived from Jombang. It is common for followers from other regions to attend the rituals held in Jombang.

[26] It is a cultural ritual of traditionalist Muslims to visit the grave of great *'ulama* such as a *murshid* or a saint. To have a description of 'visting grave', see Fox (1991), "Ziarah Visits to the Tombs of the Wali, the Founders of Islam on Java". In Ricklefs, M.C. *Islam in the Indonesian Context*. Clayton, Victoria: Centre for Southeast Asian Studies, Monash University.

[27] Concerning the pattern of leadership in this *tarekat* I found a difference between Kiai Musta'in and Kiai Rifai. When Kiai Musta'in led the *tarekat*, *bai'a* for followers could be conducted by himself as the *murshid* or his *khalifa*. On the other hand, Kiai Rifai centralised the authority so that only he could do *bai'a* for his followers. Kiai Rifai was hence very busy since he had to do *bai'a* for his followers who lived in Jombang as well as in other regions of Indonesia. I do not know the reasons underlying his policy. I assume that Kiai Rifai had learned from the failure of the leadership of Kiai Musta'in. Kiai Musta'in often gave authority to some of his *khalifa* to do *bai'a* for his followers as he could not attend all the local *khususiya* held by his *khalifa* because his leadership was not confined to his *tarekat* in Jombang. This situation gave the *khalifa* a chance to build a close relationship with the followers. In the *tarekat* world, there seems to be no differentiation between the respect given to the *murshid* and his *khalifa*, since both are religiously good Muslims. Discriminating against them would bear a consequence for the *baraka* (divine grace) the followers might receive from practising the *tarekat*. Accordingly, the closeness of the *khalifa* and the followers built through "giving *bai'a*" and the continuous social encounter during the local rituals of *khususiya*, can result in loyalty to the *khalifa*

3.3 The Jam'iyah Ahli Thoriqoh Al-Mu'tabaroh An-Nahdliyah: Tarekat Cukir

The *Tarekat Qadiriyah Wa Naqsyabandiyah* split into two after its leader, Kiai Musta'in, joined Golkar in the second half of the 1970s. To coordinate especially followers of the *Tarekat Qadiriyah Wa Naqsyabandiyah* who were disappointed with Kiai Musta'in's political actions, NU subsequently formally established another *tarekat* organisation called the *Jam'iyah Ahli Thoriqoh Al-Mu'tabaroh An-Nahdliyah*. Although this organisation is coordinating various *tarekat*, it is mainly represented and managed by followers of the *Qadiriyah Wa Naqsyabandiyah*. In Jombang, the *Jam'iyah Ahli Thoriqoh Al-Mu'tabaroh An-Nahdliyah is represented only by* the followers of the *Qadiriyah Wa Naqsyabandiyah* who separated from Kiai Musta'in's leadership.

Although the establishment of the *Tarekat Cukir* was a reaction against Kiai Musta'in, its ritual practices are those of *Qadiriyah Wa Naqsyabandiyah*. The formation of this *tarekat* initially served to coordinate those former followers of Kiai Musta'in who were bewildered and disappointed with his political steps. Therefore, the formation of *Tarekat Cukir* and the *Jam'iyah Ahli Thoriqoh Al-Mu'tabaroh An-Nahdliyah* was just a slight transformation of the same *Qadiriyah Wa Naqsyabandiyah* formerly led by Kiai Musta'in and a similar association established in 1957 by NU respectively.

The embryo of the *Jam'iyah Ahli Thoriqoh Al-Mu'tabaroh An-Nahdliyah* was created in Jombang. Many *kiai* asked NU to do something following their dissatisfaction with the political actions of Kiai Musta'in. Muhammad Baidlowi, the NU leader in Jombang, then initiated the formation of another association, the *Tarekat Nahdlatul Ulama*. Muhammad Baidlowi was uncomfortable with this since he had a close relationship with Kiai Musta'in (his wife is a sister of Kiai Musta'in's wife). Muhammad Baidlowi thus tried to involve other NU leading figures, who also had close relations with Kiai Musta'in, to reduce the possible negative reaction of Kiai Musta'in. The document for the formation of the *Tarekat Nahdlatul Ulama* in Jombang was therefore signed by Muhammad Baidlowi (chairman), Najib Wahab (president) and Khatib (secretary). Muhammad Baildowi

---

being greater than that to the *murshid* himself. That was why when some of the *khalifa* withdrew their allegiance from Kiai Musta'in, some followers at the grassroots level easily followed their *khalifa* in leaving the *murshid*. Kiai Rifai was aware of this and did not want what happened to Kiai Musta'in happening again to himself. Hence, he alone gave *bai'a* to his followers. In addition, he often attended local *khususiya* conducted by his *khalifa* or *imam*. The leadership of Kiai Dimyati, however, may change the pattern laid down by Kiai Rifai in regard to such centralisation of power. According to Kiai Arwani, it is very possible that Kiai Dimyati will give more opportunity to his *khalifa* to conduct *bai'a* for followers, not only because it is customary but also because the number of his *tarekat* followers is increasing. I carried out my research in Jombang from November 1992 to October 1993. After I attended the NU congress in December 1994 in Tasikmalaya, I went to Jombang to conduct interviews. In the second week of December 1994, Kiai Rifai died. Kiai Dimyati was then promoted to *murshid* I left Jombang at the end of December. I can not therefore discuss the Kiai Dimyati's leadership in any detail because I did not have much time to see it.

chose Najib Wahab instead of Kiai Adlan Ali, who was formally more appropriate since he was higher in rank than Najib, because Najib Wahab was the brother of Kiai Musta'in's wife. Khatib, on the other hand, had a familial relationship with Kiai Musta'in, since his father was Kiai Musta'in's uncle[28]. The establishment of the *Tarekat Nahdlatul Ulama* in Jombang was then put forward to the NU congress in Semarang in 1979. It then became the stimulus for the formation of the *Jam'iyah Ahli Thoriqoh Al-Mu'tabaroh An-Nahdliyah*.

Kiai Adlan Ali from Jombang was promoted to be the main *murshid* of the *Qadiriyah Wa Naqsyabandiyah* (the *Jam'iyah Ahli Thoriqoh Al-Mu'tabaroh An-Nahdliyah* version). When he joined the *Tarekat Rejoso*, he was a *khalifa* of Kiai Musta'in. He received his *ijaza irshad* from Kiai Muslih Abdurrahman (Mranggen, Semarang). With this *ijaza irshad* Kiai Adlan established another *Tarekat Qadiriyah Wa Naqsyabandiyah* organisation with a *silsila* which was separate from the *Tarekat Qadiriyah Wa naqsyabandiyah* led by Kiai Musta'in.

The Silsilah of the Murshid of the Tarekat Qadiriyah Wa Naqsyabandiyah (Tarekat Cukir Version):

1. The Prophet Muhammad
2. 'Ali Ibn Abi Thalib
3. Husein Ibn Ali
4. Zainal-Abidin
5. Muhammad Al-Baqir
6. Ja'far Al-Sadiq
7. Musa al-Kazim
8. Abu Hasan 'Ali Ibn Musa Al-Riza
9. Ma'ruf Al-Karkhi
10. Sari A-Saqati
11. Abu Qasim Al-Junaid Al-Baghdadi
12. Abu Bakr Al-Shibli
13. 'Abdul Wahid Al-Tamimi
14. 'Abdul Faraj Al-Tartusi
15. Abu Hasan 'Ali Al-Hakkari
16. Abu Sa'id Al-Makhzumi
17. 'Abdul Qadir Al-Jailani
18. 'Abdul Aziz
19. Muhammad Al-Hattak
20. Syams Al-Din
21. Syarif Al-Din
22. Zain Al-Din
23. Nur Al-Din

---

[28] Interview with Muhammad Baidlowi, 10 September 1993.

24. Wali Al-Din
25. Husam Al-Din
26. Yahya
27. Abi Bakr
28. 'Abd Rahim
29. 'Usman
30. Kamal Al-Din
31. 'Abdul Fattah
32. Muhammad Murad
33. Syams Al-Din
34. Ahmad Khatib Al-Sambasi
35. 'Abdul Karim

36. Asnawi Banten	36. Ahmad Hasbullah ibn Muhammad Madura
37. 'Abdul Lathif Banten	37. (Muhammad) Khalil
38. Muslih Abdurrahman	38. (Muhammad) Romly Tamim
	39. (Muhammad) Adlan Ali

In addition, the promotion of Kiai Adlan to the *murshid* of this new *tarekat* organisation automatically excluded Kiai Musta'in in his *silsilah* of the *Qadiriyah Wa Naqsyabandiyah*. This was because the *ijaza irshad* received by Kiai Muslih Abdurrahman was not derived from Kiai Musta'in. Kiai Muslih Abdurrahman, instead, received his *ijaza irshad* from Kiai 'Abdul Latief; and Kiai 'Abdul Latief obtained his *ijaza irshad* from Kiai Asnawi Banten, who, together with Kiai Ahmad Chasbullah received his *ijaza irshad* from Kiai 'Abdul Karim Banten. According to another source[29], Kiai Adlan also received *ijaza irshad* from Kiai Romly Tamim, Kiai Musta'in's father (see the *silsilah* above).

Kiai Adlan Ali was also promoted to the national leader of the *Jam'iyah Ahli Thoriqoh Al-Mu'tabaroh An-Nahdliyah*. He died in 1991. There are now three *murshid* of the *Tarekat Cukir* in Jombang who can conduct *bai'a* for followers or give *ijaza irshad* to a *murshid* candidate. The three *murshid* are Kiai Makki, who used to be one of the *khalifa* of Kiai Musta'in, Kiai Hisyam and Kiai Sholihin.

---

[29] If Kiai Adlan actually had received *ijaza irshad* from Kiai Romly, why did not he directly declare his intention to establish another leadership of the *Tarekat Qadiriyah Wa Naqsyabandiyah* when he was disappointed with Kiai Musta'in's political steps (without having to go to Kiai Muslih to have an *ijaza irshad*)? Most *khalifa* in Jombang suggested that it is common for a *murshid* candidate to receive more than one *ijaza irshad*. In my judgement, the *ijaza irshad* of Kiai Adlan from Kiai Muslih was more political. It was needed to satisfy followers generally in regard to their separation from former *Qadiriyah Wa Naqsyabandiyah*. As Kiai Muslih's *murshidship* was not received through Rejoso *kiai*, the reformation of this *Tarekat Qadiriyah Wa Naqsyabandiyah* was more satisfying. It was absolutely not related to former *Qadiriyah Wa Naqsyabandiyah* which was continually passed through *murshid* from Rejoso. As we can see from the *silsila*, Kiai Muslih's *murshidship* was received not through Rejoso Kiai, that is Kiai Muhammad Khalil and Kiai Romly Tamim, but rather through Kiai Asnawi Banten.

In addition to these three *murshid*, commonly called the *khalifa kubro* (lit. major *khalifa*), the *Tarekat Cukir* has four *khalifa sughro* (lit. minor *khalifa*). They are Kiai Abdullah Sajad, Kiai Khoerul Anwar, Kiai Rifai Marzuki and Kiai Abdul Hamid. While the *khalifa kubro* are classified as *murshid*, the *khalifa sughro* cannot conduct *bai'a* for the followers. The *khalifa sughro* are the main assistants to the *murshid*, either in regard to running the *tarekat* organisationally or performing the *tarekat* ritually. It is evident therefore that, in terms of the structure of either *murshidship* or *khalifaship*, the *Tarekat Cukir* is different from the *Tarekat Rejoso*, which does not acknowledge such a division in regard to its *khalifaship*[30].

In conducting its *khususiya*, the *Tarekat Cukir* follows the same patterns as the *Tarekat Rejoso*, since they have the same roots and history. Although the formation of the *Tarekat Qadiriyah Wa Naqsyabandiyah (Cukir version)* was a reaction against Kiai Musta'in's political actions, its *khalifa* throughout East Java have continued to be successful in managing and coordinating (recruiting) former followers of the *Tarekat Qadiriyah Wa Naqsyabandiyah* led by Kiai Musta'in. A significant number of former followers of Kiai Musta'in have joined this *tarekat*. In Jombang, the number of followers of this *tarekat* seems to be higher than that of the *Tarekat Rejoso*. According to its *khalifa*, Kiai Abdullah Sajad, there are about 40,000 people affiliated (as members) with this *tarekat* in Jombang. This compares with about ten to fifteen thousand followers of *Tarekat Rejoso*, a figure suggested by one of its staff. It is, however, difficult to get exact numbers, since neither *tarekat* has accurate data about followers. The figures may therefore be exaggerated. The followers are spread out in all regions of Jombang, and they are involved in local *khususiya*. The *Tarekat Cukir* has around 73 places of *khususiya*, each of which is led by an *imam* who is assisted by one to three *badal* (lit. a substitute)[31].

Another important note in regard to *Tarekat Cukir* is that it continues to support PPP although this party has changed its Islamic base with *Pancasila*, and NU has formally freed its members from affiliation with PPP. The consistency of this sufi organisation in regard to its support for PPP seems to be related to the circumstances of its origin. Since it has been affiliated with PPP for a long time, and the PPP symbol was often used in its big ritual events, this sufi order in Jombang is also known as the 'Tarekat PPP'[32]. On the other hand, the *Tarekat*

---

[30] In addition, some of the *khalifa* of both *Tarekat Rejoso* and *Tarekat Cukir* have been promoted to hold positions in the leadership of the *Jam'iyah Ahli Thoriqoh Al-Mu'tabaroh Indonesia* and the *Jam'iyah Ahli Thoriqoh Al-Mu'tabaroh An-Nahdliyah* respectively either at the regency or provincial level.
[31] Interview with Kiai Abdullah Sajad, 25 November 1994.
[32] A Few *khalifa* of this *tarekat* denied the common notion that *Tarekat Cukir* is a 'Tarekat PPP'. Kiai Khoerul Anwar, the leader of this *tarekat*, tried to change that notion. He believed that in his *tarekat* there is an increasing number of public servants who are politically affiliated with Golkar. He always emphasised this opinion when he gave his religious speech among his followers (informal telephone talk with Kiai Khoerul Anwar, 10 January 1996).

Rejoso is explicitly affiliated with Golkar, although it is very likely that the support of the followers for this party in elections varies. The *Tarekat Rejoso* is also commonly called the *Tarekat Golkar*.

This discussion shows that the organisations of *tarekat* in Jombang are related to political developments in NU. Although the formation of the *Tarekat Cukir* was legitimated politically by NU and aimed to coordinate *kiai* and followers who were disappointed with Kiai Musta'in's political actions, all *kiai* of the *Tarekat Rejoso* in present day Jombang continue to affiliate with NU. The pattern of political support of *tarekat* organisation remains the same regardless of NU's decision to free its members to affiliate with any political organisation. The *Tarekat Cukir* continues to support PPP, while the *Tarekat Rejoso* supports Golkar.

3.4 Other Tarekat Movements

3.4.1. The Tarekat Shiddiqiyah

The centre of the *Tarekat Shiddiqiyah* is in the northern region of Jombang. Kiai Muchtar Mu'thi, the *murshid* of this *tarekat* was a student of Kiai Abdul Fatah of *Pesantren Bahrul Ulum*. His educational background indicates that Kiai Muchtar was mostly influenced by NU culture. Why he formed a *tarekat* separate from the NU's is a difficult question to answer. The *Tarekat Shiddiqiyah* is classified not *mu'tabarah* from NU's point of view. The *tarekat* is hence marginal compared to other *tarekat* in Jombang. By marginal I mean that most NU members in Jombang are affiliated with either *Tarekat Rejoso* or *Tarekat Cukir*, but not *Tarekat Shiddiqiyah*. It is also marginal, because members of this *tarekat* are not involved in NU activities, whereas the main stream of Islam in Jombang is represented by NU.

Researchers such as Dhofier (1982) have noted that the origin of this *tarekat* is not clear. The *tarekat* emerged for the first time in 1958 in a district of Ploso, in the northern part of Jombang. According to Dhofier, this *tarekat* does not exist in other countries. Kiai Muchtar, however, maintains that he is not the founder but inherited the leadership of this *tarekat* from Kiai Syu'aib, who went abroad. In addition, according to Dhofier, Kiai Muchtar is also well known as a *dukun*, a person who can cure certain diseases.

The shortage of research about this *tarekat* is due to several factors. Firstly, since this *tarekat* is not classified as *mu'tabarah*, and is not involved in the cultural network of NU in Jombang, it may be regarded by some as unimportant. Secondly, the *tarekat* is regarded as being rather exclusive. The impression of exclusiveness is acknowledged by many people in Jombang. Kiai Muchtar does not respond to questions about his *tarekat*[33].

---

[33] Interview with Kiai Azis Masyhuri, 19 April 1993.

In addition, Kiai Muchtar is also regarded as controversial in regard to *Friday prayer*. NU *kiai* maintain that *Friday prayer* is performed at the mosque as a substitute for that day's *zuhr prayer* [34]. Those who perform *Friday prayer* feel that their obligation to conduct *zuhr prayer* for Friday has been met. Nevertheless, *Friday prayer* is not merely considered as an alternative which can be substituted for *zuhr*, but rather it is seen as an additional obligation which stands by itself. Only certain people, such as those who are sick, are allowed to perform *zuhr* instead of *Friday prayer*. Kiai Muchtar, on the other hand, contends that those who perform *Friday prayer* still have to conduct *zuhr prayer*. *Kiai* in Jombang have tried to discuss the problem with Kiai Muchtar. They have also invited Kiai Muchtar to explain his *tarekat*, since NU has indicated an intention to examine it. I was told by a *kiai* that Kiai Muchtar has never responded to such an invitation.

The exclusivity of Kiai Muchtar also impressed me when I tried to visit him at his house. Unfortunately he was not at home when I called. It was then recommended that I meet Kiai Muchtar's assistant, who lives nearby. What was surprising to me was that the assistant told me that I must have Kiai Muchtar's approval to get information about his *tarekat*, and refused to give me information. After a few days of waiting I was told by the assistant that Kiai Muchtar refused to be interviewed and had not given me permission to research either his *tarekat* or his *pesantren*. Kiai Muchtar had reasons for his refusal. According to the assistant, some university students had come to research Kiai Muchtar's *tarekat* and *pesantren*, but their description (in their theses) had deviated from the facts. Kiai Muchtar contended that such attitude was unfair and dishonest, and that he would feel it sinful to give me a chance to act in a similar way to the previous researchers. I understood enough of his reasons and appreciated them. I thus had to be satisfied with information about this *tarekat* gained from outside the *Tarekat Shiddiqiyah* followers.

This does not mean that Kiai Muchtar never reacts to negative responses from *kiai* and Muslims criticising his *tarekat*. He has written some short *risala* (lit. writing). Kiai Muchtar insists that he did not create a novel *tarekat*. His *tarekat*, he maintains, is similar to other (*mu'tabarah*) *tarekat* which have chains of *murshid* to the Prophet Muhammad. His *risala can easily be obtained by anyone who is interested. Although the risala* are provided for his followers, they are also sold publicly on big ritual occasions. In his *risala* entitled *Informasi tentang Thoriqoh Shiddiqiyah* (Information on *Tarekat Shiddiqiyah*), Kiai Muchtar explains that his *tarekat* traces its chain to Abu Bakr Al-Siddiq, one of the main four companions of the Prophet Muhammad. He claims that his *tarekat* was also

---

[34] A Muslim is obliged to perform prayer five times a day, that is *zuhr, 'asr, magreb, 'isha and subh*. He is also obliged to perform *Friday prayer* once in a week. This prayer is usually carried out at the same time as *zuhr prayer*

practised by such a great sufi as Al-Syadhili, the founder of the *Tarekat Syadhiliyah* (Mu'thi, 1992:24).

The word *shiddiqiyah* is related to Abu Bakr, who was called *Al-Shiddiq* by the Prophet Muhammad. This was because Abu Bakr accepted as true everything spoken by the Prophet in regard to the Prophet's *mi'raj* [35] (lit. to ascend). *Shiddiqiyah*, according to Kiai Muchtar, is nothing but a *silsila* through which the *wird* practised by followers were passed from the Prophet Muhammad through Abu Bakr. This standpoint is derived from *Mu'jam Al-Buldan* written by Sheikh Al-Imam Syihabuddin Abi Abdillah Yaquti Ibn Abdillah Al-Rumi (Mu'thi, 1992:16). It is said in this book that a great sufi, Sheikh Muhammad Amin Al-Kurdi Al-Ibrili mentioned that the *silsila* which started with Abu Bakr and passed down to Sheikh Thoifur Ibn Isa Abi Yazid Al-Busthomi was called *Shiddiqiyah*. Kiai Muchtar explains further that the *silsila* of *Shiddiqiyah* was passed from Abu Bakr through either Ali Ibn Abi Thalib or Salman Al-Farisi.

With this explanation, Kiai Muchtar shed light on the origin of his *tarekat*, but he did not explain how the *murshidship* of this *tarekat* was passed to him. As commonly emphasised by those involved in the *tarekat*, proper *silsila* through which (the *wird* of) the *tarekat* is passed on is a necessity. Otherwise, the *tarekat* will be regarded as *munqati* (cut off). The *silsila* is one prerequisite that determines whether a *tarekat* is *mu'tabarah* or not.

The Silsilah of Mursyidship of the Tarekat Shiddiqiyah (through Salman Al-Farisi)

1. Allah
2. Gabriel 'Alaihissalam
3. Prophet Muhammad
4. Abu Bakar
5. Salman Al-Farisi
6. Qasim bin Muhammad bin Abu Bakar Ashshiddiq
7. Ja'far Al-Shadiq

<u>Thoriqoh Shiddiqiyah</u>

8. Abi Yazid Thoifur bin Isa
9. Abi Al-Hasan Ali bin Abi Ja'far Al-Khorqoni
10. Abi Ali Al-Fadlol bin Muhammad Ath-Thusi Al-Farmadi
11. Abi Ya'qub Yusuf Al-Hamdani

---

[35] One night the Prophet was requested by Allah to attend Him. In this session the Prophet received among other things the obligation to pray five times a day. The journey to Allah was very very long, since the Prophet started it from mosque *al-haram* in Mecca through mosque *al-aqsa* in Jerusalem and finished his journey in the 7th layer of the sky (where he came to Allah). He then returned to Mecca. This journey was done in one night. People of Mecca were bewildered by the Prophet's story because it was beyond common sense, but Abu Bakr did not hesitate to acknowledge it as true. That was why the Prophet called Abu Bakr *ash-shiddiq*, he who believes without question.

Thoriqoh Ath-Thoifuriyah

12. Abdul Kholiq Al-Ghojduwani ibn Al-Imam Abdul Jalil
13. 'Arif Arriwikari
14. Mahmud Al-Anjiri Faghnawi
15. Ali Ar-Rumaitani Al Masyhur Bil 'Azizaani
16. Muhammad Baabas Samaasi
17. Amir Kullali Ibn Sayyid Hamzah

Thoriqoh Al-Khuwaajikaaniyyah

18. Muhammad Bahauddin An-Naqsyabandi
19. Muhammad Ibnu 'Alaaiddin Al-Athori
20. Ya'qub Al-Jarkhi

Thoriqoh An-Naqsyabandiyah

21. Nashiruddin Ubaidillah Al-Ahror As-Samarqondi
22. Muhammad Az-Zahid
23. Darwis Muhammad Samarqondi
24. Muhammad Al-Khowaajaki
25. Muhammad Al-Baaqi Billah

Thoriqoh Ahroriyah

26. Ahmad Al-Faruqi As-Sirhindi
27. Muhammad Ma'shum
28. Muhammad Saifuddin
29. Muhammad Nurul Badwani
30. Habibullah Jaanijanaani Munthohir
31. Abdillah Addahlawi

Thoriqoh Mujaddadiyah

32. Kholid Dliya Ad-ddin
33. Utsman Siroj Al-Millah
34. Umar Al-Qothbul Irsyad
35. Muhammad Amin Al-Kurdi Al-Ibril

Thoriqoh Kholidiyah

(Source: Mu'thi, 1992:19– 21)[36]

---

[36] Kiai Muchtar Mu'thi quoted this *silsila* from the *Tanwirul Qulub*, pp. 500– 502. However, it is not clear how the *murshidship* of this *tarekat* was passed to Kiai Muchtar.

3.4.2. The Penyiar Sholawat Wahidiyah

I need to describe briefly the *tarekat*-like movement known as *Penyiar Sholawat Wahidiyah*, since it has some followers in Jombang. The *Penyiar Sholawat Wahidiah* or the *Wahidiyah* is not a sufi order. It is a religious movement which emphasises the moulding of society by encouraging its followers to perform *wird* by reciting *salawat* (prayers for the Prophet Muhammad). Like a *tarekat* movement, the *Wahidiyah* aims at approaching Allah in different ways. In Jombang, the centre of the *Wahidiyah* is located in a village in the Ngoro district in southern Jombang. The founder of the *Wahidiyah* was Kiai 'Abdul Madjid, who was from Kedunglo, Kediri. Kiai 'Abdul Madjid introduced this religious movement in 1963. In Jombang, the *Wahidiyah* is led by Kiai Ihsan Mahin, the owner of the *Pesantren at-Tahdzib*.

The formation of the *Wahidiyah* began when Kiai 'Abdul Madjid had a dream in 1959. In his dream it was as if an angel whispered to him. He was urged to improve the moral aspect of society and to mould the inner aspect of religious life. He had the same dream again twice in 1963. The third dream demanded that he act immediately. The tone of the dream alarmed Kiai 'Abdul Madjid greatly (see Sanusi, 1993). As a result, he became determined to encourage the society to practise *salawat*. He then created a number of *wird*, especially the *salawat*. A major difference between *Wahidiyah* and other *tarekat* is that its *wird* focus on reciting *salawat*, while the *tarekat's* focus on reciting *dhikr*. Another difference is that the *tarekat* is usually a long established religious movement, transfered from one *murshid* to another, starting from the Prophet Muhammad, while the *Wahidiyah* is a new and local religious movement. Its *wird* were created by Kiai 'Abdul Madjid one by one or he amended an earlier version (see, Sanusi, 1993).

The *Wahidiyah* has a very special character in terms of its ritual practices. The followers of *Wahidiyah* usually perform their *wird* in a sorrowful manner. In their *wird*, they try to acknowledge and realise their sins. In their view the essence of their *dhikr* is to ask Allah forgiveness (*tauba*). According to them, this is the main reason for the practice of *dhikr* in Islam. Because of their mode of ritual practice, one can hear the mourning of the *Wahidiyah* followers in the night when other members of society are sleeping[37].

The *Wahidiyah* initially received a rather negative response from some *kiai*. Kiai Machrus Ali from Kediri warned his *santri* not to join this Islamic religious movement. It is also important to note that while NU indirectly organised several *tarekat* movements classified as *mu'tabarah*, according to a *kiai*, it never accepted *Wahidiyah* as an Islamic organisation under its umbrella. Despite this fact,

---

[37] I was impressed by the extent of their mourning when one night I went to their 'big ritual', which was attended by *Wahidiyah* followers from various regions of Indonesia.

however, the *Wahidiyah* draws followers from various regions of Indonesia. Its followers vary from lay Muslims to government officers or even *kiai*. In Jombang, followers include the younger *santri* of Kiai Ihsan Mahin. The *kiai* has encouraged his *santri* to practise the *Sholawat Wahidiyah* rituals. In contrast to the *tarekat*, the *Wahidiyah* does not make any *bai'a* for those who want to practise its *wird*.

In brief *Wahidiyah* is a *terakat*-like movement, which receives an increasing acceptance from Muslims in Jombang and other cities. Its followers range from farmer Muslims to businessmen and Islamic organisation activists. In terms of follower attachment, this Islamic movement is different from *tarekat*. In the latter, followers' attachment either to the *tarekat* or to their *murshid* is stronger.

Chapter 4: The Social Reality of Kiaiship

This chapter discusses important aspects of *kiai* leadership. Having described two important institutions attached to *kiaiship*, that is the *pesantren* and the *tarekat*, in the previous chapters and the social conditions under which the *kiai*, as a traditionalist group, relate to other Islamic groups, I would like now to discuss the social reality of the *kiai* world. The first section of this chapter highlights the position of the *kiai* in society in general. The second section illuminates the basis for society's relationship with the *kiai*. This second section gives us a basic understanding of why the society affords the *kiai* such a respected position so that the relationship is marked by unequal position. I will then discuss general features of *kiai* leadership. As there are so many *kiai* in Jombang, either leading *tarekat* or running the *pesantren*, Jombang society is socially fragmented, since it is divided between various centres of authority. Since followers have such strong emotional ties to their *kiai*, any conflict between *kiai* is reflected in antagonism between their followers. This is salient to the field of politics (which I will discuss in Chapter VI), since the followers allegiance to their *kiai* entails agreement with their *kiai's* political views. The final section discusses the development of the *kiaiship* itself in terms of educational attainment and background and how society views these differences. I consider the question of whether the emergence of modern *kiai* has given rise to changes in society's perspective in regard to *kiaiship*. This question is important not only because some *kiai* have a modern educational background but also because this situation has led to a decrease in the number of qualified *kiai* in a more traditional sense.

4.1 The Kiai's Role in the Society

Before presenting a framework to assist in the understanding of social relations between the *kiai* and his community or between the former and society at large, let me first discuss the general picture of social and interpersonal relationships among Javanese. It is widely accepted that Javanese society acknowledges differences between individuals in their social status and that this has become the norm that governs social relations among Javanese (see Guinness, 1986). Social status is largely defined by age, wealth and occupation, so that an older Javanese in a village, for example, will receive respect from a younger person, just as wealthy Javanese receives homage from the poor. The same holds true for a highly educated individual who will receive respect from less educated Javanese.

Although differences in social status are in fact more complicated and overlap in practice, Javanese social life is typified by the operation of such norms of differentiation. A Javanese is socialised into such norms at an early age. The system works efficiently, especially in rural areas where most people know each other, so that the "social location" of any individual Javanese is easily identified. This culture of social difference among Javanese is perpetuated and institutionalised by the operation of the informal control of social sanctions. The concept of *wis Jawa* (finally become Javanese), for example, reflects the existence of idealised behaviour which requires compliance by any Javanese; and the "culture of shame", moreover, encourages a Javanese to conform to such an idealised norm of behaviour. A Javanese villager will feel ashamed if he or she does not comply with the requirements of established etiquette. A wealthy villager, for example, should not only receive respect from the poor but should also behave in certain accepted ways[1]

In line with such notions of differences in social status, the *'ulama*, especially the *kiai*, in Javanese villages receive high respect from society. Compared to other local elites, like wealthy farmers, the *kiai*, who usually run a *pesantren*, have a more respected position. This has made him a leading figure in society. His leadership, moreover, is in fact not confined to the religious sphere but also extends to the political field. His success in these leadership roles has resulted in his being regarded as a man of great worth who can easily induce social action. The *kiai* have therefore long been a powerful elite.

Two main factors have contributed to the *kiai's* powerful position. First, the *kiai* is a knowledgeable person from whom villagers learn Islamic knowledge. His erudition and higher level of knowledge of Islam mean that the *kiai* always has followers, both informal audiences, who always attend his *pengajian* or lectures, and his *santri*, who stay at *pondok* around his house. Secondly, it is common for a *kiai* to come from a well-to-do family. Even though it is not rare to find a *kiai* who was a poor *'ulama* at the time he commenced teaching Islam, as evidenced by the small size of his first *pesantren* building, the average *kiai* is classified as coming from a rich family. These two factors have led to the *kiai* being seen as an elite figure in a Javanese village. The *santri* and his obedient villagers, as his followers, constitute human resources which sustain his position and his leadership in society. Furthermore, the economic resources he usually owns have made villagers and his *santri* dependent on him in many senses. Through his wealth, a *kiai* creates a pattern of patronage which ties him to certain people in his community. Because of his huge land holdings, he can employ villagers to work either as labourers or as land tenants. In addition he strengthens his relationship with his *santri* by allowing some of them, who come from poor families, to work on his land (see Fox and Dirjosanjoto, 1989). In modern *pesantren*

---

[1] It is common that such norms are applied in any traditional society. In this society, a wealthy villager should also take care of his poor neighbours or fulfil social obligations such as holding lavish celebration at weddings. This will not only prevent malicious gossip, but strengthen and legitimise his social position in many respects (see Scott, 1977).

the patronage is evidenced in a different pattern. The *kiai* may recruit his former qualified *santri* or other members of society to work in his university and other modern educational institution. These *santri* receive a formal salary. The *kiai*, for these people, is a person who can provide economic subsistence, and a patron who can be a good friend in need. It is not accidental, however, that in few cases these *santri* were fired because they did not fulfil what was needed by the *kiai* family.

Having these two human and economic resources at hand, the *kiai* has become a respected person in a village. As the pattern of relationship between the *kiai* and villagers is not based on egalitarianism, the former often receives an exaggerated amount of respect from the latter. This unequal position is not only because the former has a higher social status, as conceptualised by Javanese culture, but also because he is a leader who has a wide network. The *kiai* who runs a *pesantren* will automatically get support from people from the surrounding villages and other cities. Since most of the *kiai* are also involved in politics in a more general sense at a higher level, their position in the eyes of society goes unchallenged.

Furthermore, it is important to add that a *kiai* is often endowed with an ability which is unusual to ordinary Muslims. The extraordinary ability is commonly found in individual *kiai* even before they commence their *kiaiship*. It is often evident when they are very young and still learning Islam at certain *pesantren*. It is a truism that a *kiai* candidate often has what is called *ilmu laduni*, that is knowledge acquired without learning. Such knowledge, which may precede one's *kiaiship* or be shown after becoming a *kiai*, gives legitimacy to the *kiai's* leadership. It seems as though God has given a sign to choose him as an Islamic leader. It is thus understandable if a *kiai* becomes a charismatic leader, since he is deemed the holder of divine authority, which in turn has made him very different from society at large.

The relationship between the *kiai* and his community (the *umma*) is bound by religious emotion which makes his legitimate power more influential. The charisma which surrounds the *kiai's* actions also imbues the relationship with emotion. Since the *kiai* has become the avenue through which people in villages solve their problems, which are not just those confined to spiritual but also to wider aspects of their lives, people also endorse the *kiai* as their leader and representative in the national system (cf. Horikoshi, 1976). His success in performing such an important role "…tends almost inevitably to lead to his being regarded not merely as a mediator of law and doctrine (of Islam), but of holy power itself" (Geertz, 1962:238).

Under these conditions, the *kiai* in a Javanese village has a very strong influence on society and plays a crucial role in inducing social and even political actions. But his important position and role are not confined to the village level. As can be seen through the NU, especially when it was a political organisation comprising a variety of members, including intellectuals and politicians, the centrality of the *kiai's* position was evidenced by his having the highest prestige and influence compared to the professional politician (Samson, 1978:201). The approval of the *kiai* guarantees popular support for a political party since the *kiai* in general "…are believed to be acting legitimately in their utilisation of power so long as they act for God" (Samson, 1978:201).

The relationship between the *kiai* and society is similar to that between *'ulama* or *saints* in other societies of the Islamic world (see Bruinessen, 1992:246– 249). This similarity may be due to the fact that Muslims share concepts and religious experiences which have created the same style of leadership. The idea influencing the establishment of such a pattern is found in Islamic precepts. The *kiai's* respected position basically derives from the fact that Islam emphasises the importance of knowledge, which should be pursued by all Muslim. In the Qur'an and hadith (the tradition of the Prophet), it is always stressed that seeking for knowledge is a necessary part of Muslim life and that knowledgable Muslims have a higher status before Allah[2]. It is no exaggeration to say that this notion has encouraged Muslims to seek knowledge. Thus, possession of scientific curiosity has become part of Muslim duty, and those who succeed in obtaining such needed knowledge will be appreciated by society. This perspective has given rise to the creation of a culture which appreciates the *'ulama* since he is a man who has acquired such knowledge.

The establishment of the *sufi* order in North Africa almost always begins with the society's acceptance of the presence of an *'ulama* (see Gellner, 1969). What is interesting to note from the sufi leadership as well as *'ulama* is the fact that the relationship between the leader and his society is cemented by close emotional ties. The intimate relationship between the *'ulama* and his society derives from the society's perception that the former leadership is the real leadership, and that the *'ulama* is the expert who can understand and explain the precepts of the Qur'an. It so happens that most of the saints or *sheikh* (leader) of the sufi orders in North Africa are *'ulama* who have a geneological linkage with the Prophet Muhammad. Their leadership is thus regarded as legitimate. Apart from the fact that genealogy plays an important part in society's recognition of one's *'ulamaship*, the Islamic concept of *'ulama* as *waratha al-anbiya* (those who inherit prophecy) is of great significance. It is this conception which encourages Muslims in Jombang to accord high respect to the *kiai* and to submit to his leadership. Furthermore, such a belief has endowed the *kiai* with certain symbolic attributes which make him different from the rest of society. The *kiai*, for example, is

---

[2] The hadith stresses that "seeking knowledge is obligatory for all Muslims". In the Qur'an it is mentioned that "Allah respects and ranks Muslims and those knowledge seekers at a higher degree".

conceived of as having grace or *baraka* which is simply given by God due to his being close to God.

The discussion helps explain why the *'ulama* in Islamic countries and the *kiai* in Java receive high respect from society and occupy powerful positions. Their central position is nonetheless very much dependent on societal recognition. In certain regions, like Madura, society's acceptance is based on genealogy, which means that a *kiai* should come from a *kiai* family (Mansurnoor, 1991). Another factor is performance by the *kiai*. This is decisive in preventing him from losing his popularity. The *kiai's* power and position therefore depend entirely on the continued recognition of society, which means that *'ulamaship* and *kiaiship* are not merely inherited but also need to be achieved.

In addition to similarities, it is important to acknowledge that *'ulamaship* and the social relationship between an *'ulama* and society can vary from one country or region to another. In Java, for example, the emotion which characterises society's relationship with its *'ulama* is more discernible than in other regions of Indonesia. Thus, at very minimum, one would expect some variation in the nuances of meaningfulness of such relations. This notion is of great importance in understanding Muslim society in general. Muslims in Java and their relations with their *'ulama* should thus be treated, analytically, differently from those in other regions in order to avoid misleading generalisations. The difference which marks *'ulama* relations with their society in various regions results from different factors which influence and shape such relationships. It is also related to the existing situation when Islam was introduced to those regions. It is commonly suggested that the coming of a religion into a society not only results in changes in the belief system of that society, but also in shifts in some aspects of that religion as adopted by that society. This is so because the religion is locally coloured by cultures of that society. These two process, that is the adoption of a new religion and subsequent changes to that religion, are commonly found when a world religion, like Islam or Christianity, spreads and is accepted by a local people. As the Islamic concepts written in the Qur'an are revealed in more general terms, it is common for them to be localised or nativised when they are accepted by local people without destroying their essential meaning. It is therefore understandable that Islam in various regions is marked by differences in practice and others aspects of local culture.

4.2 The Underlying Principle of Relationship: Baraka

The *kiai* in Java usually have supra-village influence. Some have national influence. A *kiai's* position in a *pesantren* and involvement in NU can make him a national leader of the Islamic community in Indonesia. The *pesantren* is an important institution attached to one's *kiaiship*. It is through the *pesantren* that a *kiai* builds a pattern of patronage which relates him to his community. The pattern of patronage can easily be established since most, if not all, *pesantren* are privately owned by *kiai*, a fact which can tie society to its *kiai*.

The *kiai's* wider influence and his supra-village pattern of leadership have enabled him to keep in touch with private and government agencies. The *kiai* sometimes plays a brokerage role in transmitting development messages, and the society may accept a government program more easily when they are approached by the *kiai*. The elevated position of the *kiai* is indeed inherent in the nature of Islamic society, since in a society where religious knowledge constitutes an important part of life, the *kiai* is the source of this necessary knowledge. The *kiai* also fulfils societal needs in relation to religious life. He performs birth and death rituals and other religious ceremonies. It is evident that the crititical role of the *kiai* stems from his position as both religious leader and teacher, often coupled with charismatic leadership. The *kiai*, as a group, try to bring their communities into an idealised situation as it is conceptualised by Islam. They also try to interpret all developments and changes in the socio-cultural and political fields in order that Muslims, especially in the villages, can understand the situation.

I would argue that there is no *kiai* whose death is not followed by the society's sadness or, at least, a sense of loss at his death. Institutionally, the *kiaiship* ideally comprises those Muslims who are very close to their God, happy to undertake the duty given by God to do His will. They can be grouped with those holy men who always relate worldly matters to religious norms. It is understandable, therefore, that *kiaiship* has a respectable place at the heart of the society, since it is through the *kiai* that the spirituality of the society is established and guarded. *Al-'ulama waratha al-anbiya* (lit. the *'ulama* is the inheritor of the Prophets), said the hadith (saying of the prophet). The hadith suggests that characteristics that commonly attach to the Prophets, such as honesty and cleverness and even the willingness to save society, either on earth or beyond, are part of the *'ulama*'s personality. Due to these characteristics and the power of his leadership, the *kiai* is always surrounded by loyal and trusted followers who ask him to lead them in religious and worldly matters. In addition, the leadership of certain *kiai* is reinforced through their leadership role in the *pesantren*, since they are not only spiritual agents but also intellectuals who provide knowledge. The *kiai* can therefore become a centre of power. However, this situation can also create a polarisation of power since the existence of many *kiai* in a village can create several centres of power. In Jombang, for example, no one *kiai* has overarching influence. Each *kiai's* influence is limited by location and political factors. A *kiai* in Jombang is usually popular only in certain districts, especially his own. A common phrase among Muslims in Jombang, *bukan kiai saya* ("not my *kiai*"), expresses the limited sphere of influence of each *kiai*.

This situation, however, does not necessarily mean that a certain group in society will only give respect to the *kiai* they call 'my *kiai*'. All *kiai* in Jombang are generally respected. It should nonetheless be emphasised that there is a difference in the pattern between the relationship of the *pesantren kiai* and society, and that of the *tarekat kiai* and his followers. The level of submission of *tarekat* followers to their *murshid* in the *tarekat* is greater than that in the general *kiai* world. The *tarekat* followers give exaggerated respect to their *kiai*. In the *tarekat* world the loyalty or submission of the *murid* (pupil, but is used to mean 'follower') to his *murshid* comes close to absolute. Accordingly, in all circumstances, the *tarekat* followers would support the action of their *murshid*.

The difference between this attitude and the attitude of the followers of *pesantren kiai* can be seen in the case of the *Pesantren Darul Ulum* when Kiai Musta'in, the former leader of this *pesantren*, joined the government political party (I will discuss this matter at length in Chapter V). Joining government party during the 1970s seemed to be taboo for Indonesian Muslims. Some parents of children studying in the *pesantren* of Kiai Musta'in tried to withdraw their children and send them to another *pesantren*.

Although Kiai Musta'in was condemned by Muslim society in general in Jombang, he was still respected by thousands of followers of the *Tarekat Qadiriyah Wa Naqsyabandiyah* which he led. These followers remained loyal and supported his leadership in the *tarekat*. It can even be assumed that the latter followed Kiai Musta'in's steps and supported the government party, an action which was deemed as *haram* (religiously prohibited) at the time, since it deviated from what was called 'the struggle for Islam'. It is interesting to note further that those followers who left him did not regard the action of Kiai Musta'in as wrong; at least no *tarekat* follower dared to express such an attitude. Accordingly, Kiai Musta'in still received respect from them although they were no longer his formal followers.

One can ask the question: what actually bound Kiai Musta'in and his followers together? The answer lies in the 'Islamic'[3] concepts of *baraka* and *karama*, which are deeply embedded in the belief of the people in general and in that of the *santri* in *pesantren* and the followers of the *tarekat* in particular. *Baraka*[4] (cf. Ahmed, 1976) is usually related to the *karama*. *Karama* is a characteristic attributed to a holy man, who can transfer God's blessing to the people who need it. Due to his being *karama*[5], a saint can do things *khawariqu'l-'ada*

---

[3] My use of the word 'Islamic' with quotation marks is to emphasise that this understanding of *baraka* is not held by all Islamic groups. In Indonesia, only traditionalist Muslims believe in *baraka*.
[4] Ahmed in his *Millenium and Charisma among Pathans* (1976:103– 130) equates the concept of *baraka* with that of charisma.
[5] The subordination of the society to the *kiai* is commonly expressed by people kissing his hand. 'Kissing the hand' is culturally meant to signal high respect. Moreover, at the same time, it aims to obtain *baraka*. 'Kissing the hand' never seems to occur among the Muhammadiyah members. This may indicate that

(contradictory to the normal human situation). In the traditional orthodox perspective, the *hijab* (lit. curtain) hides divine things or creatures from human sight. The secrets of Allah were only revealed by Allah to certain chosen people such as the saints. With the power they receive from Allah, saints can thus do things which from the normal human perspective are unusual. Folklore or local Muslim stories tell us, for example, that those who reach the stage of saintship can perform their *Friday prayer* in Mecca, while at the same time they are also seen visibly conducting the prayer at their local mosques. Because of this, it is believed that one can receive God's blessing through the intermediary of a holyman such as a saint or the *murshid*. Some Muslims believe that "a great saint's *karama* is effective even after his death"[6] (Bruinessen, 1992:215). Since the *kiai* and *'ulama* in general are close to God, they can reach the stage of *karama*. As a result, a request by a *kiai* to God either for himself or for others, may be more readily received.

Those who have *karama* can give *baraka*, that is the positive effect which arises from interaction with a holy man. A life filled with *baraka* can be exemplified in a *hidup yang cukup* (a life where we make ends meet). My informant gave me the following example. A poor man might be living at subsistence level, but because of *baraka* this condition does not result in any trouble. On the other hand, a rich man, who lives *serba kecukupan* (lit. at a higher standard), could have problems that disturb his mental condition due to his not having *baraka*. An informant told me about a person who graduated from the faculty of economics but had been jobless for a couple of years. One might have thought, from his discipline, the person would have had more chance of being recruited into an administrative positions than graduates from other disciplines. It appeared that this person was the son of a policeman who often accepted money from people working in a 'dirty place'. The money was used by the policeman to fund his son's education. In the opinion of this informant, such money did not incur *baraka*. As a result, his son could not get a job, despite the fact that he had graduated from university. The informant ever considered that this tainted education had even hindered the son in his attempts to find employment.

---

they are more egalitarian since kissing another's hand may imply an unequal position. In their opinion, exaggerated respect is not encouraged by the Prophet. Even the Prophet himself did not want to be treated exaggeratedly by his followers. For example, the Prophet said: "do not call me *sayyid*". *Sayyid* is a term referring a very respected person. The NU members, on the other hand, do not interpret such a hadith as a prohibition. It just illustrates the low profile attitude of the Prophet. In the view of NU members, therefore, it is not prohibited to call him *sayyid*, which shows the high respect which the Prophet deserved. Respecting others is a matter of degree. It is not different from the case when a Catholic bowed down, kissing the pope's feet. The *kiai* or the *murshid*, they suggest, deserves high respect from society due to their knowledge and dedication in developing and guarding Islam.

[6] Among *kiai* and, especially, *tarekat* followers in Jombang there is a tradition of attending the grave of *keramat kiai*, i.e. the *kiai* having *karama*. This is the *ziyara* (a spiritual journey to the grave of the dead). Hundreds of Muslims from Jombang, led by their *kiai*, come to the grave of *walisongo*, the nine saints, who are buried in different cities. The *ziyara walisongo* is carried out once a year. The aim is among other things to get *baraka*. For more detail about this tradition, see Fox (1991).

In brief, *baraka* is a quality which is reflected through people, such as the *kiai*, who are endowed with *karama*. The *kiai's* followers believe that he can give *baraka*, especially if he himself says a prayer. In any *ziara* (visit) to a *kiai*, the *tarekat* followers usually ask for his prayers for a secure life. In addition, they try to avoid disappointing the *kiai*, and certainly avoid opposing him, since either could result in the loss of *baraka* in their lives. In an extreme case, a follower could even become *kualat* (fairly cursed). It is acknowledged that the state of *baraka* may stem from having a good relationship with the *kiai* or other holy men who have *karama*. However, *baraka* can also be derived from the prayer of common people, who perform extremely good religious acts, such as those returning from *hajj*. Such a prayer is easily accepted by God. This is a tradition, of course, but it also relates to people's belief systems which underly their actions.

On two evenings I visited two Javanese Muslims who had just arrived from undertaking *hajj*. The first one was a *lurah* (village head), and the other was a *kiai*, who heads a *pesantren* under the collective leadership of other *kiai* on the west side of Jombang. When I arrived at the *lurah's* house, there were some people chatting with him. I then became involved in a conversation with them. When a young mother among them was about to leave, she asked the *lurah* for a prayer. She said: *Pak lurah, kulo nyuwun barakahipun lan do'ane panjenengan* (Mr. Lurah, I would like to get *baraka* from your having undertaken the *hajj*. Please say a prayer for me). The same situation occurred when I visited the *kiai* in his house. People who came there shook the *kiai's* right hand (some kissed it) and then embraced him, an action indicating closeness or brotherhood. It should be noted first that such embraces happened only between the *kiai* and male Muslims, or between *nyai* (the *kiai's* wife) and female Javanese, and only between Muslims and those just finishing their *hajj*. On this occasion, I also noticed that before people left the *kiai*, they always begged for his prayer, just to get *baraka*.

The happenings in the *kiai's* house were not too surprising me, since begging *kiai* for *baraka* is very common. However, asking the *lurah* for *baraka* led me to ask certain questions. I later received an answer which, although not satisfying, gave me a logical understanding of these actions. The Javanese Muslims believe that doing *hajj* is symbolically similar to cleaning the soul of sin. At the very least, those who do the *hajj* have completed their Islamic obligation[7]. For a short

---

[7] Islam has five pillars according to which Muslims perform their religious rituals. These are *shahada*, that is stating that there is 'No God but Allah and Muhammad is his messenger', performing *salat* (prayer), giving religious alms, fasting during *ramadan* (the name of a month in the Muslim calendar), and finally, performing *hajj*. Of the five pillars, four are reachable by any Muslim because they are common practice. One pillar, that is doing *hajj*, needs a lot of money to carry out. For most Muslims doing *hajj* is very difficult because of its economic dimension. That is why Islam only asks its adherents to conduct *hajj* once during one's life time. Due to its special place in Islam, performing *hajj* is highly rewarded by Allah. Those who perform it have a high social position among Muslims.

time after one completes his *hajj*, this being clean enables him to be a person whose prayer is easily accepted by Allah.

The tradition of *baraka* is more prevalent among those Muslims who orient their ideologies through the traditionalist Islamic organisation, NU. Among Muhammadiyah[8] followers or sympathisers, such a tradition is less known. In the NU's tradition such beliefs and practices of *baraka* have been embedded for a long time. My informant (a lecturer at the *Universitas Darul Ulum*, who used to be a *santri* of Kiai Musta'in) told me about a *santri* of *Pesantren Darul Ulum* who disagreed with his *kiai* (Musta'in) because of the latter's affiliation with Golkar. He was one of those *santri* who sharply criticised his *kiai*. This *santri* was a *muballigh* (preacher). While PPP was the Islamic party, such criticism could impinge on an area that could discredit the *kiai*. Some years later, the *santri* had a psychological problem, which according to some sources had no clear cause. Since he was a *muballigh* his mental illness was known to many people, who often came or heard his preaching. Some people thought that his illness was due to the *kualat* (indirect curse) that resulted from his discrediting his teacher, Kiai Musta'in. Hence, the *muballigh* was sent to face Kiai Musta'in and beg for his forgiveness. After this visit, the *muballigh* recovered from his mental ilness.

The problem of *baraka* or *karama* has indeed been embedded in the practice and culture of Javanese Islam. These practices have produced attitudes that might be exaggerated and 'not allowed', from an Islamic perspective[9]. The Javanese Muslims, for example, differentiate some things in terms of their *karama*, incurring *baraka*. A respondent who used to be the *khaddam* (servant) of a well known *kiai* in Jombang, but is now a lecturer at the *Universitas Darul Ulum* after obtaining his M.A from the government university, Gadjahmada, gave me an illustration drawn from a Javanese whom he had interviewed. This

---

[8] Some scholars have conceptualised the terms traditional and modern orthodox Muslims to refer to the Islamic organisations represented by NU and the Muhammadiyah respectively. This conceptualisation, however, is no longer adequate. The basis for this conceptualisation was initially the educational background of both groups, NU society being more *pesantren* oriented and Muhammadiyah tending to be modern educated. However, this situation has changed significantly. Both societies are now modern in terms of their education. Many NU leaders both locally and nationally are university graduates; and their concern for modern education for NU members is great. As I discussed earlier, some *pesantren* provide their *santri* with university and other modern institutions.

[9] This heretical situation is what worries the Muhammadiyah members. The Muhammadiyah movement tries to throw away any practice classified as *khurafat* (heretical), even though, as I discuss in another part of this thesis, they are in essence also involved in such things as *bid'a*, which is beyond their awareness. The words *khurafat* and *bid'a* are Arabic. They mean heresy respectively. Nevertheless, there is a different understanding between NU and Muhammadiyah concerning how *bid'a* things are seen from the Islamic perspective. NU grounds its understanding in the principle of *al-muhafaza bi'l-qadim al-salih wa'l-akhdhu bi'l-jadid al-aslah* (maintaining existing good religious practice, and adopting any new practice which is religiously better). It thus encourages the spread of Islam and even the adoption of other practices as far as they can be coloured by Islam. On the other hand, Muhammadiyah is more concerned with purification, and tries to remove any heretical practice from Islam.

Javanese, who works in the Jogyakarta palace, considered his salary to have a special value. While realising that his salary was not sufficient to support his family, he was convinced that accepting such a salary would incur *baraka*, which might give him a chance to obtain additional employment outside the palace. He thus deemed the salary a sacred thing that merited special treatment. A person with such a belief would not put the salary into the same pocket or wallet as money coming from other sources. He would physically separate such salary from other money if he put them in the same pocket.

In Jombang my field assistant told me about a *kiai* who has a *karama*. The *karama* of this *kiai*, however, is often related to a certain accident experienced by someone but which was not known by the *kiai* himself. This example is to indicate that the result of a *kiai's karama*, either *baraka* or *kualat*, is automatic. The *karama* responds to a certain attitude of a Muslim in accordance with his relation with the *kiai*. Thus, any good perception about *kiai* would incur *baraka* on the Muslim's part, and any bad attitude (*kurang ajar*) would cause *kualat*. Thus, the *baraka* is not only obtained by the *kiai's* prayers, but can also be elicited by those who have good relations with the *kiai*.

This culture of subordination does not seem to be characteristic only of traditional Javanese, since we can find its parallels in the culture of sainthood in general, such as in North Africa. The notion of *baraka* has resulted not only in the existence of small kingdom-like groupings established by a *kiai* or saint, but has also created a culture of inequality in social relations. The *kiaiship* in Java has become a small kingdom-like entity that exerts a type of informal rulership; and gatherings to obtain the *kiai's baraka* have become a routine ritual. In Jombang, where people's emotional attachment to the *kiai* is sufficiently strong, the culture of subordination not only marks the relationship between the *kiai* and his society but is extended to the society's relationship with the *kiai's* family. The people's view of the *kiaiship* leads them to foster good relations with the *kiai's* family as well. Treating the *kiai's* family well, in one informant's opinion, is a necessity since the family is the inheritor of one's integrity (cf. Sukamto, 1992).

There are several media through which the relationship between the *kiai* and his community is perpetuated. Firstly, it is important to look at the *pesantren* culture (see Dhofier, 1982) within which the *kiai* provides Islamic studies for his *santri*. The relationship between the *kiai* and his *santri* is very close and, in some cases, very emotionally laden because of the charismatic position of the *kiai* in his community, informed by a culture of subordination. Since these close relationships are not confined to the *pesantren* but continue after the *santri* become members of society, the perpetuation and the spread of such culture is assured. This unequal relationship is perpetuated because former *santri* continue to visit their *kiai* regularly. The alumni of a *pesantren* commonly make regular visits to former *kiai* just to do *silaturrahmi* (lit. to connect one's kindness to others) and obtain the *kiai's* blessing. Such regular visits do not stop even after a *kiai*'s son succeeds his father in leading the *pesantren*. This is because the position of the *kiai* and his son is the same in the *santri* perspective. In addition, by the time the the son occupies the *kiaiship*, the former *santri* are usually sending their own sons to the *pesantren* now managed by the *kiai*'s son.

A second factor which helps bind the *santri* to the *kiai* relates to certain important religious rituals, which are held by the *kiai* and are attended by former *santri*, including those from other provinces. These rituals range from the commemoration of the death of the founder of the *pesantren* to the festival at the end of schooling. In the *tarekat* world, there are religious rituals, like *mujahada kubro* (great ritual) which are attended by thousands of followers. On the one hand, such rituals provide a forum where people can practise their religious beliefs. On the other hand, it is the medium through which the relationship between the *kiai* and his *santri* or followers can be strengthened. A number of people, some of them very young, whom I met in Jombang, had come from other provinces just to attend such religious rituals. "I feel I must attend such an important event as the *mujahada kubro*", said a young member of the *Penyiar Sholawat Wahidiyah* who had come from Jakarta. Although he had to spend four nights attending this ritual, he was very happy. What was important for him was that his attendance at this ritual would incur *baraka*.

However, we can find some changes in this culture of submission with regard to people's relationships with their *kiai* and in relation to the notion of *baraka* itself among the younger *santri* community. The more secularly educated young *santri* have different notions, reflecting changes in society and general attitudes toward the institution of the *kiaiship* itself. The changing pattern of *pesantren* education, especially in relation to the motivation brought by the *santri* to the *pesantren*, has given rise to changes in their perception of the *kiaiship*. Although such changes have not been pronounced, they affect the pattern of relationships between members of the community and the *kiai*. I will discuss this further in a later chapter of this thesis.

4.3 The Fragmented Organisation of Islam

The *pesantren* in Jombang are well developed in comparison to those in other cities. It is thus understandable that Indonesian Muslims call Jombang the *city of santri*. This development is related to the efforts of the *kiai* to spread Islam. These efforts were initially begun by individual *kiai* who extended *pesantren* education through familial connections. Thus the increase in the number of *pesantren* in Jombang is in many respects a result of the expansion of the *kiai* families. It is common for a son of a *kiai* to establish another *pesantren* after he is mature and has his own family. This pattern of expansion usually occurs when the *kiai* has many children. As the leadership of most *pesantren* is inherited, with the leadership being passed down from father to son, the availability of many children has enabled the *kiai* to extend the *pesantren* through the establishment (by their children) of other *pesantren* in nearby villages or other cities.

Despite the familial connections between many *pesantren* in Jombang, the authority of individual *pesantren kiai* is autonomous in that each has unfettered rights in terms of the management of his *pesantren*. He is not influenced by other *kiai*. Such independence is more in evidence when we consider the political affiliation of various *pesantren*. Since 1977, for example, the *Pesantren Darul Ulum* has had a different political orientation from that of the *Pesantren Bahrul Ulum*, despite the fact that both have close familial connections.

Each *kiai* has certain *santri* and a section of society as his followers. This leads to a situation where Muslims in Jombang are socially fragmented. There are various groups in society, each following the leadership of their *kiai*. However, these groupings, in many respects are not acknowledged, since in people's daily lives there are few situations of open conflict. Nevertheless, the existence of such groupings becomes apparent if one compares the present situation to that of the 1950s, when the conflicts in society were obvious. Each group tried to humiliate each other, so that people called this conflictual situation in the 1950s *zaman poyok-poyokan*, a period of humiliation (Pranowo, 1991).

There are two interesting points concerning the leadership of the *kiai* and the grouping of Muslim society in Jombang. The first concerns the institution of *kiaiship* which acts as a 'small kingdom', independent of others in terms of the connection with its community and its structural existence in relation to NU. The followers of, or sympathisers with, such a 'kingdom' are not only derived from the local area but also from other districts of Jombang. There is no spatial limitation concerning the influence of a local *kiai* since he can attract followers from other areas which might be within the sphere of influence of another *kiai*. By the same token, it is very likely that some people living in the same district as a *kiai* would be followers of other *kiai* living in other districts. I need to stress this point because in Jombang there are a large number of *kiai*[10]. One result of this is that individuals in Jombang often move beyond their district boundaries. This situation is promoted by NU, especially its *tarekat* groups, which often hold ritual activities attended by thousands of members from different parts of Jombang. In this situation people from other districts are introduced to the local *kiai* leadership, which makes it possible for them to come under this local *kiai's* influence.

The same holds true in the *tarekat* world. In Jombang, there are at least four *tarekat* movements, each with its own followers. Although there is no open conflict between members of these *tarekat*, the allegiance of the members would

---

[10] As I mentioned there are three categories of *kiai, the stage kiai* (preacher) also has strong influence in society. Due to the mobility of the *stage kiai*, his followers are spread throughout Jombang.

be definitely given to their respective leaders, the *murshid*. Members always regard their *tarekat* as the best. Their allegiance has been strengthened through ritual practices led by the *murshid* which assist the establishment of an emotional relationship. The relationship between *tarekat* members and their *murshid* is stronger than that between the *pesantren kiai* and their followers (see the case of Kiai Musta'in's joining Golkar).

The emergence of local authority and its strong influence among its followers was encouraged after the internal conflict which occurred in NU early in the 1970s and in the second half of the 1980s. The phrase *kiai saya* (my *kiai*) is commonly uttered to show allegiance toward certain *kiai* and indifference toward others. This fact, on the other hand, shows us that in present-day Jombang no one *kiai* has influence which extends throughout the entire society. The emerging local powers of the *pesantren kiai*, independent of each other, could lay the seeds of social tension or even conflict if each of them directs its followers in different directions. A *kiai* in Jombang told me that there is no one *kiai* who has the power to unify these local authorities, so that tension often occurs when they take different political stands. This statement indicates that familial connectedness notwithstanding, the relationship between the *pesantren kiai* in regard to politics is rather fragile. NU, to which most are affiliated, only coordinates the *pesantren*. It is incapable of directing the *kiai* politics.

From the fact that NU has two (informal) affiliated institutions, the *pesantren* and the *tarekat*, we can infer that within NU there exist various sub-cultures, each of which is different from the other in many respects. The world of the *santri* in the *pesantren*, for example, may be different from that of *tarekat* followers. Although all of these institutions remain under the umbrella of NU, their performance as expressed through the attitude and behaviour of their followers, especially with respect to politics, continues to indicate differences. This situation means that the NU's strength in practice lies in its sub-institutions. In other words, the strength of NU leadership has been established and centred on the *kiai* leadership in these two institutions.

Thus I would venture to say that the situation in regard to the *kiai*-followers relationship in Jombang might be different from other regions in Java where the role of the *pesantren* and the *tarekat* is less dominant. In Jombang, the allegiance of the NU members is given to the *pesantren* and the *tarekat* rather than to NU itself. Popular emotional attachment toward NU has for a long time been built through the *pesantren* and *tarekat*. It is the *kiai*, as leaders of the *pesantren* and *tarekat* with close ties to local society, who have established an ideological commitment among their followers and related them to NU as an organisation. Accordingly, it is the *kiai* who run the *pesantren* or lead the *tarekat*, not NU, who have mass followers identified as NU members. We can understand from this perspective that NU in Jombang as an organisation of *kiai* does not have a monopoly on power. In certain cases it may even be powerless, since the existing power is spread among *kiai* running the *pesantren* or heading the *tarekat*. The equilibrium of this structure can easily be disturbed by social tension or even conflict, when the different attitudes of the *kiai* of *pesantren* or the *kiai* of *tarekat* cannot be reconciled.

This perspective is significant if we want to understand the social tension occurring at the grassroots level in Jombang. Such tension, which usually does not impinge on the ideological domain, actually constitutes an expression of the tension existing among the *kiai*. NU as an organisation would be powerless to induce societal action unless the *kiai* gave their approval. In the case of deciding the day of the *'idu'l-fitr* festival, for example, Muslims in Jombang would not follow any decision made by NU unless their *kiai* were in accord. Accordingly, if there is any contradiction between a decision made by NU[11] and that of local *kiai*, the Islamic society in Jombang would turn to the *kiai*.

I need to emphasise and give further detail of the existing power dispersion, especially in the *tarekat*. In contrast to *tarekat kiai*, the *pesantren kiai* does not delegate his power to his assistants, so that he is not threatened by the power of others. His assistants in many respects lack direct relations with the society. The assistant's position in a *pesantren* differs from that of *khalifa* in the *tarekat*. The *kiai's* assistant's position in the *pesantren* is a formal structural position in the management of the *pesantren*, which may include teaching, while the position of the *khalifa* involves serving the followers' spiritual needs, moulding their unity under the leadership of the *murshid* and promoting emotional attachment toward the leaders of the *tarekat* in general. Furthermore the relationship between the *pesantren kiai* and society is less formal and looser than that of *tarekat kiai*. The assistant in the *pesantren* does not have an intense relationship with the society. The *khalifa*, on the other hand, devote themselves to the *tarekat* and assist the *murshid* in running any *istighatha* (religious ritual in the *tarekat*) and building emotional unity among the followers. It is the *khalifa* who actually have direct relationships with members since, with dozens of places for ritual practice established in Jombang, where *istighatha* is held once a week, the *murshid* cannot attend all sessions. He needs the *khalifa* to fulfill his duty in conducting the *istighatha*. The establishment of one's membership in the *tarekat* is thus dependent on the efforts of the *khalifa* through their public practice of *istighatha*; and the internal conflicts that occur in the *tarekat* in Jombang are very much fostered by the attitudes of these *khalifa*.

---

[11] One needs to differentiate between the *kiaiship* and NU institutionally. NU is a socio-religious organisation run by the *kiai*; but since not all the personnel in the NU leadership are *kiai*, the influence of NU is not dominant. That is why in Jombang it is the individual *kiai*, not the NU, who are more influential in inducing popular action.

Within the existing structure, the centralisation of a *murshid's* leadership in a *tarekat* is not provided with adequate power, since the charismatic authority accrued by his being the leader is, among other things, determined by the *khalifa's* assessment of his legitimacy. The situation means that the *murshid*, as the sole leader[12], distributes his charismatic authority to his *khalifa*. Although the *khalifa* are actually only the conductors of *tarekat* rituals and do not occupy a position which determines the legitimacy of the *tarekat* as the *murshid* does, they still have power. Their religious authority to conduct *istighatha*, which is given by the *murshid*, can be the means of opposing the charismatic power of the *murshid* himself.

Compared to that of the *pesantren kiai*, the relationship between the *tarekat kiai* and their followers is stronger. The emotional attachment, imbued with religious colour, is more clearly expressed. The *murshid* in the *tarekat*, being seen as a spiritual guide who can bring the society or those individuals involved in the *tarekat* closer to Allah, is very decisive in establishing this relationship. The ideology of *murshidship* is institutionalised through the process of 'indoctrination'. The *murshid* or his assistants, the *khalifa*, usually give brief talks before any *istighatha* is held, emphasising the importance of obedience to the *murshid* and the need to follow in the *murshid* steps. The *guru* or the *murshid* is not only regarded as a means for society to approach Allah, but he is also deemed to be a kind of 'doctor'[13] who can cure social diseases. That is why the influence of the *murshid* in the *tarekat* is so strong, enabling the *mursyi* and his *khalifa* to build a cohesive community, held together by strong emotions.

Due to this emotion, it is understandable if religious gatherings held by the *tarekat*, not to mention the gathering to commemorate the *haul* (a yearly religious commemoration for the death) of the previous *murshid*, are always attended by a huge number of followers. A *tarekat kiai*[14] told me one day that the *haul* for Kiai Wahab Chasbullah, one of the NU founders, was usually attended by an insignificant number of people, despite the fact that Kiai Wahab was a great *kiai*. One of his sons contacted this *kiai*, asking him to encourage the Jombang population to come to the next *haul*. Due to the *kiai* invitation, the *haul* was attended by thousands of people, the majority of them *tarekat* members.

Nevertheless, there are some interesting points to explore in terms of the close relationship between the *murshid* and his followers and the *kiai* and Muslim

---

[12] During Kiai Musta'in's leadership in the *Tarekat Qadiriyah Wa Naqsyabandiyah*, he was the sole *murshid* of this sufi order in Jombang. The same held true with Kiai Rifai and Kiai Dimyati. It should be noted, however, that the *Tarekat Qadiriyah Wa Naqsyabandiyah* centred in Cukir, Jombang, currently has three *murshid*. Nevertheless, the *murshid* cannot attend all *istighatha* attended by members. They, too, have to delegate their *khalifa* to lead such *istighatha*.

[13] I received this explanation when I attended a religious sermon delivered by a *khalifa* of the *Tarekat Qadiriyah Wa Naqsyabandiyah* in the *Pesantren Darul Ulum*.

[14] Interview with Kiai Khoerul Anwar, 28 May 1993.

society in general. The split of the *Tarekat Qadiriyah Wa Naqsyabandiyah* into two groups[15] has great significance for our understanding and reviewing of conceptual frameworks which relate to the limitation of charismatic authority, as modeled by Weber, or to the fragility of the norms inducing social action. The charismatic authority, as applied through the leadership of a *murshid*[16] in the *tarekat*, has some boundaries which determine the areas or circumstances for its legitimate application. The holder of charismatic authority is usually deemed as powerful. However, such authority in certain situations can be powerless when its entrenched usage is overstepped. At this point the followers have "a possible basis for a challenge to the leader's legitimacy and sometimes a motive for his replacement" (Hill, 1987:154).

For the *tarekat* followers, these boundaries are fairly normative although blurred. It is loosely formulated in the concept of *memperjuangkan Islam* (to struggle for Islam). According to this concept, tacit evaluation is made by any *tarekat* member or society in general of a *tarekat kiai*. The exaggerated respect, or even 'kissing the hand' to gain *baraka* from a *kiai*, afforded by a member of a *tarekat*, would cease if the *kiai* was devoid of this *memperjuangkan Islam* attitude. Possession of this quality is sustained by the leadership structure of the *tarekat* itself. The *tarekat* followers in Jombang are grouped according to different *istighatha* headed by the *khalifa*. The *khalifa*, through conducting weekly local *istighatha* have cemented good relationships with their *tarekat* members, an intimacy which might be stronger than that which marks members' closeness to their *murshid*. Any deviation by a *khalifa* would hence affect the followers' attitude towards their *murshid*[17].

From the above discussion it is evident that the decline of legitimacy of the *murshid* in the *tarekat* derives mostly from his overstepping the boundary; and the *khalifa*[18], because of their closeness to the members, have responded to the *murshid's* excesses by challenging his leadership. So it is very likely that the

---

[15] As I discussed in Chapter II, the former *Tarekat Qadiriyah Wa Naqsyabandiyah* in Jombang is now divided into two, that is the *Tarekat Qadiriyah Wa Naqsyabandiyah* organised by the *Jam'iyah Ahli Thoriqoh Al-Mu'tabaroh An-Nahdliyah*, which was established through the NU congress in Semarang in 1979, and the *Tarekat Qadiriyah Wa Naqsyabandiyah* coordinated by the *Jam'iyah Ahli Thoriqoh Al-Mu'tabaroh Indonesia* which was formally headed by Kiai Musta'in.

[16] I apply the charismatic authority to the leadership of a *murshid* since he is regarded as a holy man through whom people can obtain *baraka*. See discussion in section 2 of this chapter.

[17] In addition, I do not rule out the possibility of direct evaluation from members themselves in regard to the attitude of *memperjuangkan Islam* of the *murshid*. Such a possibility, however, seems to be hindered by the existence of a culture of 'obedience' to the *murshid* which exists among the *tarekat* members.

[18] It is interesting to compare the *khalifaship* in the *tarekat* in Jombang and in Indonesia in general with that in Kurdistan as noted by Bruinessen (1992). In the latter the political dynamic of *khalifaship* is apparent. In the former the *khalifaship* is merely concerned with assisting with religious rituals in the *tarekat* which are mostly those which cannot be conducted by the *murshid*. In the latter the function of the *khalifa* is the same as in the former. However, in the latter it is very likely that a *khalifa*, in Bruinessen's (1992:245) words, "declared himself a sheikh against the wish of his murshid" for his own political interests.

exodus of the followers of Kiai Musta'in, which will be discussed in Chapter V, was motivated by some of his *khalifa*, whose political perspective was different from Kiai Musta'in's. By the same token, the continuous allegiance of some followers in the *tarekat* led by Kiai Musta'in was because some of his *khalifa* were very loyal to him. The political defection of Kiai Musta'in, in the view of this loyal group of followers, did not have any connection with the *tarekat*, since their loyalty to him did not necessarily mean that they had to follow his political steps. Such a structural perspective holds only for our understanding of the leadership in the *tarekat* movement.

4.4 The Modern Kiai and Santri

There are two types of *kiai* in the *pesantren* based on their educational background, that is the traditional *kiai* who have undertaken Islamic studies in traditional *pesantren* and modern *kiai* whose Islamic knowledge was acquired through a formal modern Islamic tertiary institution. The traditional *kiai* usually has more knowledge of Islam than a modern *kiai*. The modern *kiai*, on the other hand, has a better methodology in teaching Islam than a traditional *kiai*. The difference is generational. Most of the traditional *kiai* derive from an older generation who had no opportunity to acquire a formal modern education. It was not until the second half of the 1960s that the *pesantren* in Jombang and other parts of Indonesia provided the *santri* with a modern system of education (see discussion on *pesantren* in Chapter II). Although this categorisation may be blurred in the sense that both traditional and modern *kiai* can have the same quality in their teaching, their difference in educational background has created a different image of them among the *santri*. In the future it is probable that all *kiai* in any modern *pesantren* will be modern *kiai*. This is because modern Islamic learning at a formal university or other institution is becoming a necessity from the perspective of the *santri*. Modern *santri* need modern *kiai* who have a broader educational background and range of skills. In addition, there is a trend among *kiai* families to obtain a formal degree from a university.

The presence of some modern *kiai* in the *pesantren* has hence resulted in no problems. Although their knowledge of Islam is doubted by their senior *kiai*, they are accepted by the *santri* and society in general. In my observation, some of them (people call them 'secular *kiai*') are equal in ability to senior *kiai*, since they have acquired sufficient knowledge of Islam. The *santri* give them the same respect as they do to the traditional *kiai*. The point is not whether a *kiai* is secularised in the sense of being educated in a modern Islamic institution, but whether or not he is equipped with Islamic knowledge. According to Idham[19], a current *santri* at the *Pesantren Tebuireng*, the respect given by a *santri* to his

---

[19] Interview with Idham Khalid, a student of the *Institut Keislaman Hasyim Asy'ari* and a local leader of PMII, 15 September 1994.

kiai has nothing to do with formal educational attainment. Idham feels he has to give homage to any *kiai* to the extent that he is well equipped with Islamic knowledge. In the view of other *santri*, it is essential for a *kiai* to have received a modern Islamic education, which can raise the position of the *kiai* in the eyes of his *santri*. Exposure to modern education makes the *kiai* more open and gives him a wider perspective than those traditional *kiai* who completed their education in traditional *pesantren*. These are qualities appreciated by modern *santri*.

It should nonetheless be noted that the leadership of a modern *kiai* is different from that of a normal traditional *kiai*. The emotional attachment between him and his following is less strong in many respects. Some modern *kiai*, however, still invoke strong emotional feelings in their followers in so far as they are supported by other factors, such as the genealogy of *kiaiship* or certain institutions with which they are affiliated. I found, for example, that a *santri* kissed the hand of a younger modern *kiai* who had graduated from a certain university. Although this *kiai* is not particularly erudite in Islam, he is treated the same as the older traditional *kiai*. This is so because he is the son of a well known *kiai* in Jombang. In certain institutions, such as the *tarekat*, the position of the modern *kiai* does not incur any problem in the sense that they hold the same position in the eyes of their followers. Kiai Rifai Romly, to mention only one example, was a modern *kiai* who was able to build emotional ties with his followers. He was a modern *kiai* for he graduated from a modern Islamic institution, obtaining a degree of *Sarjana Hukum* (Master of Law). He also assumed a *murshidship* in the *Tarekat Qadiriyah Wa Naqsyabandiyah*, and his leadership in this *tarekat* ran well.

Although there is little difference between traditional and modern *kiai* in respect of the attitude of the *santri* in general toward them, the perspective of the *santri* on *kiaiship* in general is changing. This change not only relates to the *santri* interpretation of *pesantren* education but also impinges on their world view, especially the values underlying their social relationship with their master, the *kiai*.

While the perspective of the *santri* toward their *kiai* within the context of the *pesantren* is changing, the change in the perspective of Muslim society towards the *kiai* is taken for granted. The modernising process which contributes to such change is greater in society generally than in the *pesantren* world. The changing pattern of *kiai* relationships within the broader society relates especially to the continuing process of social mobility in Muslim society in Indonesia. The emergence of more educated individuals, who have either graduated from Islamic or secular universities, has made available agents other than *kiai* who can give professional religious advice and who possess Islamic learning. The *kiai* is no longer the sole agent who provides Islamic learning, since society can obtain such learning from other agents, such as Muslim scholars[20] who teach in tertiary educational institutions. Another important factor which impinges on existing norms of relationship, especially between the *santri* and their *kiai*, is the availability of a greater flow of information which can give rise to the emergence of modern values. The *santri* now have access to a variety of books, magazines or newspapers provided by the *pesantren*, a situation which exposes the *santri* to a modernising world outside the world of the *pesantren*.

The following account describes the change in the attitude of a *santri* in terms of his relationship with the *kiai*:

Barghowi is a lecturer at the *Universitas Darul Ulum*. He has just finished his MA in sociology at the Gadjahmada University, one of the few prestigious universities in Indonesia. He used to be a *khaddam* of Kiai Musta'in. His promotion to his current job at the university is due to his closeness to this *kiai* who established the university. *Khaddam* is an Arabic term which literally means servant; but the term is commonly used to refer to a special servant, since the *khaddam* serves the *kiai* in such matters as taking his drink or receiving his guests. Barghowi's position as a *khaddam* indicates that he did not come from a well-to-do family. Becoming a *khaddam* was thus a way by which Barghowi could afford his life and education during his stay in the *kiai's pesantren*. In addition, being a *khaddam* enables one to obtain *baraka*. Being a *khaddam* not only involves being in a subordinate position (facing the *kiai*) but also being part of the culture of obedience or giving exaggerated homage to the *kiai* and his family.

Together with other *khaddam*, Barghowi was sent to the local school owned by the *kiai* until he finished high school. Later the *kiai* married him to a woman of Barghowi's choice. While he was working as a teacher in a local *madrasa*, he continued his study at the university owned by the *kiai*. Again, due to his closeness to the *kiai* family, he was accepted as a lecturer at the *Universitas Darul Ulum* after he finished his sociology study at this university.

Teaching at the university and living in a Javanese social environment as head of a family has introduced Barghowi to life which is different from that of the *pesantren*. His involvement in academic activities widened his perspective, a situation which encouraged him gradually to change his accustomed behaviour as a *santri* formed during his service as a *khaddam*. He dared to propose more openness in the university environment, making some criticisms about undemocratic practices occurring in it. This is an action which he was unlikely

---

[20] It is even often suggested that the service or explanation of Muslim scholars concerned with Islam is more satisfying. They usually give explanations which are acceptable to common sense and the logic of the educated. There is also no superior-subordinate pattern in their relationship with society in contrast to the relationship between a *kiai* and his followers or his *santri*. The role of these scholars can be seen in the religious activities on some campuses, which are organised by Muslim scholars rather than by *kiai*.

to have undertaken while he was a *khaddam*. Barghowi made his criticism at a meeting presided over by the *kiai's* wife (who happened to be the one who had sent him to school during his service to her husband). When he was told that the *nyai* was disappointed and even felt offended by his criticism, Barghowi just smiled. He did not feel uncomfortable when the *nyai* called him *kemelinti* (a Javanese term which means *tidak tahu diri*, that is one who does not acknowledge that he was supported by the person whom he criticised). Later he came to the *nyai*, asking her apology. He said: "Nyai, saya mohon maaf karena saya kemelinti" (I apologise for my being *kemelinti*). It is said that when he said *kemelinti*, he emphasised the word (by stressing its sound and displaying no shyness), an attitude which in *santri* culture expresses a rather rude and arrogant manner. He emphasised the word *kemelinti* because it was the word which was spoken by the *nyai* to someone else when she talked about Barghowi's unacceptable behaviour.

This example shows how the change in attitude of the modern *santri* toward the *kiai* can occur. Barghowi is the personification of those who grew up and were socialised in a culture of respect but have subsequently changed. The Barghowi case also provides an example of the response of a *kiai* family to such change.

Such occurrences are becoming less rare. At the end of February 1994, according to a fortnightly magazine[21], hundreds of high school (SMA) students of the *Pesantren Darul Ulum* in Jombang held a demonstration. They asked the *pesantren* leader to establish a more democratic situation in their school environment. The leader of the *pesantren* responded to this action by expelling 15 of the students involved. "Diukur dengan uang puluhan milyaran pun tak cukup untuk mengobati kekecewaan kami. Di pondok tidak pernah ada demonstrasi" ("Millions of rupiah cannot heal our disappointment. In the *pesantren* no demonstration has ever been carried out"), he said. Furthermore, a senior *kiai* of this *pesantren* suggested that "Kalau murid sudah berani menilai gurunya, hubungan rohani antara mereka bisa tertutup. Murid tidak akan tambah pandai, tapi akan bodoh" ("If a student evaluates his teacher, the spiritual relationship between them is closed off. The student will not become clever but become stupid").

The action taken by the *kiai* to expell some of the students involved did not stop other *santri* from holding similar protests. As reported by a newspaper[22], a number of students of the *Universitas Darul Ulum* held a similar protest at the *Pesantren Darul Ulum*. The protest was clearly directed at the head of the *pesantren*, Kiai As'ad Umar. The *kiai* was reported to have given political support to President Suharto's candidacy for another term in office (1998). Not only did the student consider that the support had been given too early, but they also

---

[21] Forum Keadilan, 2 March 1995.
[22] Media Indonesia, 2 July 1995.

saw such support as the *kiai's* effort to gain certain political ends. The student thus felt that the *kiai* had exploited Islam for political purposes[23].

What I have described above is a new phenomenon in the *pesantren* world. Modernisation of the *pesantren* has not only produced a favourable condition for the emergence of modern *santri*, but has also distorted the character of the *pesantren* world. The characteristics of *keihklasan* (lit. willingness to serve for Islam), which have for a long time been the foundation of *pesantren* education, have been replaced by a more profit-making one. The secular school-based system, which has been established in the *pesantren*, differs on a basic level from that of the traditional *pesantren*. The former stresses the transference of skill based knowledge, while the latter emphasises character building. The relationship between the teacher and the student in traditional *pesantren* is marked by exaggerated respect. In modern schools, however, such a pattern of relationship is less likely to occur, making it feasible for a teacher to be criticised by his students.

---

[23] As the *kiai's* influence on Muslim society is still great, the *kiai's* decision (*kebulatan tekad*, means political determination) to support Suharto's next presidency, from the *santri's* point of view, will influence Muslim society's political attitude. The political manoeuvre of Kiai As'ad Umar was launched after he held a meeting with around 70 *kiai* throughout Jombang, discussing the possibilities of accepting some funding which would be offered by the government and Golkar for the *pesantren*. Some *kiai* protested against Kiai As'ad Umar since such political support was not discussed at the meeting. It is important to note that this protest which was held by the students of *Universitas Darul Ulum* incurred reaction from the *santri* of the *Pesantren Darul Ulum*. Some of the students of the *Universitas Darul Ulum* are *santri* who stay at the *Pesantren Darul Ulum*. Many of them, however, live outside the *pesantren* environment.

Chapter 5: The Kiai and the Dynamics of Politics at the Local Level

This chapter tries to highlight the problems of the *kiai* leadership in the *tarekat* world. It examines how the *kiai* exercises his power. It explores other principles, in addition to the concept of *baraka* discussed in Chapter IV, which underlie the followers relationship with their *kiai*. There are general guide lines which a *kiai* must follow in order to legitimise his political position in the eyes of his followers and society in general. Despite the close relations with his followers, a *kiai* is vulnerable to their evaluation. The split of the *Tarekat Qadiriyah Wa Naqsyabandiyah* in Jombang clearly demonstrates how a great *kiai* with a large number of followers was shaken and his legitimacy to lead the *tarekat* was questioned. This case, morover, is sociologically important in terms of the breakdown of the existing order and the introduction of another. The main actor in the split presented a new perspective on Islamic politics in Indonesia. Despite being sharply criticised by his *kiai* colleagues, his political standpoint was eventually followed by other *kiai* ten years later when NU introduced its policy of 'back to khittah'.

In addition, the chapter also discusses local formal *kiai* leadership through NU. It highlights the conflict which occured among the local elite of NU. The local conflict between *kiai* in Jombang has occurred in the first half of the 1960s when a *kiai* in NU leadership was forced to resign. As a *kiai* has his own followers, his conflict with other *kiai* in NU has sharpened the nature of organisational fragmentation of Muslim society in Jombang.

5.1 The Kiai's Politics in the Tarekat

NU, as the largest Islamic organisation in Indonesia, dominated the politics of Islam until 1984. As a political party, from 1952 to 1973, the direction of its politics was clear. The same held true when NU merged with other Islamic organisations to form the Masjumi or with other Islamic political parties to form the United Development Party, PPP (both Islamic political parties). All the institutions under NU, including its members and sympathisers, followed its politics of Islam. There was a harmonious relationship among the *kiai* in Jombang at that time. Not only did they feel themselves to be representatives of the same organisation, NU, but they also moved in the same direction, pursuing Islamic politics.

This situation created a political ethos which not only strengthened the unity of the *umma* (the transnational Islamic community), but also raised the significance of the political struggle that must be carried out by a Muslim. It is this ethos that has enlivened Jombang society, though it has lately been marked by different ideological orientations. Since the legitimacy given by the *kiai* in regard to politics contributes significantly to building the orientation of the *umma*, the various current political affiliations of the *kiai* tend to create divisions within the *umma*. I will discuss this later in Chapter VI.

The first break that disturbed the harmonious situation in Jombang Muslim society happened when Kiai Musta'in, the former head of both the *Pesantren Darul Ulum* and the *Tarekat Qadiriyah Wa Naqsyabandiyah* defected quietly to the government party, Golkar, preceding the 1977 general election. This defection not only marked a disaffection with, and a disturbance of the existing social structure, but also created the beginning of a split between *kiai* in Jombang, which was followed by hidden conflict between their followers. The conflict occurred between the NU's *kiai*, who maintained affiliation with the only Islamic party, PPP, and Kiai Musta'in and his close *kiai* colleagues. It gave rise to a situation where mutual abuse occurred between *kiai* with each group accusing the other of being *kafir* (infidel)[1]. The Muslim society of Jombang, who had been united by a single Islamic political ethos, was split. Only the most obedient followers of the *tarekat* led by Kiai Musta'in himself and *the santri* in his *pesantren* followed him. For these obedient followers, the *kiai's* defection did not raise any problem. They believed that Kiai Musta'in's teaching remained correct. They also emphasised an absolute obedience to the *guru* (master, the *murshid*) provided that he was not *shirk* (claiming partnership with God; or attributing God's qualities to someone other than Him). The word 'obedient' here needs to be emphasised, since it has significant implications in understanding the subsequent conflict.

The situation was unfavourable for the other *tarekat* members since Kiai Musta'in's joining Golkar marked the breakdown of their *bai'a* (religious following) of him. Some hesitant members did not even attend monthly *istighatha* conducted by Kiai Musta'in himself. They felt it better to gather at the weekly *istighatha* carried out by the *khalifa* who still persisted in their allegiance for the Islamic political party. Some *kiai* in Jombang tried to establish another leadership of the existing *Tarekat Qadiriyah Wa Naqsyabandiyah*, since they no longer regarded the leadership of Kiai Musta'in as legitimate. They promoted Kiai Adlan Ali as the new leader. His leadership in the new *tarekat* was legitimised when he was authorised (through a *bai'a* and *ijaza irshad*) by Kiai Muslih of Mranggen (Semarang). Kiai Adlan's leadership was formally legitimised by NU when he was also chosen as a leader of the *Jam'iyah Ahli Thoriqoh Al-Mu'tabaroh An-Nahdliyah* at its conference in Semarang in 1979.

There are two important points in regard to the formation of the *Jam'iyah Ahli Thoriqoh Al-Mu'tabaroh An-Nahdliyah* by NU. Firstly, this event indicated a

---

[1] Interview with Kiai Aziz Masyhuri, 9 April 1993.

loss of legitimacy for Kiai Musta'in both as the leader of a large *tarekat* organisation, the *Jam'iyah Ahli Thoriqoh Al-Mu'tabaroh* which he had managed since 1975 and the leader of the *Tarekat Qadiriyah Wa Naqsyabandiyah*. NU no longer formally acknowledged the *tarekat* organisation headed by Kiai Musta'in as its *tarekat* although the *kiai* continued to lead his *tarekat* after he joined Golkar. Secondly, the very term *An-Nahdliyyah* (lit. means affiliated with NU) emphasised that this new organisation was NU's *tarekat*. There have hence arisen two *Tarekat Qadiriyah Wa Naqsyabandiyah* and two large *tarekat* organisations, the *Jam'iyah Ahli Thoriqoh Al-Mu'tabaroh* and the *Jam'iyah Ahli Thoriqoh Al-Mu'tabaroh An-Nahdliyah* managing various *tarekat aliran*. The *Tarekat Qadiriyah Wa Naqsyabandiyah* led by Kiai Musta'in was affiliated with the *Jam'iyah Ahli Thoriqoh Al-Mu'tabaroh*, while the *Tarekat Qadiriyah Wa Naqsyabandiyah* headed by Kiai Adlan was affiliated with the *Jam'iyah Ahli Thoriqoh Al-Mu'tabaroh An-Nahdliyah*. Both Kiai Musta'in and Adlan were also the leaders of *Jam'iyah Ahli Thoriqoh Al-Mu'tabaroh* and the *Jam'iyah Ahli Thoriqoh Al-Mu'tabaroh An-Nahdliyah* respectively. Kiai Musta'in *tarekat* was centred in Rejoso, while Kiai Adlan's *tarekat* was centred in Cukir.

The strong reaction of the *kiai* in Jombang against Kiai Musta'in was based on the fact that, at that time, NU was directing Islamic politics, which it articulated through PPP. Their reaction was followed by a sharp decrease in popular loyalty towards Kiai Musta'in. This was expressed by the withdrawal of children from Kiai Musta'in's *pesantren*, and the hesitancy of parents throughout East Java to send their children to his *pesantren*. Moreover, a significant number of the *Tarekat Qadiriyah Wa Naqsyabandiyah* members withdrew from *istighatha* conducted by the *khalifa* of Kiai Musta'in, and some followers joined Kiai Adlan's *tarekat*. Although it is not easy to ascertain all the underlying reasons for such an exodus, the perceived loss of legitimacy of Kiai Musta'in in the eyes of his followers at the grassroot level can be attributed largely to his joining Golkar.

Seen from the perspective of the *kiai* in Jombang, the cause of the conflict can easily be understood. As the Jombang *kiai* had become the guardians of Islamic politics, the line that demarcated Muslim politics from others was clear during the 1970s. The Islamic leaders in Indonesia, especially in NU, had made encouraging noises that sounded very religious, to support the Islamic political parties. In the 1977 general election, the Javanese *kiai* suggested that it was religiously obligatory for a Muslim to vote for the Islamic political party. Such a notion actually had been prevalent during the 1955 and the 1971 general election when Muslims in Indonesia could join one of four Islamic political parties. This notion spread widely, reaching the ears of even very young Muslims[2]. The defection of Kiai Musta'in had great consequences for the political

---

[2] I still remember when I was sixteen and voted for the first time in the 1971 general election. A friend of mine who seemed to have more information suggested that I had to vote for NU to bolster the Muslim

unity of the *umma*, since his defection to Golkar was imitated by some of his followers, especially those who were *tarekat* members.

In the 1971 general election, Golkar was the main rival of NU, as it attempted to gain more popular support from Muslim population. The same held true in the 1977 general election, when NU merged with other Islamic political parties to form PPP. It is thus clear that Kiai Musta'in had broken the tradition of 'not supporting the government party'. The Javanese *kiai* promulgated religious justification about the inappropriateness of his steps. The aspirations of Muslim society in Indonesia had been articulated through the Islamic political party, PPP. What made Kiai Musta'in's steps wrong in the eyes of his critics was a *fatwa* (religious advice) from a senior NU *kiai*, who happened to come from Jombang, suggesting that it was a religious obligation to vote for PPP. The *fatwa* was applied nationally, so that Kiai Musta'in was severely condemned and expelled from NU[3]. The defection of Kiai Musta'in had made some followers doubtful of the necessity to vote for the Islamic political party as suggested by the *fatwa*, or to follow the *murshid* or *guru* who by now joined the government party.

In short, the defection of Kiai Musta'in was clearly against the political efforts being articulated through PPP. The *kiai* in Jombang and East Java generally felt morally obliged to support PPP and its efforts. From this perspective it is understandable that the defection of Kiai Musta'in became a source of humiliation for his fellow *kiai*. So, although most of Kiai Musta'in's followers did not fully know why they should leave him, his political actions gave them enough reason for their exodus. It was commonly believed that the *kiai* should support the Islamic political party, because almost all *kiai* in Indonesia supported the Islamic party of PPP at the time.

However, it is important to note that Kiai Musta'in's reasons for joining the government party seem to have been based on his interpretation of Islam or on

---

position in Indonesian politics. However, the encouragement did not stop there, but was followed by a prohibition to vote for any other party, especially a non-Islamic political party. The prohibition was easily understood, even by those who, at sixteen, knew nothing about politics. In a campaign rally held by NU, a tape of a well known verse from the Qur'an was played to justify not voting for other political parties. In the *pesantren* where I was taking Islamic studies, the verse was played constantly, just to remind the *santri* and the Muslim society nearby of the political demands of their religion. The verse tells of Adam who was asked by God not to eat of the fruits from a certain tree. The result of not obeying the prohibition was very severe. Allah promised Adam and Eve would be classified as *zalim* (unjust doer). "O Adam! dwell thou and thy wife in Paradise, and eat ye whence ye will, but to this tree approach not, lest ye become of the unjust doer" (Sura 2:33). It was clear that the tree mentioned in this verse was identical (politically) to the banyan tree, the symbol of the government political party, Golkar. Islamic politicians were using this verse to remind the *umma* not to support Golkar.

[3] An informant who was very close to NU leadership at that time told me that Kiai Musta'in was fired from NU. Kiai As'ad, the current leader of the *Pesantren Darul Ulum* who joined Golkar at the same time with Kiai Musta'in told me the same information although he did not mention explicitly about Kiai Musta'in but himself. However, Muhammad Baidlowi, who was the NU chairman during this time suggested that no such action was carried out by national NU leader.

his view of what is called the 'Islamic struggle'. The defection of Kiai Musta'in occured because he saw another way to achieve the political ends in regard to the 'Islamic struggle'. His wife[4] told me that he judged as a failure the strategy laid down by the Indonesian *'ulama* in general. He did not wish to further divide Islamic society into a variety of groupings based on ideological orientation[5].

The political interest of Muslim society at that time was represented by the established perspective of the *kiai*, so that those Muslims who were less devout, like the *abangan*, or those who happened to be outside the preferred organisation, like those who were in PDI, were not represented by the *kiai*'s political efforts. That was why to *bekerja di ladang yang tidak dikerjakan kiai lain* (to work in a field not worked by other *kiai*) became an important reason for Kiai Musta'in' defection. A loyal follower of his told me that PPP could be regarded as representing the larger part of the political interest of Indonesian Muslim society, but it was not the only one. Not only were some Muslims affiliated with parties other than PPP, but it is also recognised that it is human to have different interests and perspectives, which can include affiliation with a variety of political organisations. In her opinion, this human trait is actually indicated in the Qur'an, which suggests that Muslims are actually grouped into various clusters, each of which is happy with the way it is. In addition, Kiai Musta'in also tried to give a rationale for his political actions, and also to legitimise it through the use of metaphor. He told his followers that he saw in his sleep that he was playing with a kite with a world globe circled by nine stars (the NU's symbol). He also saw a big banyan tree shadowing his *pesantren* in Jombang[6].

In spite of the fact that few other *kiai* in other regions of Indonesia had already joined the government party by that time, Kiai Musta'in's joining Golkar was of considerable national importance since it led not only to the fragmentation of the *Tarekat Qadiriyah Wa Naqsyabandiyah*, but also to a political split among the *kiai* in NU. The importance of such an event lay in the fact that Kiai Musta'in was the paramount leader of the *Tarekat Qadiriyah Wa Naqsyabandiyah*, the head of the *Pesantren Darul Ulum* and one of the NU leaders in Jombang. His joining Golkar impacted on the unity of the 'Islamic struggle' pursued by the Muslim society in Indonesia through PPP because of his huge number of followers, both in his *tarekat* and in his *pesantren*.

One can thus see the importance of Kiai Musta'in's defection on the existing socio-political grouping within the *tarekat* world and the NU society in general

---

[4] Interview with Kiai Musta'in's wife, 22 June 1993.
[5] There was a strong view among the Indonesian *'ulama* suggesting that only devout Muslims who supported PPP. Less devout Muslims either supported Golkar or PDI. Kiai Musta'in tried to breach this view. His actions implied that all devout Muslims could have free political affiliation.
[6] Interview with Sukamto, 12 August 1993.

in Jombang and East Java. The formal[7] discursive interpretation of Islamic politics, which was represented by the NU's affiliation with the Islamic political party, PPP, was disturbed by the emergence of another interpretation pioneered by Kiai Musta'in. The decision of Kiai Musta'in to join Golkar was the starting point of the acknowledgement of the existence of another interpretation of Islamic politics. This is not to say that his defection was the first of its kind to occur, since similar actions had been taken by few other *kiai*. However, the significance of Kiai Musta'in's action was that it was supported by many of his followers. The defection of other *kiai* had not been. Kiai Musta'in was supported by his followers because he was a great *kiai*. He was the *murshid* of the largest *tarekat* in terms of number of followers in East Java. The others who had defected in a similar way were typically local *kiai*.

The significance of Kiai Musta'in defection thus lay in his introduction of a new interpretation concerning Islamic politics. He inculcated a new understanding, suggesting that Islamic politics need not be restricted to the politics of PPP, the only Islamic political party, but could be any politics which allowed Islamic ideals to be pursued. Kiai Musta'in was delegitimising the existing social order in regard to politics. He tried to rebuild this order through a wider perspective, seeing an Islamic political party as only one means among several in the 'struggle for the *umma*'.

Another significant consequence of his defection was that *tarekat* followers and NU society in general, either in Jombang or East Java and other regions, became divided. This was of course a negative result of Kiai Musta'in's action. In the *tarekat*, those who followed the NU *kiai* joined the *Tarekat Qadiriyah Wa Naqsyabandiyah* led by Kiai Adlan and his *Jam'iyah Ahli Thoriqoh Al-Mu'tabaroh An-Nahdliyyah*, while those who followed Kiai Musta'in remained in his *tarekat* which was affiliated with the *Jam'iyah Ahli Thoriqoh Al-Mu'tabaroh*. It should be emphasised that political affiliation did not have clear-cut relations with *tarekat* membership in the case of Kiai Musta'in's followers. Some followers who were affiliated with and supported PPP continued to support this party without altering their loyalty to Kiai Musta'in and their membership in his *tarekat*.

This interpretation of Kiai Musta'in's motives indicates that what he did was beyond politics. He was more concerned with the 'struggle for Islam' in a wider sense. He was a *kiai* and a *murshid* who was concerned more with the religiosity

---

[7] In any religious society there are always formal and non-formal interpretations either in regard to the doctrine or to the normative values used by the society. The formal interpretation is usually institutionalised and accepted by the members of the society as a whole, so that it becomes the legitimate order. The existing order is supported or built through such formal interpretations. What is also important to note is that a formal interpretation is typically made by a formal (authorised) leader, such as the priest in the Christian world or the *'ulama* in the Islamic world. On the other hand, non-formal interpretations are usually made by individuals and their level of acceptance is more limited. Such interpretation could be a reaction to the more established formal interpretation and hence rather marginal in terms of acceptance by society in general.

of Indonesians than with the power structure in which they lived. This contrasts with the majority of Indonesian *kiai* who tried to focus their struggles through politics on changing the power structure. This situation shows that the obsession about the power of Islam, as it had been conceptualised by some Indonesian *'ulama* in the past, still affected the NU's *kiai* in Jombang. Kiai Musta'in, on the other hand, sought to give more attention to inculcating or giving an understanding of Islam and its values to those Muslims who were marginal in terms of Islamic knowledge. He tried, for example, to combine the *tarekat*, the *pesantren* and the university which he managed. He introduced *tarekat* practice not only into *pesantren* life (since not all *pesantren* were affiliated with the *tarekat* organisation or practised its *wird* and rituals) but also into university life. He introduced his *tarekat* teaching to his *santri* in the *pesantren* and his students at the *Universitas Darul Ulum*. Kiai Musta'in hoped that he created modern-but-religious intellectuals (all those[8] who graduated from his university must stay for two weeks in his *pesantren* to get to know the *pesantren* life. If they did not, they could not get their university certificate). He said that he wanted to create *pesantren* graduates *yang berotak Jerman tapi berhati Masjidil Haram* (lit. with German brains but with hearts attached to the Mosque Al-Haram in Mecca). He desired to establish a modern system of Islamic education that could produce brilliant intellectuals who remained emotionally steeped in Islam. Thus, following the principle of "working the land which was not worked by other *kiai*" Kiai Musta'in was encouraged to join the government party. In other words, he wanted to widen his field of *da'wa*[9]. By being in Golkar, in his view, he could do more for Islam. Not only was the government party the largest organisation in terms of number of members and supporters but it was the party of the ruling elites. By joining that party, Kiai Musta'in intended to introduce Islam to the ruling elites[10]. This helps explain what Kiai Musta'in hoped to gain by risking his position in Islamic society.

However, it should be acknowledged that Kiai Musta'in's defection resulted in his being used by the government for its own political ends. The government

---

[8] It is important to note that not all students of the *Universitas Darul Ulum* were *santri*. Also not all *santri* are familiar with the *tarekat*.
[9] His reason for spreading his *da'wa* among the non-*santri* society became clear when he joined Golkar. He approached Chinese people in Jombang, who then converted to Islam. In Rif'ah's opinion, Kiai Musta'in always adapted to the existing situation. His style of *da'wa* was not strict. Although he was leader of the *tarekat*, he did not mind not wearing his turban when he faced the Chinese whom he tried to convert to Islam. For Rif'ah, this was a proof that Kiai Musta'in was also *luwes* (flexible) in his politics (Interview with Nur Rif'ah, 20 June 1993).
[10] It is interesting to note that a similar argument was given by Kiai As'ad Umar who joined Golkar at the same time as Kiai Musta'in. Kiai As'ad argues that joining Golkar is a necessity if one wants to struggle for Islam. He said, "saya akan membawa pondok melalui orang yang punya wewenang" (I will bring the *pesantren* through those in authority). He meant that Muslims should be accommodating to authority. The Prophet Muhammad, according to As'ad, was the head of a state, and Islam cannot develop without its cooperation with the power holder. As'ad quoted a saying of the *'ulama*, "al-nasu 'ala dini mulkihim" (people are dependent upon the religion of their King).

received an increase in support from the wider society as a result of his defection[11] and its politics were legitimised. In addition, his defection contributed to the weakening of Islamic politics as pursued by the Indonesian *'ulama* in general. Kiai Musta'in was often asked by Golkar to become involved in political campaigns, a situation which created a dilemma for him. But Kiai Musta'in never deviated from his purpose to 'work the land not worked by other *kiai*'. It is said that in his first campaign for Golkar in the 1977 general election in Surabaya, he stood for just two minutes on the stage. His main speech consisted of just asking the audiences to say 'Allahu Akbar' (Allah is the Great) together.

Many *santri* in his *pesantren* and members of his family initially could not believe what they heard in relation to Kiai Musta'in's defection. They were surprised by the way he had breached the existing social order in regard to politics. Rif'ah, a female *santri* who was very close to Kiai Musta'in's family wondered how a *kiai* in the forefront of the Islamic struggle through the Islamic party could defect to another party, a political action that might weaken the politics of Islam. Kiai Musta'in's wife, who was an important supporter of PPP, was equally surprised[12].

5.2 The Followers' Perspective

Most people in Jombang relate the split in the *Tarekat Qadiriyah Wa Naqsyabandiyah* to politics. To join the government party was seen as deviating from the politics of the *umma*, which at that time, from a Muslim perspective, had to be articulated through the Islamic party, PPP, since it was deemed to be the only party trying to articulate Muslim aspirations. As the perception of the necessity of Muslims to affiliate with PPP was very strong, it is easy to see how Kiai Musta'in's political steps could delegitimise his position in the eyes of the *umma*. The formation of the *Jam'iyah Ahli Thoriqoh Al-Mu'tabaroh An-Nahdliyah* by NU confirmed this demotion of Kiai Musta'in and the withdrawal of NU's recognition of his *tarekat* organisation.

Some people who were disappointed with Kiai Musta'in's action tried to discredit him. Various stories undermining Kiai Musta'in's position emerged. According to an informant, there was even someone within his family who tried to discredit him and encouraged *tarekat* followers to forsake him. Whether it was true or not, such an insult seems credible because of the conflict which emerged after his joining Golkar. The informant told me further that such actions by a family

---

[11] My discussion in Chapter VI shows that PPP experienced a decrease in its vote share in almost all *kecamatan* in Jombang in the 1977 general election, while Golkar received an increase in its vote share.

[12] As his wife was an important PPP figure, Kiai Musta'in did not ask her to follow his political action. His wife remained in PPP, but she felt uncomfortable campaigning for her party. But as far as his wife is concerned, she deemed Kiai Musta'in was right in what he did after she had a car accident. She felt that the accident happened because she did not follow his example. This suggestion was denied by her husband. In his opinion, the accident was unrelated to her desicion not to follow him. The accident was merely her destiny decided by God.

member and other *kiai* only occurred after Kiai Musta'in joined Golkar; it had never happened before.

The failure of Kiai Musta'in to retain control of his *tarekat* and its members did not result from processes within the *tarekat* itself but rather was caused by external worldly matters. There was no fundamental problem in regard to Kiai Musta'in's *tarekat* in terms of its religious legitimacy. This is especially evident when we relate those events to the more recent socio-political situation in which some *kiai* have not only allowed their followers to support political parties other than PPP, but have encouraged them to vote for Golkar[13], leaving PPP. Of more interest, however, is how the *tarekat* followers, especially those in the *Tarekat Cukir* see the leadership of the *Tarekat Qadiriyah Wa Naqsyabandiyah* (formerly led by Kiai Musta'in) today. The latest *murshid* is Kiai Dimyati Romly, who succeeded his brother, Kiai Rifai Romly, who died in a car accident in December 1994. I will focus my discussion on Kiai Rifai's leadership since Kiai Dimyati's leadership is new and when I did my field work, this *tarekat* was still led by Kiai Rifai.

My fieldwork indicates mixed reactions. Despite the fact that NU formally tried to exclude the *Tarekat Qadiriyah Wa Naqsyabandiyah* led by Kiai Musta'in from its umbrella[14], by establishing the *Jam'iyah Ahli Thoriqoh Al-Mu'tabaroh An-Nahdliyah*, the legitimacy of the Kiai Musta'in's *tarekat* was still recognised since it was formed by NU's *kiai*. Some prominent *tarekat* figures, however, expressed concern about this *tarekat*. This concern not only related to the *murshidship* of Kiai Musta'in which was deemed defective after he joined the government party, but also to the way his *murshidship* was obtained or passed on from the former *murshid*, his father[15]. A former *khalifa* of Kiai Musta'in, suggested that the chain of *murshidship* of the *Tarekat Qadiriyah Wa Naqsyabandiyah* (*Tarekat Rejoso*) had been broken. The *tarekat* is less *mu'tabarah* because one person in the chain of its *murshidship* was missing. The chain of *murshidship* of the *Tarekat Qadiriyah Wa Naqsyabandiyah* acknowledged by the NU's *kiai* is different from that introduced by Kiai Musta'in after 1977 (See Sukamto, 1992)[16].

Kiai Musta'in in an effort to develop his *tarekat* and at the same time strengthen his position, had published some materials in the form of calendars and others publications. The publication indicated that Kiai Musta'in was given *ijaza irshad*

---

[13] In the 1987 general election a few well known *kiai* in Jombang encouraged Muslims to vote for Golkar. See my discussion about this matter in Chapter VI.
[14] The majority of *kiai* in Jombang did not interpret the formation of the *Jam'iyah Ahli Thoriqoh Almu'tabaroh An-Nahdliyah* as NU's policy to exclude the *tarekat* led by Kiai Musta'in, despite the fact that such formation was a political reaction of NU in conjunction with Kiai Musta'in's political action.
[15] It is important to note, however, that such concern only emerged after Kiai Musta'in joined Golkar. It did not exist before.
[16] See my discussion in Chapter III.

directly by his father, Kiai Romly. In the opinion of some other *kiai*, however, Kiai Romly never gave *ijaza irshad* to his son because the latter was still very young. The *ijaza irshad* received by Kiai Musta'in was passed on from Kiai 'Usman who received *ijaza irshad* from Kiai Romly.

This *kiai's* opinion is not held by the followers of the *Tarekat Rejoso*, who see the situation from a different angle. According to a version of events suggested by one follower, the *murshidship* of Kiai Musta'in and his *tarekat* are absolutely legitimate. In his opinion, Kiai Musta'in received the *bai'a* three times from his father, Kiai Romly, the *murshid* of the *Tarekat Qadiriyah Wa Naqsyabandiyah* at that time. The rest of the *bai'a* were done by Kiai 'Usman after the death of Kiai Romly. Kiai 'Usman was a *khalifa* of Kiai Romly, whose duty was giving *bai'a* to the *tarekat* followers. In this follower's opinion, Kiai 'Usman was not a *murshid* and did not have the right to hold a *murshidship* (even though he was the senior *khalifa*), since the *murshidship* cannot be obtained by just any follower. The *murshidship*, this follower explained further, is inherited (like the authority of a King is inherited by his son); and it was Kiai Musta'in who had the right to receive the transfer of *murshidship* from his father. This transfer of authority (*ijaza irshad*) occurred when the father was on the point of death. According to this follower, the father said: "..'In (a diminutive for Kiai Musta'in) teruskan *tarekat* ini" (lit. "Musta'in, you go on with this *tarekat*"). It is this exchange, in this follower's opinion, which decisively legitimised the *murshidship* of Kiai Musta'in and his *tarekat*. This follower went on to suggest that conflict occurred because of the uncontrolled action of Kiai 'Usman. Kiai 'Usman was assumed to have wanted to be a *murshid*. He felt it was appropriate to achieve *murshidship* since he was the most senior *khalifa* of Kiai Romly, Kiai Musta'in's father. However, it seems that this follower did not know that the NU's *kiai* had accepted Kiai 'Usman as one of the *murshid* of the *Qadiriyah Wa Naqsyabandiyah* order before Kiai Musta'in joined Golkar.

This follower suggested further that the transfer of *murshidship* must be performed by the former *murshid* for his successor, the former giving authority for the latter's succession. It is not legitimate for a senior *khalifa* to receive directly a *murshidship* after the death of a former *murshid*. In his opinion, Kiai 'Usman, Kiai Adlan and Kiai Makki (Makki is one of the three curret *murshid* of the *Tarekat Cukir*) who at that time constituted the senior *khalifa* of Kiai Romly had no right to succeed to the *murshidship*. They did not receive the authority of Kiai Romly to lead this *tarekat*. Although this opinion may not be representative of all *Tarekat Rejoso* followers[17], it gives an indication of their view on both their own *tarekat* and the *Tarekat Cukir*. Such an opinion seems

---

[17] It is hard to find a lay follower who dares to deliver his opinion about the legitimacy of both the *Tarekat Rejoso* and the *Tarekat Cukir*. I interviewed this follower during his presence at the big rituals of his *tarekat* held at the *Pesantren Darul Ulum*.

common among *Tarekat Rejoso* followers. It is doubtful, however, whether they dare to say that the *murshidship* of the *Tarekat Cukir* is not legitimate. In the *tarekat* tradition, no overt action should be taken in regard to perceived errors in 'grey' areas, especially if these impinge on the *murshidship* domain.

Based on the evaluation of Kiai Musta'in's *tarekat*, *tarekat* followers in Jombang cannot help but hold a view on the leadership of Kiai Rifai, the successor of Kiai Musta'in. Certain questions remain unanswered concerning the succession of the leadership in this sufi order[18]. Firstly, there was no *ijaza irshad* given by Kiai Musta'in to anyone to continue the leadership. The continuation or the legitimacy of a *tarekat* is, among other things, sustained by the transfer of authority from the existing *murshid* to his successor. The successor's legitimacy to the leadership is formally performed through *ijaza irshad*. He can then be called the *murshid*. In other words, Kiai Rifai, who held the leadership of the *Tarekat Qadiriyah Wa Naqsyabandiyah* (Rejoso version) was not promoted in the normal way. In the *tarekat* world the chain of *murshidship* is usually decisive, defining the legitimacy of the *tarekat* itself. Because of this, the *Tarekat Rejoso*, could be regarded as non-legitimate.

Nevertheless, according to a reliable source, Kiai Rifai actually received a symbolic *ijaza irshad*. The *ijaza irshad* which sustains the leadership of Kiai Rifai is said to be based on some hints made by Kiai Musta'in. For example, it is believed that Kiai Rifai was often asked by Kiai Musta'in to substitute for him in leading *solat* (the prayer), when Kiai Musta'in was not able to perform it. Some followers thought that Kiai Musta'in's request was an indication that he was counting on Kiai Rifai to continue the leadership of his *tarekat*. However, such hints, in the opinion of Kiai Musta'in's wife, were not very significant.

Whether the *murshidship* of Kiai Rifai is legitimately strong or not, his followers treat him as they should treat the *murshid* of the *tarekat*. The same holds true for his *khalifa*. A senior *khalifa* who received *bai'a* from Kiai Romly acknowledges that he does not have any idea whether or not Kiai Rifai received an *ijaza irshad* from his brother, Kiai Musta'in. For him, what is important is that he is now able to continue what was asked of him by his teacher, who was the father of Kiai Musta'in and Kiai Rifai. His teacher asked him to build *umma* religiousity through the *tarekat*. In other words, this *khalifa* is not concerned about the

---

[18] According to a reliable source, there was a little dispute in the family in regard to the *tarekat* leadership following Kiai Musta'in's death. The dispute was between the promotion of Mudjib, the son of Kiai Musta'in, and Rifai, a brother of Kiai Musta'in and a younger *kiai* but older than Mudjib in the *Pesantren Darul Ulum*, for the leadership in the *tarekat*. The followers wanted Mudjib, who was ready to perform the leadership in the *tarekat*. However, his youth and immaturity in Islamic understanding, made the followers uncomfortable to accept him as a *murshid*. They chose Rifai because he was mature enough, although he actually had a lower claim on the position than Mudjib, from the *tarekat* perspective. Nevertheless, neither Mudjib nor Rifai were actually ready to assume such spiritual leadership of the *tarekat* when Kiai Musta'in died.

status of the *murshidship* of Kiai Rifai. What is important for him is to develop the *tarekat* by performing its rituals.

From this *khalifa's* perspective we can see some variations among the attitudes of the *tarekat* followers in regard to *murshidship*. There are a number of factors which affect the attitude of Kiai Rifai's *khalifa*. Firstly, there is a tendency among the *khalifa* to avoid any chaos or confusion on the part of the followers which could occur if they knew the details of the *murshidship* of Kiai Rifai. This viewpoint encourages some *khalifa* to support the leadership of Kiai Rifai. Secondly, *khalifa* support Kiai Rifai's leadership as an indirect means to protect the reputation of Kiai Musta'in. In so doing they are defending the controversial (political) decisions made by Kiai Musta'in, which were so criticised by some colleagues and much of society. The support of Kiai Musta'in's successor is an indirect justification of Kiai Musta'in's political actions[19]. Thirdly, Kiai Rifai did not change any ritual practices, especially the *wird*, in the *tarekat*. Despite doubts about his *murshidship*, therefore, the *khalifa* regard such practices as religiously positive. While the leadership of Kiai Rifai might not be legitimate from the *tarekat* perspective, attending the rituals held by his *tarekat* and practising its *wird* in general still incur *pahala* (rewards from Allah).

The decrease in number of *Tarekat Rejoso* followers after Kiai Musta'in joined Golkar occurred gradually, since most of them did not have sufficient information about Kiai Musta'in's political action from the *tarekat* perspective to alter their opinion of the *tarekat*. The followers' interpretation of Kiai Musta'in's defection depended on their allegiance to certain *khalifa* and other *kiai*. The followers' attitudes towards Kiai Musta'in and his *tarekat* was very much affected by the perspective of the *khalifa*. Since there were two groups of *khalifa*, those who stayed loyal to Kiai Musta'in and those who left him, the followers' view were also of two kinds. When the conflict between Kiai Musta'in and the majority of other *kiai* occured, some of his followers did not automatically leave him. It took some time for them to be convinced. Their decision was dependent on and supported by explanations from various sources, including the *khalifa*, the majority of whom were motivated by politics. This explains why those who left Kiai Musta'in share no single unanimous reason to justify their actions. A common reason given by them, and their *kiai* who are now the *Tarekat Cukir* followers, concerns Kiai Musta'in's joining Golkar. Other *Tarekat Cukir* followers are even doubtful if they had a reason for leaving the *Tarekat Rejoso*. The majority even confirm that the *Tarekat Rejoso* is legitimate, without any defect. Their decision to join the *Tarekat Cukir* was just based on the fact that this was the decision of NU.

---

[19] Interview with Kiai Arwani, 12 December 1994.

The various reasons given by different groups of *Tarekat Cukir* followers can be illuminated by recourse to recent socio-political developments. When Kiai Bisri Syansuri launched a *fatwa* nationally, making it a religious obligation for Muslims to support PPP, all *kiai* in Jombang were expected to support the Islamic political party of PPP. Kiai Musta'in's joining Golkar hence triggered some internal problems in the *kiai* world and Muslim society in Jombang and East Java. This factor must have been significant in inducing 'the action of leaving' of some of Kiai Musta'in's followers. However, when this *fatwa* was cancelled by the NU's 'back to khittah' decision made at its conference in 1984, allowing its members to affiliate with any political party, the political reasons undermining the legitimacy of Kiai Musta'in's leadership were invalidated. Very few *Tarekat Cukir* followers would dare say that there is a defect in the *Tarekat Rejoso*. One follower[20] suggested that all *tarekat* are good since they are a means to reach Allah. In general, therefore, it should be acknowledged that there is no real religious basis which delegitimises the *Tarekat Rejoso*. If its illegitimacy was due to its *murshid* joining the government party, it became legitimate again when NU launched its policy of 'back to khittah'. If the prohibition of NU members against supporting non-Islamic parties was based on religious factors, the encouragement to support the 'back to khittah' policy, which allows NU's members to affiliate with any political party, is also supported by religious factors.

Thus no follower of the *Tarekat Cukir* regards the *Tarekat Qadiriyah Wa Naqsyabandiyah* led by Kiai Rifai as not *mu'tabarah*. This perspective, however, is not shared by other *kiai*. A former *khalifa* of Kiai Musta'in who left him because of the omission of one person in the *murshidship* chain of this *tarekat*, contends that he still cannot accept the leadership of the *Tarekat Qadiriyah Wa Naqsyabandiyah* (at that time led by Kiai Rifai) since it was *menyesatkan* (misleading). "Saya kasihan dengan ummat" (I feel sorry for the *umma*). In his opinion, the legitimacy of a *tarekat* is not only sustained by the correct *wird* and other rituals performed by the followers, but also by the legitimacy of the *murshid* who leads the *tarekat*. If the *murshid* is not legitimate, the rituals conducted in his *tarekat* would not incur any *baraka*. This *kiai* quoted other *kiai* who mentioned the possible *bahala* (disaster) which could befall the *umma* due to the illegitimacy of the *murshidship*. According to this view, the illegitimate nature of the *Tarekat Rejoso* derives from two factors, the improper action of Kiai Musta'in in omitting one link in the chain of the *murshidship* and the absence of direct *ijaza irshad* from Kiai Musta'in to Kiai Rifai. Because of this fact, this

---

[20] This follower was influenced by the existing culture of the *tarekat* world, which stresses the importance of the *murshid*. He used to be a follower of Kiai Musta'in and was taught by him, so that he did not dare to say that the leadership of Kiai Musta'in was not legitimate. Not only was the *wird* performed by this *tarekat* legitimate, but also the allegiance to the *murshid* was a necessity. What was done by a *murshid* could be wrong, but the *murshid* would continue to be the *murshid* as long as he did not do wrong from the Islamic perspective, such as *shirk* (ascribing partners to God).

former *khalifa* of Kiai Musta'in is hesitant to acknowledge the legitimacy of the *Tarekat Rejoso*.

5.3 NU at National Politics

In this section I would like to describe briefly the conflict among NU leaders in Jombang. This conflict has a close connection to the conflict in the succeeding years, especially following the introduction of 'back to khittah' in the second half of the 1980s. Familial background contributed to this conflict. What is important in regard to this description is the fact that conflict among NU leaders is common, following the political dynamic of NU itself.

Although the primary objective of the formation of NU was to develop and maintain the *ahl al-sunna wa'l-jama'a*, it had for some time also been used as a means of political struggle. At the end of Dutch colonialism in Indonesia, NU's *'ulama*, together with other Islamic organisations, established the Majlis Islam A'la Indonesia in 1937 (MIAI: the High Indonesian Islamic Council). In addition, during the Japanese occupation (1943), NU joined the Majlis Sjuro Muslimin Indonesia (Masjumi: the Consultative Council for Indonesian Muslims)[21]. These organisations were a confederation which represented Islamic political interests. Although these organisations were originally mainly socio-religious in orientation, the increase in political activity at the end of the Dutch colonial period in Indonesia and the Japanese occupation made their members, including NU's *kiai*, change their orientations to be more political[22].

NU involvement in politics seemed to be inevitable. The position of the *'ulama* at the forefront of Islamic society not only made them informal leaders who maintained *ahl al-sunna wa'l-jama'a* but also made them political leaders, since in Indonesia the relationship between politics and Islam was quite strong. The *'ulama*'s effort to develop *ahl al-sunna wa'l-jama'a* were realised by the establishment of *pesantren*, centres of Islamic learning. It was natural for a great *'ulama*, like Kiai Hasyim Asy'ari, to have a *pesantren*. On the other hand, the *'ulama*'s interest in politics was realised by their involvement in an Islamic political party. Soon after the government encouraged the establishment of political parties at the end of 1945, around two months after independence, NU's *'ulama*, together with Islamic members of other organisations established an Islamic political party, Masjumi. In 1952, NU even announced that it was a political party after a conflict with another Islamic group in the Masjumi could

---

[21] This Masjumi was distinct from the Islamic organisation of the same name established in 1945. The latter was an Islamic political party.
[22] At the second half of the 1930s, the threat to Indonesian Islam also came from native Indonesians. The formation of MIAI was prompted by the political atmosphere which mostly discredited Islam. In 1938, an article was written by a Western educated young lady. She attacked polygamy practised by Muslims and that practised by the Prophet Muhammad himself. The reaction from Indonesian Muslims was very strong, resulting, among other things, in the strengthening of the MIAI (see Alfian, 1989).

not be resolved. As a political party, NU took part in the 1955 and 1971 general elections.

In 1973, however, the Indonesian government tried to reduce the existing ten political organisations which took part in the 1971 general election, to three. Four Islamic political organisations, NU, Parmusi, PSII and Perti, were merged to form the United Development Party (PPP). Other political organisations with nationalist, Catholic and Christian backgrounds merged to form the Indonesian Democratic Party (PDI). In contrast, Golkar, the organisation of professionals which won the most seats in the 1971 general election, merged with no other party. Although the merging of the Islamic parties into PPP was initially opposed by NU leaders, NU was at the forefront of the new party since it constituted the biggest component of the party. This was due to the fact that of the four Islamic parties, NU received the highest proportion of votes in the 1971 general election (18.5 percent compared to Parmusi, PSII and Perti which obtained 6.3, 2.3 and 0.7 percent respectively).

Although the formation of PPP was initially opposed by some Muslim leaders, it became a 'blessing in disguise'. Its formation seemed to unify and strengthen Islamic politics. In the first general election after its formation, that is in the 1977 general election, PPP succeeded in increasing its votes by 1.2 percent compared to that of the four Islamic parties in the 1971 general election. Although the increase was small when compared to the votes received by Islamic parties in the 1955 general election, it gave a hope for Muslims in Indonesia that the party could represent their political interests.

However, the expectation that PPP was the medium for Indonesian Muslim politics may have been too optimistic, since the merger was a government policy which was not intended to unify the politics of Indonesian Muslims - but aimed at reducing general political conflict, which had frequently destabilised the existing government during the Old Order. In addition, the difficulty of accommodating the political interests of the party's various components made the party unable to function as was hoped. There was inevitable conflict within the party, a factor which contributed later to a weakening of the party. Any hope that Indonesian Muslims might have had to unify their politics through this party after its success in increasing its share of votes in the 1977 general election ceased after the emergence of an ongoing conflict between the NU and MI (former Parmusi) components, preceding the 1982 general election. The MI component, led first by Sudarji and later by Naro, tried to change the decision on the composition of PPP which underpined the formation of the party in 1973. This decision had made NU dominant both in the structure of the party leadership and in the representation of PPP in parliament. This conflict was resolved by the reduction of NU personnel in the party and the transfer of some of them to unimportant positions, after Naro assumed leadership of the party in 1984. Naro was trying to change the power composition of the party's components[23]. For NU members, the leadership of Naro was an embarrasing incident, since it marked a decrease in their position in the party. Their dissatisfaction with Naro was due to the fact that he was seen to be disadvantaging NU. The great reaction of NU exponents at both the national and provincial level aimed not only at confronting Naro, but also NU's exponents who continued to occupy positions in PPP, signalling their acceptance of Naro. Nevertheless, Naro's position was stronger than that of his NU critics, since his leadership in the party was nonetheless accepted by the government.

This change in the pattern of power among the components of PPP gave rise to a change in NU's politics. NU, a dominant component of the party and the biggest political group among Muslims in Indonesia, withdrew itself from politics. At its congress in 1984, NU announced its intention to return to being a socio-religious organisation as conceptualised in 1926 when NU was established. This meant that NU was no longer politically oriented. This decision, widely known as 'back to khittah', also signalled NU's dissociation from PPP. In addition, NU allowed its members to affiliate with political organisations other than PPP. Such affiliation was, however, not organisational but was an individual matter.

The change worried other components of PPP, since the main source of support for PPP derived from NU. As a result, PPP national vote attainment in the 1987 general election decreased by about 42 percent (in Jombang it fell by 36 percent) compared to that in the 1982 general election. The decrease in PPP's attainment was a general phenomenon. It was experienced by almost all branches throughout Indonesia. This was because some NU exponents, who were supported by some *kiai*, tried to weaken the party. This manoueuvre, however, gave rise to internal conflict within NU at the local level, since weakening PPP meant confronting their own friends. The conflict, in terms of its scope, served to fragment the movement[24].

5.4 Local Political Conflict

The presence of many *pesantren* in Jombang has given rise to the emergence of various local *kiai* leaderships. It has also socially fragmented Muslim life in Jombang. The influence of a certain *kiai* can be so strong for certain Muslims that they cannot give loyalty to another *kiai*. This close relationship between a *kiai* and his followers is stronger than the relationship between a *kiai* follower

---

[23] By power composition is meant the representativeness of PPP components. In the 1982 general election, some NU supporters were placed in 'nomor tidak jadi' (the number beyond the possible elected rank) on the list of PPP candidates for parliament. As people in Indonesia vote for the party, the list of ranked candidates was based on the results of the previous election. If in the previous election, PPP of East Java received 16 seats, for example, a candidate place in number 20 on the 'candidate list' would probably not be elected. This number is called 'nomor tidak jadi'.
[24] I will return to this matter later in Chapter VI.

and NU. The strength of NU in Jombang depends on the support of the *kiai* in the *pesantren*.

The fragmentation of Muslim society in Jombang becomes apparent in times of conflict. A conflict results in closer affiliation with certain *kiai* and consequent distancing from others. Despite the importance of the sources of conflict, it is also necessary to note society's perception of the conflict itself. I will return to this matter later in Chapter VI. The conflict among the NU elite in Jombang actually first occurred in the early 1960s. The conflict was attributed to and influenced by the existing local NU leadership, and the extent of the conflict was dependent on the way the main NU leader handled it.

I will briefly discuss some of the conflicts which have occurred among the NU elite in Jombang, including the conflict which emerged after NU launched its 'back to khittah' policy. This discussion not only aims to show that conflict among Muslims in Jombang has been a common phenomenon but also to explain why such conflicts take place. The first conflict among the NU elite in Jombang occurred in 1963 when NU was under the leadership of Kiai Masduqi Zein, who assumed the leadership in 1952. The conflict, which was marked by Muslim protests against, and sharp criticism of Kiai Masduqi Zein, was resolved by his replacement by Kiai Musta'in Romly, the head of the *Pesantren Darul Ulum*. Kiai Masduqi Zein was accused of recommending to the local government that some investors be allowed to provide gambling-like game at a 'Jombang fair' in 1963 (Mochtar, 1989:138).

Another conflict occurred at the end of the 1960s when NU under the leadership of Muhammad Baidlowi. Muhammad Baidlowi, the grandson of the NU founder, Kiai Hasyim Asy'ari, assumed local NU leadership in 1966. He was confronted by another local NU faction headed by Nawawi. Nawawi, who was supported by some members of society, challenged Muhammad Baidlowi's legitimate leadership. This challenge, however, was not based on any identifiable reason but simply aimed to topple Muhammad Baidlowi. Nawawi's action was merely based on his feeling that he had every right to assume NU leadership and was more appropriate than Muhammad Baidlowi[25].

Muhammad Baidlowi was associated with the *Pesantren Tebuireng*, while Nawawi was from the *Pesantren Denanyar*. Both Muhammad Baidlowi and Nawawi received some support from Muslims in Jombang. Their family backgrounds encouraged this support. A *pesantren* has certain followers, and it is very likely that both received support from those Muslims affiliated with each of their *pesantren*. According to some sources, both received support from some NU leaders at the national level. The support for Muhammad Baidlowi stemmed from his being a legitimate NU leader, chosen by a local NU conference, while

---

[25] Interview with Hafidh Ma'shum, 15 December 1994.

the support for Nawawi was based on familial relationship with some of the national leadership in Jakarta. Although Muhammad Baidlowi also received support from some *kiai* in the NU national leadership in Jakarta, his leadership was legitimate since he had been chosen through the conference. Such endorsement had not been received by Nawawi.

This dispute over the local NU leadership in Jombang also extended to PPP. As PPP leadership in Jombang was dominated by the NU component, the competing groups led by Muhammad Baidlowi on the one hand, and Nawawi on the other, felt every right to represent NU in the party. Both tried to assume the PPP leadership. The result was that PPP also had two leaderships. The PPP leadership which represented Muhammad Baidlowi's NU faction was headed by Badawi Mahbub, while that which represented the Nawawi's NU faction was led by Nawawi himself. The emergence of this ongoing conflict in the leadership of NU in Jombang was atributed to the fact that NU was very politically oriented at that time. It was common for those who occupied a certain position in NU to occupy certain positions in PPP. Accordingly, any conflict occurring at the local NU leadership would also affect the leadership of PPP.

The Nawawi leadership of NU, commonly called 'NU-Bangladesh'[26] finally ended by itself. Not only was his leadership not legitimate, since it was not established through a conference, but also at the grassroots level, the majority of NU members and sympathisers were in favour of the legitimate leadership of Muhammad Baidlowi. Nawawi's support was limited to a few NU figures. In addition, the government did not recognise the PPP leadership of Nawawi. The NU leadership in Jombang during the 1970s was thus under Muhammad Baidlowi's control, and PPP was headed by Badawi Mahbub, Muhammad Baidlowi's man.

Although NU domination of the local leadership of PPP in Jombang continued, and the party was not disturbed by any internal conflict between its various components due to the fact that more than 95 percent of the PPP leadership derived from NU, the conflict at the national level between members of the NU and MI factions at the beginning of the 1980s, gave rise to conflict among the NU elite in Jombang. The conflict was again marked by the emergence of two NU factions. The first was led by Muhammad Baidlowi, who promoted Kiai Syamsuri Badawi as his successor, while the other was headed by Kiai Shohib Bisri, who was appointed temporarily by NU provincial office in Surabaya.

Until the first half of 1986, NU in Jombang was still under the leadership of Muhammad Baidlowi. Since Muhammad Baidlowi was close to PPP, due to his being appointed as one of the national PPP leaders in 1984 (under Naro), his leadership was not supported by the NU elite in Jombang. This was due to an NU policy which suggested that an NU leader should not simultaneously occupy

---

[26] Interview with Hafidh Ma'shum, 15 December 1994.

positions ('rangkap jabatan': hold dual positions) in PPP and NU. They should choose to manage either NU or PPP. Muhammad Baidlowi, who held an important position in PPP at the national level, however, continued to lead NU in Jombang. He then organised a local NU conference in June 1986, without the acknowledgement of the NU leadership at provincial level. The conference was held at Muhammad Baidlowi's house and chose Kiai Syamsuri Badawi to be NU top leader in Jombang[27].

As Muhammad Baidlowi was regarded as having violated NU policy on 'rangkap jabatan', the NU provincial office did not recognise Muhammad Baidlowi's leadership. It then appointed Kiai Shohib Bisri to assume NU leadership temporarily, and asked him to make all necessary preparation for a conference. Kiai Shohib came from the *Pesantren Denanyar*. His temporary appointment was not only an indication that he would be the next leader of local NU, but also hinted that the conference organised by Muhammad Baidlowi, which had chosen Kiai Syamsuri Badawi, was not recognised by the NU provincial office. Kiai Shohib then held another conference in 1986, and was chosen as a local NU head. His nomination for the leadership was accepted by the NU leadership at the provincial level. Kiai Shohib's support derived not only from NU activists who were dissatisfied with PPP leadership under Naro, but also from former Nawawi supporters, who had opposed Muhammad Baidlowi's leadership in the early 1970s. Nawawi had been defeated by Muhammad Baidlowi in his attempt to topple Muhammad Baidlowi's leadership of NU. These subsequent actions by Nawawi supporters indicate their continued opposition to Muhammad Baidlowi.

Like his predecessor, Kiai Syamsuri Badawi's leadership of NU continued regardless of the disapproval of the NU provincial office. It also continued the close relationship with PPP. Since PPP was more or less identical with NU, all the party's activities were centred in the NU's office. The NU office had been the office of PPP since its formation in 1973. The rivalry of Syamsuri Badawi and Shohib Bisri can be seen by their efforts to seize the NU office at Gatot Subroto street. The office was used simultaneously by Syamsuri Badawi and PPP. Shohib Bisri supporters then asked to use it. As the office was owned by NU, and the local NU leadership recognised by the provincial and national NU leadership was that headed by Shohib Bisri, the office was returned to Shohib. Before this, Shohib Bisri's leadership had been centred in the *Pesantren Denanyar*, his *pesantren*. It is important to note that it was Shohib Bisri's leadership of NU which then continued, since it was legitimised by the central office's acceptance. In contrast, Syamsuri Badawi's leadership of NU, which was not legitimised by the central office's acceptance, ceased.

---

[27] Interview with Hafidh Ma'shum, 15 December 1994.

A further conflict was the one among members of the *Jam'iyah Ahli Thoriqoh Al-Mu'tabaroh An-Nahdliyah*. As this *tarekat* was formed as a reaction against Kiai Musta'in, who joined Golkar, its formation hence reaffirmed NU's political orientation which by that time was articulated through PPP. That meant that NU's *tarekat* should affiliate with PPP. This situation made the *Tarekat Qadiriyah Wa Naqsyabandiyah* affiliated with the *Jam'iyah Ahli Thoriqoh Al-Mu'tabaroh An-Nahdliyah*, commonly called *Tarekat Cukir*, appear as though it was PPP's *tarekat*. This was indicated by the fact that this *tarekat* often used PPP's symbol in its big religious activities. However, when NU changed its politics in 1984, some members of the *Tarekat Cukir* in Jombang were disappointed with the *tarekat's* continued close affiliation with PPP. They began to conduct separate religious activities at locations other than those used by the *Tarekat Cukir*. This was done to show that NU's dissociation from PPP should be followed by its *tarekat's* dissociation from the party. Although only a small number of followers joined these activities, this situation indicated the beginning of a split in the *tarekat*, which mirrored the conflict among the NU elite in Jombang. The initiator of this splinter group was Kiai Zamroji. Since he did not receive popular support from *tarekat* members, however, his idea to have a group which was different from the *Tarekat Cukir* failed.

In present day Jombang, conflict seems to have disappeared from the stage. However, it has left a situation unfavourable for NU development. The elite of the *Tarekat Cukir* continue to be closely affiliated with PPP and its elites. They feel uncomfortable with other local NU leaders who, in contrast, are more comfortable to be close to Golkar. In their preparations to attend the NU national congress in West Java in 1994, for example, local NU leaders in Jombang preferred to approach Golkar's leaders rather than PPP's. They also felt more comfortable asking for travel funds from Golkar's fraction of the local parliament rather than PPP's[28].

In brief, conflicts among the NU elite in Jombang have been very common. These conflicts have always involved politics, in the sense that they followed any change in the field of politics. This is especially evident in the conflict which followed the application of NU's 'back to khittah' policy. This conflict had wide social consequences. I will return to this matter in the next chapter. Several factors contributed to the conflict among the NU elite in Jombang following the application of the 'back to khittah' policy. Firstly, the conflict was triggered by the application of NU's policy of *rangkap jabatan* (lit. dual position), which prohibited NU members from occupying leadership positions in both NU and in PPP simultaneously. They were advised to take either a position in the party or in NU. It was very common for an NU activist also to be a PPP activist. He could hold a position in NU and in the party. The policy aimed to disengage NU

---

[28] Interview with Hafidh Ma'shum, 15 December 1994.

members from PPP and to consolidate NU. It was hoped that those who were recruited into the NU administration would give full attention to the development of NU. At the time, many NU activists were more concerned with the party's problem than NU's. However, as the disappointment with the behaviour of Naro, the national PPP leader, was great among NU activists, the policy of 'dual position' was exaggeratedly applied in Jombang. The activists not only condemned other NU activists who occupied positions in both NU and PPP, but also any NU member who was affiliated with the party.

The second factor contributing to conflict was the lack of acceptance of different political affiliations within NU. Such differences have traditionally led to fragmentation. Take the case of Kiai Musta'in. The difference between his and other *kiai's* politics led to an organisational split. Political difference typically result in the development of an 'in and out-group'. Disappointment with Naro, for example, led to those holding positions or active in PPP being regarded by NU activists as the out-group. A third factor was the continued hostility of Nawawi's supporters towards the leadership of Muhammad Baidlowi when NU launched its 'back to khittah' policy. Since Muhammad Baidlowi remained close to PPP and tried to control the NU leadership by promoting Kiai Syamsuri Badawi, Nawawi's supporters used his conflict with the NU elite to expel him.

Chapter 6: Islam and Politics: Implications in Electoral Behaviour

There are two viewpoints concerning the relationship between religion and political behaviour (Hammond, 1979:20). One argues that religious membership and the activities of members with distinctive values and orientations have a formative influence on political behaviour. The other suggests that the political preference of any group in society does not need to be motivated by its religious beliefs and that any relationship in this sense is 'spurious'. Scholars who hold the first view take religious loyalty into consideration in their examination of political participation. Religious loyalty and affiliation are regarded as factors that affect the political behaviour of society. This perspective further suggests that religious group membership is a source of identity which differentiates one group from another, since such involvement can provide members with particular norms and values that form a particular group culture. In democratic countries, people's advocacy of their religious aims can be realised through politics, since the system allows political parties to function as the means through which people can articulate their interests, including religious interests. Thus, a religious political party constitutes a means of bridging religious ideals and the reality experienced by believers. Through such a party, believers can articulate their religious ideas to regulate their worldly lives.

This chapter tries to analyse the relationship between the religious affiliation of Muslims in Java and their political actions. It stresses the role of ideas which affect socio-political action. The analysis will focus on voting behaviour which gives support to a particular political party in general elections. In Jombang, the Islamic political party was dominant in core *kecamatan* of the regency. The results of the 1955 general election indicate that together NU and Masjumi obtained an almost 50 percent share of the votes in Jombang. In the 1971 general election, although the share of the votes of these Islamic parties decreased compared to that of the 1955 general election, they were significantly dominant in five *kecamatan*. In these *kecamatan*, the Islamic parties received more than 50 percent of the votes. The basic questions being considered are: why do Muslims give support to one political party and not to others, and what makes certain political attitudes legitimate from their perspective? In looking at the pattern of support given by Muslim society in Jombang, analysis will also focus on the role of the *'ulama* or *kiai* who are assumed to be dominant and able to induce socio-political action within society to determine how far their charisma influence political action.

6.1 The Islamic Political Party

Before discussing the role of Islam and of the *kiai* in Javanese politics, I would like to give a general history of the Islamic political party, PPP, which was established in 1973. As I am going to discuss the electoral pattern of behaviour, I need to describe the place of Islamic parties in Indonesian politics. PPP was resulted from the merger of four Islamic political parties which took part in the 1971 general election. It was hoped that it would accommodate various political interests of Muslim society in Indonesia. As the character of the party has been discussed in a previous chapter, I will briefly focus here on its development in the context of the government's general political agenda. To this end, I should highlight two aspects: the nature of government politics and how Islam was viewed especially by authority.

The New Order government under Suharto, who came to power in 1966, is very different from the Old Order government under Soekarno. The New Order is more concerned with economic development. This concern has had definite implications for Indonesian politics since the emphasis on development necessitated particular political circumstances conducive to economic growth. The effort to pursue this growth has meant that other aspects of Indonesian development have been neglected. Politics, therefore, did not develop in a natural sense but was used to ensure programs of economic development. Accordingly, government politics was in general characterised by an emphasis on security and aimed at achieving political stability.

Armed with 'the ideology of development' and seeking stability, the government has presented itself as a strong political regime which is repressive in many respects. Repression has been seen as a necessary element in the march towards economic development. The state has tried to monopolise power, and has imposed control over potentially disintegrative and destructive social and political forces. The government learned from the experience of the Old Order, whose instability mostly derived from politics. That was why the main concern set in motion by the New Order government was to engineer people's socio-political lives.

Among government fears of possible dangers which might disturb the socio-political order was fear of Islamic political parties and other Muslim groups. Fear of Islamic radicalist movements, such as *Darul Islam* [1] (1948–1962), had forced the Suharto government to be strict and repressive towards any political movement backed by religious ideas. The government had reasonable grounds to be worried, particularly about any political movement by Indonesian Muslims,

---

[1] *Darul Islam* (Daru'l-Islam, Arabic) literally means 'The abode (or House) of Islam'. "The term is used, particularly, in Islamic jurisprudence, to denote the totality of those regions or countries which are subject to Islamic law". It may be contrasted with *Daru'l-Harb*, 'the abode of war' or non-Islamic regions (see Netton, 1992:67). In Indonesia, *Darul Islam* was a separatist movement which tried to establish an Islamic state. It rebelled against the Soekarno government. The movement was brought to an end in 1962.

since attempts to have Islamic ideology applied in the Indonesian state, for instance, have been made by both separatist movements, like *Darul Islam*, and also by Muslim political leaders. Such attempts were made openly, for example, when members of BPKI (the body which investigated measures to prepare for Indonesian independence), which was dominated by those with a secularist nationalist cast of mind, included debate on the place of Islam in the Indonesian state (Jenkins, 1984:6). This idea, which was still nurtured by some Islamic leaders in the 1970s, was used by the army for its own political ends to exert pressure on Muslims. In any political turmoil, for instance, Indonesian Muslims became objects of government accusations that they were supporters of the idea of Islamic state, which was regarded as subversive. McVey (1971:139) points out that:

> the long years of warfare against Muslim rebellion encouraged a tradition of army distrust of militant Islam, and the many Javanese officers of abangan persuasion were strengthened in their objection to Muslim aggressiveness.

Determination to preserve social order, together with a fear of the idea of an Islamic state, led the government to put increasing pressure on political parties. Political parties were forced to regroup into only two parties, under leaders acceptable to the government. In addition, they were undermined by the government which cut off their base support through implementation of the 'floating mass' program of depoliticisation, especially in rural areas (Crouch, 1980:659).

The New Order government stance in relation to Muslims, expressed by its fear manoeuvered through its politics, was an overreaction. According to Jenkins (1984:11), the government "…ignored the great changes that were taking place among Muslims… as …many of the younger Muslim intellectuals had left the idea of an Islamic state behind them". The exaggerated stance of the government has been politically perpetuated. It has also been sustained by the political stance of groups other than Muslims. Since Muslims are the majority, and account for about 90 per cent of Indonesia's population, political groups other than Muslims, which also fear the existence of an Islamic state, have given tacit support to the military stance against Muslim dissidents. One Indonesian scholar is anonymously quoted by Jenkins, as saying:

> it is a fact that there is enough combustible material in our society to keep alive the fear of Islam. What kept Soekarno in power so long? It was the fact that the abangan, the Catholics and the Protestants were more afraid of Islam than of the Communists. The same groups support the army and I think that fear is being manipulated for power reasons. Many seriously fear it [Islam] but a leadership that would know how to

handle the Muslims and had closer cooperation with them would be able to reduce the fear to more manageable proportions (Jenkins, 1984:12).

Although the government was successful in excluding Muslim political leaders from national decision-making as well as from any reasonable opportunity to increase their power, the persistence of political Islam in Indonesia was apparent during 1970s. The effort to eliminate or to weaken political Islam was contrary to the aspirations of a large segment of the Indonesian people.

Conflict between the regime and Indonesian Muslims was seen soon after the 1977 general election. Based on its experience during this election, the government increased its pressure upon political parties, forcing them change their ideological base to Pancasila. This policy resulted in a decrease in the strength of political Islam and pushed it into a weak position. The political parties[2] were also disturbed by internal conflict. Both PPP and PDI had been experiencing ongoing internal conflicts since the second half of 1970s. Continuous internal conflict finally came to the point where government involvement at reconciliation it was inevitable. This situation impacted greatly on Indonesian politics. Since Golkar has been in power, the government involvement in the internal conflicts of other political parties created an unconducive situation for the development of politics in Indonesia. It gave the impression that political parties could indirectly be managed and engineered by the government, and that the government was 'the reconciliator father'. This further enhanced the culture of paternalism which has long been a feature of Indonesian life. The elites of the parties tended not to be critical of the government. Even when the government refused candidates proposed by the parties, they could do nothing, so the government could easily control parliament. This decreased role of political parties in Indonesia also seemed inevitable since the military's political role was so strong (Almond, 1978:49– 69). Sundhaussen (1978:50) in his analysis of the military in Indonesia said:

> The weakness of the political parties almost matches that of the parliament. First of all, parliament is fully controlled by the government through the military and Golkar factions. In addition, the few supervisory functions formally left to parliament often are abused and circumvented by those in the center of power.

In addition, before the internal conflict characterised the political parties' existence, and before the government introduced its policy of 'floating mass' launched in 1975 and of 'Azas Tunggal' (sole ideology) applied in 1985, both of which particularly cut off political Islam in Indonesia, the government has made efforts to engineer bureaucracy since 1970. The government introduced a concept

---

[2] Of the three political organisations, only PPP and PDI are called political parties although Golkar has the same function as a political party.

of 'mono-loyalty', by which all civil servants in all departments had to have one loyalty, that is loyalty to the government. The application of this concept has gradually undermined support for the Islamic political party from civil servants.

The concept of 'monoloyalty' which was introduced by General Amir Mahmud as the Minister of Home Affairs, aimed to avoid any internal conflict within the bureaucracy due to different ideologies such as occurred under Soekarno. To strengthen this effort, the government also set up KORPRI (lit. the Corps of Indonesian Public Servants) in 1971 with the purpose of enhancing "l'esprit de corps" among civil servants[3]. Since Golkar represented the government, supporters or sympathisers of Islamic and other parties were faced with a problem when KORPRI was formed. They had to choose between supporting their preferred party and the necessity of being loyal to the government, which meant supporting Golkar. Although the concept does not necessarily mean that civil servants are prevented from being members of any political party, it has had a psychological effect. This is because civil servants organised within KORPRI must indirectly be members of Golkar, since KORPRI is one of the pillars that sustains Golkar. In addition, there is a regulation suggesting that civil servants occupying certain positions must have a permit from their superiors, if they want to be members of political parties and functional groups (Indonesia, 1988:65).

Since the structure of KORPRI could hardly be more top-down, as shown by its executive council which comprises the Minister of Home Affairs, with all departmental Secretaries General and State Secretaries as its members, the government's important effort to stretch a web, which indirectly forces all civil servants to be Golkar members or supporters, has been effective. This happens not only because all the heads of government, from the national to the village level are automatically KORPRI chairmen, but also because all civil servants, through presidential regulation number 6/1970, as interpreted by Amir Mahmud, were denied the right to engage in political party activities.

Monoloyalty and its imposition throughout the bureaucracy has brought about great success for Golkar. Political parties, which during the Soekarno government received their support from their members or supporters in the government departments, suffered a large decline. PNI, for example, which had electorally been the strongest party in 1955 and had enjoyed the greatest bureaucratic base under Soekarno, suffered the greatest decline in 1971. According to Emerson

---

[3] However, the government's efforts to build a structure that knows only a single loyalty is not new. It had previously been sought through KOKARMINDAGRI, the Home Government Functional Staff Corps. This was introduced in conjunction with a historic consensus between civilian experts and army officers and lies at the heart of the New Order's antipathy to party politics (Emerson, 1978:105). The difference is that KOKARMINDAGRI was limited to Home Affairs employees, while KORPRI has spread a much wider net encompassing "all civilian public employees in the country, at every level, from national to village government, and in every kind of agency, from public schools to state corporations" (Emerson, 1978:107).

(1978:107), "comparing the 1955 and 1971 elections, despite a 45 percent increase in the voting electorate, PNI lost a staggering 4.6 million votes". It should be acknowledged that political parties during the liberal democracy period had grown strong enough to challenge the ruling authority on many occasions, and make the latter compromise with them to avoid tension. Accordingly, the 1971 election was a turning point for the power of political parties. In this election, N.U, one of the 'big four parties', which had enjoyed a strong bureaucratic base under Soekarno, also suffered a decline. Nevertheless, its decline was different from the PNI's, since NU still received support from its grassroots in villages in Indonesia. However, the government's efforts in 'social engineering' replaced many NU members and sympathisers in the Department of Religious Affairs, and made its entrenchment in that department less secure. For the first time, the Minister of Religious Affairs, who had traditionally been appointed from NU, was occupied by a technocrat Muslim, Professor Mukti Ali.

Thus political parties during the New Order no longer received support from civil servants. Also they have not been represented in the Suharto cabinet since the 1971 general election. The government bureaucracy linkage created through KORPRI is an effective way to weaken political parties. The appointment of village heads, for example, needs to be approved by district heads (camat), even though the former are conventionally elected by society. In addition, the government created 'Dharma Wanita', an organisation of civil servants' wives which can be used as political means to muster votes for Golkar in a general election, even down to the village. Through these bureaucratic networks, the government mobilises the masses.

Although the government was worried about Islam, it still needed support from Muslim society. Thus the government's pressure on Muslims aimed both to establish political stability in accordance with its economic development plan and also to gain Muslim support. The introduction of the 'Azas Tunggal', according to which all political and other organisations were obliged to use Pancasila as their ideological base, resulted in increased support from Muslim groups. This in effect dissolved the Islamic base of the Islamic party, so that for some PPP supporters to change their support to Golkar raised no problem.

Amidst the increased support of Indonesian Muslims towards the government party, the beginning of the 1990s saw a change in the government stance against Muslims in general. The government now tends to be more accommodative towards them. Nevertheless, this does not help Muslims to have a particular means for the realisation of their politics. PPP cannot remould itself as an Islamic party. Its position in politics continues to decline as expressed through its vote share in the last two general elections. Variation at the local level occurred in regard to PPP's political position, but in general it is not comparable to its position during the 1970s. In all regions in Indonesia, PPP's vote share declined significantly. In the next section I will discuss PPP politics at the local level in Jombang. I will look particularly at Muslims' support towards this party, and examine how their views developed after it changed its ideological base to Pancasila.

6.2 The Politics of Javanese Muslims

Before discussing my findings concerning the relationship between Islam and politics in Jombang, I would like to describe briefly the characteristics of Jombang society in general which relate to the political attitudes of its members. First, the population of Jombang has long been supported by a strong Islamic environment. One of the factors contributing to this is the existence of *pesantren*. Although not all *kecamatan* (district) have had a *pesantren* for a long time, the development of education generally in Jombang has made it possible for numerous *pesantren* and *madrasa* to be established in various *kecamatan* since the second half of this century. Secondly, the influence of the *kiai* on this society is sufficiently strong to ensure that the *kiai* are socially followed by Muslims at the grassroots level. As the *kiai* always try to apply Islamic concepts in their socio-political life, the Islamic environment has flourished in the life of Jombang society affecting Muslims' political behaviour in various ways. Thirdly, *tarekat* practice is embedded strongly in the life of many Jombang Muslims. As the *tarekat* focuses on exercising people's religiosity, the religious attachment resulting from this exercise influences the political attitude of its members. The wider practice of *tarekat* by Muslims in Jombang has enabled their actions to be inspired and influenced by Islamic values and norms.

Nevertheless, the question of the extent to which Islamic tenets and ideas influence the socio-political behaviour of the society can still be posed. I will begin to answer this question by referring to what is understood of politics by Muslims in Jombang. As commonly stated by Islamic leaders, Islam should play a comprehensive role in all aspects of human life. Thus politics is inseparable from Islam itself (cf. Samson, 1978), and Muslim society needs to establish a political system which is grounded on an Islamic framework[4]. In the *kiai's* view,

---

[4] Islamic ideas influence political behaviour of Indonesian political leaders and adherents generally. Some ideas pursued by some Islamic leaders, such as their dream of an Islamic state, or other efforts to apply Islamic values, are proof of strong Islamic influence. This religious orientation has been established through Muslims' understanding of Islamic values and Qur'anic precepts. But a general type of orientation presented by Geertz (1959a, 1965), who categorised religious orientations among Muslims into three kinds of subcultures, marked by differences in their political behaviour, was an expression of how varied the political behaviours of Indonesian Muslims were. Although Geertz's categorisation of *santri*, *priyayi* and *abangan*, has been criticised, it depicts the intensity and quality of Islam's influence on the ethos of cultural groupings and how a certain religious outlook establishes a certain political orientation. From the three categories, it was only the *santri* who were strongly influenced by Islam, so that they made this religion a guide for their lives and used Islamic political parties as a vehicle to realise the ideals of Islam. It is understandable that they belonged to or 'leaned toward' either Masjumi or Nahdlatul Ulama (NU) as the two big Islamic political parties during 1950s. On the other hand, the *abangan*, who were represented by a large number of rural Javanese and more syncretic in their Islam, leaned to the

Islam and politics are like two sides of the same coin: Islam is the ideal and politics is the means to implement or realise that ideal in the life of the society.

In Jombang, the political orientation of society is expressed clearly through the people's affiliation with Islamic political parties. From the composition of the seats in the local parliament in 1957, it is evident that NU as an Islamic party was dominant in comparison to the other parties in Jombang. NU had won 14 out of 35 seats (Ward, 1974:167) in the local parliament. If we combine the number of seats obtained by NU and Masjumi[5], using Geertz's (1965) and Feith's (1974) frameworks that relate society's religiosity to their (relative) political support, we can surmise that around half of Jombang voters were Muslims devoted enough to commit themselves to Islamic parties.

Despite variation between all the *kecamatan* in Jombang in terms of people's attachment to Islam, the greater share of the vote for Islamic parties in that election is understandable since Islam in Jombang was supported by the existence of so many *pesantren*. The *kiai* played a significant role in getting support from the Muslim society since a *kiai* has generally been a charismatic figure whose authority is greatly acknowledged (cf. Dhofier, 1982). Through his own charisma, a *kiai* could induce political action since the power of his charisma was imbued with religious legitimacy. The *kiai* in Jombang were members of NU at that time, so that it was NU (as a political party) that obtained higher votes in the 1955 election in Jombang.

The crushing of the PKI in late 1966 could have contributed to increased support for NU and other Islamic parties in the following elections. As most people involved in the crushing in Jombang were Muslims, it seemed to those supporters of the former Communist party, whose Muslimness was nominally acknowledged, that to join Muslim groups, especially NU, was a necessity, since Islam could be a safe haven[6]. In addition, some *kiai* offered a protection for those communist

---

Indonesian National Party (PNI) or to the Indonesian Communist Party (PKI). Also the *priyayi*, who were white collar civil servants, were inclined to be supporters either of PNI or PKI. These three categories were called *aliran* political orientations. The political manoeuvre set in motion through this *aliran* system had condensed the four political parties into two blocks: one was the Islamic block represented by Masjumi and NU and the other was the nominal or syncretic Muslim block, including non-Muslims, represented by PNI and PKI. During the New Order government, the *aliran* system does not work well because of the change in the political constellation.

[5] I had some difficulty in obtaining data on the 1955 local election. But an interview with Muhammad Baidlowi, the former chairman of NU in Jombang, indicated that Masjumi, which represented modernist Muslims in Jombang, had only won 3 seats. The rest of the seats were shared by PNI (Indonesian National Party) and PKI (Indonesian Communist Party), that is 8 and 10 respectively.

[6] The situation in East Java after 1966 was marked by a political crack-down in regard to former Communist Party supporters who converted to Islam. In his research in villages near Mt. Bromo, East Java, Hefner (1987) found evidence of forced destruction of all the existing *abangan* religious institutions. A place of prayer, for example, was demolished by village officers and other Muslim villagers. Although the devout Muslim society in Jombang in general did not destroy everything *abangan*, the pressure could be seen in the way young Muslims in Jombang treated the PKI members and its symphatisers. This pressure made it possible to identify who among former communist members could be accepted as members of society and who could not. NU and its ANSOR (youth organisation affiliated with NU)

members who wanted to reassert their Islam. The *kiai* could guarantee the safety of these people against their 'pengganyang' (lit. destroyers). In Ngepeh village, for example, all communist members were saved from death, because they were helped by a *kiai* who protected them from violence. However, the unavoidable killing of so many PKI members in Jombang has led them to support parties other than the Islamic one. A feeling of enmity among those people whose parents were killed has been kept alive. I was told by an informant that a number of children of former PKI members in Mojowarno converted to Catholicism. It is therefore understandable that many former PKI members and sympathisers did not support the Islamic parties in the elections during the New Order government.

The emergence of Golkar in the 1971 general election has changed the Islamic parties' vote shares. This election was marked by a decrease in the Islamic vote generally. This decrease not only initiated this tendency but also indicated a change in support of former Islamic party voters. In this election, the NU political party only obtained 13 seats in Jombang, while another Islamic party, Parmusi[7], obtained only 1 seat. The decrease in NU's vote was in line with its decrease at the national level. In the 1971 general election, the government party, Golkar, had to compete with NU as the biggest Islamic political party. Furthermore the politics of non-cooperation launched by one of NU's leaders, Subchan Z.E,

---

had a prominent role in this movement. According to a Muslim involved, the movement was actually confined to efforts to 'mengislamkan kembali' (to reassert their Islam, or reislamisation). Reislamising former communist members, who were mostly Javanese *abangan* in Jombang, was meant to reacknowledge them as Muslims, since they were already nominal Muslims. Young Muslims asked these communist sympathisers to reassert their Islam identity by reciting the *shahada*, which they might have recited before they became communist members. The *shahada* is the Profession of Faith. The Profession runs as follows: "there is no God but Allah and Muhammad is His Messenger". The 'shahada' is one of the five pillars of Islam. Anyone who converts to Islam should firstly recite the *shahada*. Because of this situation, village mosques were always attended by huge numbers for prayers during the second half of the 1960s. However, as some communist members refused to reassert their Islam, some killings were inevitable. This is because some former communist members had also threatened Muslims. It is hard to obtain the exact number of victims.

[7] Golkar which took part for the first time in a general election, received 18 seats, while PNI received only 2. Compare the seats obtained by Islamic parties in this election with that obtained in the 1955 general election mentioned above. Two other Islamic parties, Perti and SI, did not receive any seats in the 1971 general election in Jombang. They had only a few members or sympathisers (see Table 6.2). In 1960, the Soekarno government banned Masjumi. The government based this action on the fact that some Masjumi leaders were involved in the PRRI separatist rebellion in Sumatra. Under Suharto's New Order government, some former Masjumi leaders intended to revive the party, but the government did not permit this. They therefore established another party, the Parmusi. In the 1971 general election, this party could not regain the popularity of the former Masjumi. The party then changed its name to 'Muslimin Indonesia' (MI) after it merged with other Islamic political parties to form the Partai Persatuan Pembangunan (PPP). Some former Masjumi leaders, however, did not acknowledge Parmusi or MI as neo-Masjumi.

resulted in government pressure on NU[8]. The *kiai* in villages[9], for example, were often subjected to psychological pressures. Very often NU members could not hold any *pengajian* (religious gathering), unless they received approval from the local police office, which was usually hard to obtain. The *kiai* were usually approached by village officers who asked them to support Golkar. This political pressure resulted in a situation where many people did not dare to express their support for NU and other Islamic parties.

In the following years, Islamic political parties in Jombang experienced a continuous decline. After the four Islamic parties, that is NU, Parmusi, SI and Perti, merged to form PPP in 1973, PPP never regained the vote which NU attained in the 1955 general election in Jombang. The decline in the PPP vote was even more evident when some *kiai* supported the political manoeuvre of 'penggembosan' (lit. to deflate as in deflating a tyre; to weaken) during the 1987 general election campaign. The local PPP in Jombang, which received 13 seats (40 percent of the 32 seats) in the 1977 and 1982 general elections[10], also experienced a significant decline in the 1987 election by getting only 9 (25 percent) of the 36 seats available in the local parliament. Although in the 1992 election, this party increased its share to 11 seats (30 percent), it was not comparable to NU's performance in the 1955 general election.

It is interesting to note that general elections in Jombang have been marked by competition between the Islamic party and Golkar since 1971. Campaigners for both parties strived to increase their party's share of the votes. Similar to PPP, Golkar in Jombang oscillated in its vote attainment. On the other hand, the Indonesian Democratic Party (PDI), a amalgam of five nationalist and other religious parties, obtained a significant increase from 1 seat in the 1977 election to 2, 4 and 8 seats in the 1982, 1987 and 1992 elections respectively.

---

[8] The process of de-NUisation was carried out by the New Order government especially in NU's bastion, the Department of Religious Affairs. The top position in the Ministry of Religion was given to a Muhammadiyah member, Professor Mukti Ali. This change indicated the government's dislike of NU. The political engineering in the Department of Religious Affairs replaced its elites from NU background with those from Muhammadiyah. This process was seriously disadvantageous to NU, since it was conducted in all sections throughout Indonesia. Since the appointment of Mukti Ali, NU's domination in the local office of the Department of Religious Affairs in Jombang was replaced by the Muhammadiyah's, although the majority of Muslims in Jombang had been affiliated with NU. According to Abdurrahman Wahid, the current national chairman of NU, there are three positions which would not be given by the government to NU. These are the Minister of Religious Affairs, the head of MUI (the Indonesian Council of Ulama) and the leader of the PPP (see Forum Keadilan, 24/1994).

[9] According to Ken E Ward (1974), six NU activists in Jombang were imprisoned preceding the 1971 general election. What disappointed many Muslims in Jombang was a statement made by the local Sarbumusi (Muslim trade union affiliated with NU) head who suggested that those who were detained in jail did not commit political, but rather criminal acts. The 1971 general election saw great political pressure on NU members. This was repeated in the 1977 and 1982 general elections.

[10] In the 1977 and 1982 general election, the number of seats in the local parliament was 32, while in the 1987 and 1992 general election the number was increased to 36.

Figure 6.1. Results of the General Election in Jombang

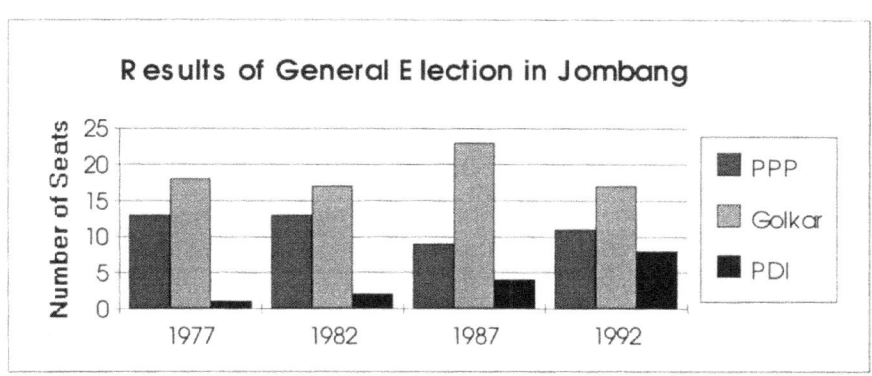

Table 6.1 shows that Golkar's decrease in the 1982 general election was balanced by an increase in PDI's vote share to 6.2 percent, while the PPP's decrease in the 1987 election was balanced by the increase in Golkar's and PDI's vote shares to 62.8 percent and 11.4 percent respectively. Although Golkar received a majority of the votes in the 1987 general election, it experienced a significant decrease in the 1992 general election. The decrease not only marked the return of some former PPP voters, who had supported Golkar in the 1987 general election to support PPP, but also marked a general loss of Golkar supporters (compare with its vote attainment in the 1977 and 1982 general elections). Thus PDI's increase in the 1992 general election was matched by a decrease in Golkar's votes.

Table 6.1. Percentage of Votes Shared by Political Parties in Jombang in General Elections

	PPP	Golkar	PDI
1971	42.9[11]	52.0	5.0
1977	40.6	56.2	3.1
1982	40.6	53.1	6.2
1987	25.7	62.8	11.4
1992	31.4	45.7	22.8

[11] This percentage is based on the vote shares of three Islamic parties which took part in the 1971 general election, i.e. NU, Parmusi, and SI (see Table 6.2). As PPP resulted from a merger of these parties and Perti (this party's share of votes is not included in this figure because it received a very small number of votes in this election in various *kecamatan*), and represented the only Islamic party in the 1977 and 1982 general elections, I took this figure as PPP's just to make the comparison between its vote share in the elections easier.

(Source: Partai Persatuan Pembangunan, 1982 and 1982a)

Table 6.2. Number of Votes of the Major Parties in the 1971 General Election in Jombang

No. Districts	NU	SI	Parmusi	Golkar	PNI
1. Jombang	13,196	127	821	23,497	1,292
2. Diwek	17,538	82	243	12,227	582
3. Gudo	5,350	79	267	11,536	2,196
4. Perak	14,845	80	369	14,721	224
5. Tembelang	4,362	79	597	17,433	1,797
6. Ploso	2,963	46	155	9,635	1,340
7. Plandaan	4,322	65	56	9,134	2,025
8. Kabuh	799	47	46	12,438	2,525
9. Kudu	4,639	44	74	13,169	360
10. Mojoagung	8,720	43	425	12,006	147
11. Sumobito	10,917	77	903	11,819	88
12. Kesamben	9,722	49	665	10,557	368
13. Peterongan	24,567	52	948	10,006	640
14. Ngoro	11,603	66	167	10,764	1,018
15. Mojowarno	13,777	420	587	9,243	3,009
16. Bareng	4,776	58	398	10,146	1,524
17. Wonosalam	138	14	7	8,037	876
Total	162,434	1,428	6,726	206,823	20,011

(Source: Dewan Pimpinan Cabang PPP, 1982)

These figures therefore indicate that while the competing Islamic party and Golkar oscillated and both sustained a decline in their share of votes, PDI, a minor party, as expressed by its share of votes in the 1971 general election, experienced a very impressive increase during general elections under the New Order government in Jombang. The factors which contributed to PPP's decrease were the change in its ideological base and the *penggembosan* by NU activists, while the factor which contributed to Golkar's decrease was the emergence of dissatisfaction among its supporters. An analysis by a political activist in Jombang reveals that these dissatisfied supporters, such as the Chinese[12], changed their support to PDI, especially in the 1992 general election. They were unlikely to change their support to PPP because they had historically never given their support to this party. PDI in the 1992 general election also received support from former PPP supporters who had voted Golkar in the 1987 general election, although traditionally this was less likely since former PPP supporters, who were largely devout Muslims, felt uncomfortable supporting PDI, a party with Catholic and other religious background. The fact that PPP did not regain all its lost supporters in the 1992 general election indicated that some of its supporters

---

[12] This activist told me that some Chinese in Jombang complained because Golkar often asked for 'sumbangan' (donation). In his opinion, the Chinese in Jombang were vulnerable to being exploited financially as their dependence on the government for security was great. However, as they then felt dissatisfied with such treatment, they changed their votes to PDI in the 1992 general election.

who had voted Golkar in the 1987 general election might have given their support to PDI in the 1992 general election[13].

While the pattern of electoral behaviour of Muslims in Jombang indicates a continuous but slight change on the part of the former Islamic party, PPP, with the exception of the 1987 general election results[14], the pattern of voting in each *kecamatan* remained the same. The general change in electoral pattern in terms of attachment to Islamic and non-Islamic parties showed little regional variation. The strength of the Islamic party shown in certain *kecamatan* since the 1971 general election has remained, while the strength of non-Islamic parties has remained in other *kecamatan*. The continuous slight decrease in PPP's vote share occured evenly in all *kecamatan*, a situation which made its relative strength between regions constant.

In the 1971, 1977 and 1982 general elections, the Islamic parties obtained more than 40 percent of the votes in nine *kecamatan*. These *kecamatan* were Diwek, Perak, Tembelang, Mojoagung, Sumobito, Kesamben, Peterongan, Ngoro and Mojowarno (see Table 6.3). In five of these *kecamatan* the Islamic parties received the majority of votes, that is more than 50 percent. On the other hand, the Islamic parties received fewest votes (30 percent and less) in seven *kecamatan*. These *kecamatan* were Gudo, Ploso, Plandaan, Kabuh, Kudu, Bareng and Wonosalam. I have labelled the former group *kecamatan hijau* (green *kecamatan*) and the latter *kecamatan merah* (red *kecamatan*)[15]. The term *kecamatan hijau* indicates that the Islamic party in these areas received strong support. Green (*hijau*) is often used as a symbol of Islam. On the other hand, *kecamatan merah* are areas where the Islamic party did not receive significant support. Although red generally represents PDI, I use the term here to simply indicate all *kecamatan* in which the Islamic party lacked support. Furthermore I have given no colour designation to Kecamatan Jombang to indicate that here the support for Islamic party was in balance with that for the non-Islamic parties (see Figure 6.2).

---

[13] My findings indicate that a few fomer PPP supporters voted PDI in the 1992 general election. I will discuss this later in this section.
[14] In this election PPP experienced a sharp decrease for about 36 percent.
[15] I adopted these terms after I had a discussion with Professor Fox (my supervisor). This is a classification used by some villagers in Jombang who were key informants in the 1980s when Professor Fox did research in Ngoro.

Figure 6.2. Muslim Support for Political Parties in Various Kecamatan in Jombang in the 1971 General Election

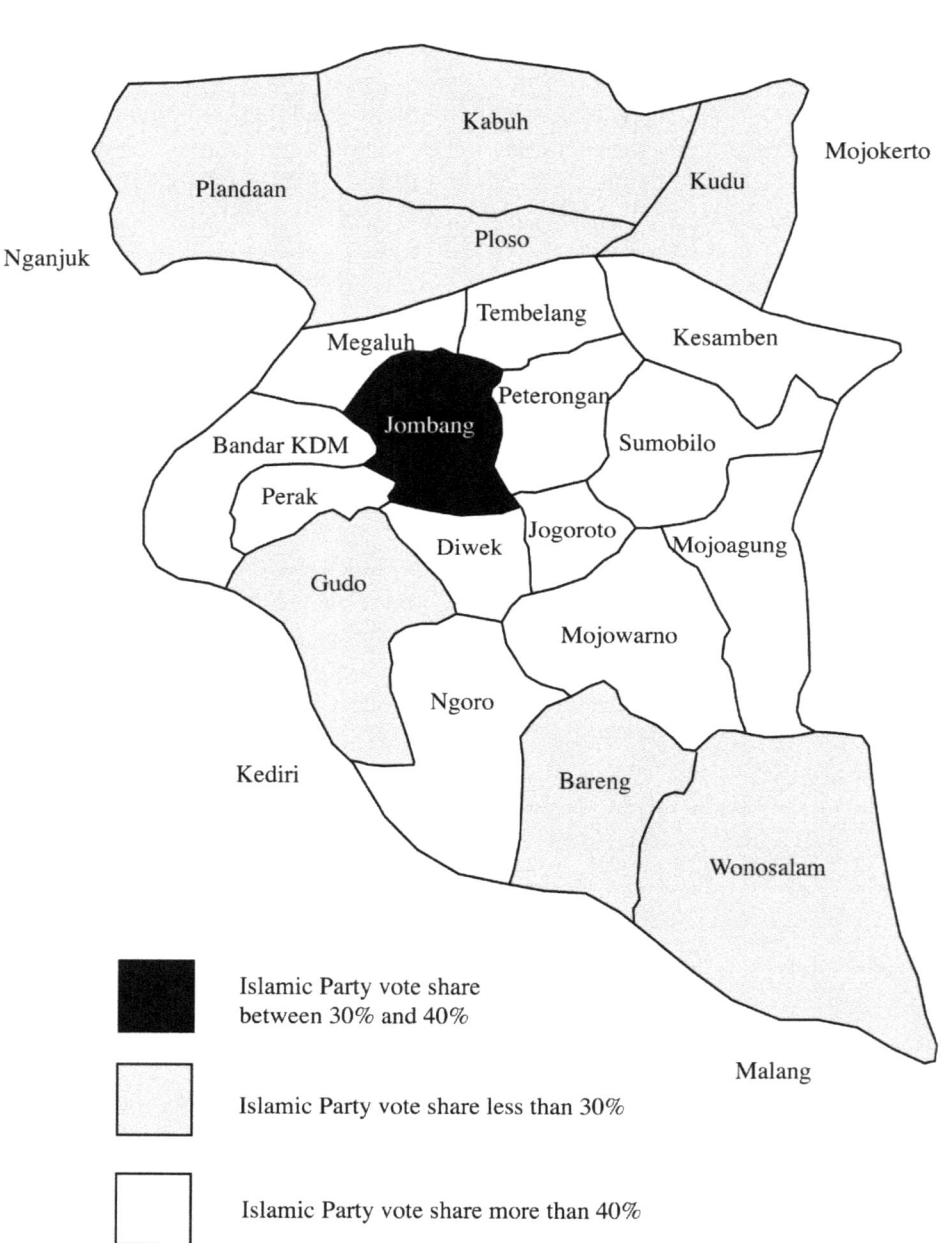

The figures in Table 6.3 indicate that all *kecamatan* in the northern region of Jombang could be categorised as *kecamatan merah* (see Figure 6.2). These regions, which are located on the northern side of the Brantas river, are less developed economically compared to those in the southern region. Kabuh, for example, is well known as "daerah minus" (a deficient area). Although economic conditions might not determine the support for a political party, it is interesting that PPP received the highest support in economically well developed regions. In Wonosalam, also known as 'daerah minus' although it is located in the southern region of Jombang, PPP also did not receive large support; while in Diwek and Ngoro, which are well developed *kecamatan*, its support from Muslims was greater. In addition, the highest Islamic parties vote share in the 1971 general election occurred in the *kecamatan* where *pesantren* had been established for a long time. It is interesting that almost all *kecamatan hijau* have *pesantren* which were established before 1960. Only Kecamatan Kesamben does not have a *pesantren*. Some of these *kecamatan* have two to three *pesantren*, which were established long before Indonesian independence.

Table 6.3. Percentage of Islamic Parties' and PPP's Share of Votes in Various Kecamatan in Jombang

Kecamatan	General Elections				
	1971	1977	1982	1987	1992
1. Jombang	36.3	33.6	35.4	20.2	23.6
2. Diwek	58.2	52.9	55.6	39.9	42.7
3. Gudo	29.3	26.0	27.5	16.0	18.8
4. Perak	50.5	47.9	48.7	20.0	28.2
5. Tembelang	43.8	40.2	42.9	25.9	28.0
6. Ploso	22.3	19.6	19.1	10.4	12.0
7. Plandaan	28.4	24.3	21.4	9.8	10.4
8. Kabuh	5.6	3.9	4.3	1.9	3.4
9. Kudu	26.0	20.4	21.3	13.4	16.8
10. Mojoagung	43.0	44.8	46.4	28.2	34.4
11. Sumobito	49.9	54.9	57.2	38.4	40.5
12. Kesamben	48.8	44.6	44.4	20.8	27.0
13. Peterongan	70.6	65.5	62.7	35.8	40.4
14. Ngoro	50.1	48.7	51.5	33.9	37.1
15. Mojowarno	54.6	48.1	51.5	39.7	43.1
16. Bareng	30.9	27.6	29.5	18.4	25.0
17. Wonosalam	1.7	3.4	5.4	1.6	4.7
18. Megaluh				25.0	27.9
19. Bandar KDM.				39.3	48.5
20. Jogoroto				45.8	51.5

(Source: Partai Persatuan Pembangunan, 1982 and 1982a)[16]

[16] These figures are based on the three Islamic parties' vote shares, i.e. NU, Parmusi and SI, in Jombang. In the next elections, the figures above represent PPP's vote share. It is important to note that until the second half of the 1980s, Megaluh, Bandar KDM and Jogoroto were under the jurisdiction of Kecamatan Tembelang, Perak and Peterongan respectively.

In the *kecamatan merah*, only two have *pesantren*, that is Ploso and Bareng. These *pesantren* are relatively recent, since they were built in 1974 and 1985 respectively. However, the presence of a *pesantren* in a certain *kecamatan* was not the sole factor which contributed to support for the Islamic parties. Kecamatan Jombang, for example, had two great *pesantren* established long before Indonesian independence. In this region, however, the Islamic parties only received 36.3 percent of the votes in the 1971 general election. This *kecamatan* is the most urbanised of all *kecamatan*[17], so that although its *pesantren* have been established for a long time, other factors contributed to people's electoral behaviour there.

It is interesting to note that the 1977 general election showed an increase in the national vote share of PPP as the Islamic party. Despite general NU disappointment, the merger of four Islamic political parties in 1973 unified Muslim politics and was successful in increasing the vote share of the Islamic political party, so that some regarded the merger as a "blessing in disguise". However, the Islamic party's vote share in various *kecamatan* in Jombang showed a decrease in the 1977 general election. In this election, the Islamic party in Jombang only succeeded in increasing its votes in two *kecamatan*, Mojoagung and Sumobito. It seemed that this situation was affected by NU disappointment with the merger. Nevertheless, in all *kecamatan* in which it received more than 40 percent of votes in 1977, PPP succeeded in increasing its votes share in the 1982 general election with the exception of Peterongan and Kesamben. In both these *kecamatan* PPP continued to decline until the 1987 general election. It is not easy to explain this exception. The only obvious thing is that in Peterongan a great *'ulama*, Kiai Musta'in (the head of *Pesantren Darul Ulum*), joined Golkar prior to the 1977 general election. Because of his large influence, his defection might have contributed to the decrease in the Islamic party's votes in the following general elections in his *kecamatan*.

The same pattern held true for PPP in the 1977 general election in *kecamatan merah*. It experienced a decrease in all *kecamatan*. Similar to its experience in *kecamatan hijau*, in the 1982 general election PPP succeeded in regaining some of the votes it lost in the 1977 general election in all *kecamatan merah,* with the exception of Ploso and Plandaan. Despite being *merah* in social environment, Muslims in Ploso have actually had an influencial *kiai*, Kiai Muchtar Mu'thi, who established a *pesantren* in 1974 and has been the *murshid* of *Tarekat Shiddiqiyah*. Since he has been close to Golkar for a long time, his political lead might not only have hindered PPP from increasing its vote share in this region but may have caused a decrease in its vote share, since some Muslims might follow his political lead.

---

[17] This *kecamatan* is centre of local government and high Chinese population.

In the 1987 general election, PPP in all *kecamatan* in Jombang received a smaller share of the vote compared to its vote attainment in the 1982 general election. The average decrease in PPP's vote share in *kecamatan hijau* was 34 percent. The highest decrease in these *kecamatan* occurred in Perak (58.9 percent), followed by Kesamben and Peterongan, with falls of 53.1 and 42.9 percent respectively (see Table 6.4). On the other hand, the average decrease in PPP vote share in *kecamatan merah* in the 1987 general election was about 49 percent. As the decrease in PPP's vote in this election related to NU's policy of 'back to khittah' and to the politics of deflating PPP (*penggembosan*) carried out by NU activists who were supported by a few *kiai*, the higher average level of decrease in *kecamatan merah* compared to *kecamatan hijau* reflected the lower conflict among NU *kiai* here. People support for PPP here was not so strong. Thus when some NU activists encouraged Muslims here to leave PPP, these PPP supporters could easily follow such encouragement, since there was no *kiai* who consistently prevented these people from leaving the party.

Table 6.4. Percentage of the Decline in PPP's Vote Share in Various Kecamatan in the 1987 General Election

	1982	1987	Decline
1. Jombang	35.4	20.2	42.9
2. Diwek	55.6	39.9	28.2
3. Gudo	27.5	16.0	41.8
4. Perak	48.7	20.0	58.9
5. Tembelang	42.9	25.9	39.6
6. Ploso	19.1	10.4	45.5
7. Plandaan	21.4	9.8	54.2
8. Kabuh	4.3	1.9	55.8
9. Kudu	21.3	13.4	37.1
10. Mojoagung	46.4	28.2	39.2
11. Sumobito	57.2	38.4	32.9
12. Kesamben	44.4	20.8	53.1
13. Peterongan	62.7	35.8	42.9
14. Ngoro	51.5	33.9	22.5
15. Mojowarno	51.5	39.7	22.9
16. Bareng	29.5	18.4	37.6
17. Wonosalam	5.4	1.6	70.4

(Source: Panitia Pemilihan Daerah Tingkat II Jombang, 1977, 1987 and 1992).

In 1992, PPP in Jombang succeeded in increasing its vote share to 31.4 percent, an increase of about 22.2 percent from its vote attainment in the 1987 general election (see Table 6.1). This increase occurred in all *kecamatan*, both *hijau* and *merah*. Several factors contributed to this situation. The first was the absence of *penggembosan*. The few *kiai* who were *pengembosan* supporters not only let Muslims support PPP but also gave tacit support to this party. A tacit understanding between PPP and NU leaders also occurred[18]. This was not only because they came from the same roots, that is NU, but also because the politics of *penggembosan* aimed mainly to show MI politicians that PPP would be powerless without NU's support. Nevertheless, this does not mean that PPP position in Jombang was similar to that in 1977. PPP was no longer formally an Islamic party, and NU members in Jombang did not feel uncomfortable supporting parties other than PPP. Some Muslims in Jombang began to view PPP differently, a situation which made it difficult for PPP to regain a position comparable to that gained by the Islamic parties in the 1971 general election.

Nevertheless, PPP remained an important means for Muslims to articulate their political interests. Many PPP supporters in villages in Jombang continued to maintain their earlier view of PPP. I would like to examine this situation in the last section of this chapter when I discuss Muslim motivations in supporting PPP and how they saw this party after it changed its Islamic base with Pancasila.

6.3 The Penggembosan and Changing Muslims Political Support

A large number of NU members in Jombang and Indonesia in general were disappointed with the leadership of PPP under Naro, an MI exponent, since he created an unfavourable situation which resulted in deep conflicts between the various PPP factions. It is commonly perceived that under his leadership, the ideals of the party were replaced by personal ambition. He was thus deemed not to be struggling for Muslim society but rather for his individual benefit. PPP was hence more a medium for personal gain rather than a medium of Islamic struggle.

After NU launched its policy of 'back to khittah' nationally in 1984, some *kiai* in Jombang explicitly encouraged their followers to support Golkar in the 1987 general election. This was because the essence of the policy allowed NU members to affiliate with any political organisation. As some *kiai* and NU politicians felt that NU was disadvantaged by MI in PPP, they used 'back to khittah' and NU dissociation from the party to weaken the party. This political manoeuvre was called *penggembosan*. The *penggembosan* was carried out nationally; not only by discouraging NU members to vote for PPP, but also by asking them to vote for Golkar in the 1987 general election. The leadership of NU in Jombang tended explicitly to support the politics of *penggembosan*. The 1987 general election therefore confused Muslim voters in many respects due to the different support offered by different Islamic leaders. This election was the first time the vote of

---

[18] A PPP leader, Hafidh Ma'shum told me that he asked Kiai Shohib Bisri, an influential *kiai* and one of the *penggembos* in the 1987 general election, not to conduct another *penggembosan* in the 1992 general election.

the devout Muslims, NU members in particular, was divided between various political parties.

Penggembosan was successful in reducing PPP's national share of votes from 25.8 percent in the 1982 election to 15.3 percent in the 1987. In Jombang PPP's votes in 1987 decreased by 36 percent[19] compared to that in 1982. Such a decline was caused by the influence of some *kiai* who supported *penggembosan*. It is thus evident that the launch of the 'back to khittah' policy in 1984 changed the support pattern for existing political parties in Jombang. The encouragement of some *kiai* to support the government party and their tacit support of the *penggembosan* movement were significant factors since they succeeded in turning one third of PPP supporters away from the party. Although the *penggembosan* movement was not a formal policy of NU, it was nevertheless sustained by the tacit support of some *kiai* in the mainstream of NU, either locally or nationally. Many *kiai* in the NU mainstream and their followers throughout Indonesia considered that the PPP political leadership needed to be weakened since it was deemed as being undemocratically run[20] to the disadvantage of NU, the largest component of the party.

Seen as a retaliatory political manoeuvre, the *penggembosan* movement was popular among NU activists in Jombang. Such a situation gave legitimacy, particularly for younger activists, to even press NU members to leave PPP. The attitude of these younger activists was based on their understanding of the policy launched by NU a year before. The policy actually only recommended that NU activists not occupy positions in both PPP and NU leadership. But since the majority of NU activists were disappointed with Naro's leadership, they asked their colleagues to leave PPP. A senior *kiai*, who was still affiliated with PPP, for example, was forced by ANSOR activists (Ansor is an organisation of NU youth) to leave the party. The same experience held true with a former local ANSOR president who had been very active in the party[21].

---

[19] The percentage share of the vote and that of seats received by a political party did not always match. The share of the vote was based on the number of the votes received, while the number of seats was based on the votes received divided by the number of votes per seat.

[20] NU members who took an interest in politics were unsympathetic towards or disappointed with Naro's national leadership of PPP. Not only did he disadvantage NU but he also cultivated a feeling of hostility among PPP faction members. According to an informant, the political actions of Naro, who came from the MI faction, neither derived from an *ikhlas* (honest) perspective nor the desire 'to struggle for Islam', but rather was influenced by selfish interests. The difference in the group characteristics of the former PPP components, NU, MI, Perti and SI, did not necessarily need to be forcefully diminished. In fact this was probably impossible. What needed to be done was to cultivate the same perspective on the necessity to support the Islamic struggle through politics. Naro, however, the informant added, did not try to create such a situation but rather he sharpened these differences.

[21] Interview with Kiai Khoerul Anwar and Hafidh Ma'shum on 27 July 1993 and 13 July 1993 respectively. It is surprising that ANSOR activists asked a *kiai* forcefully to leave PPP. I can speculate that they were modern educated members whose attachment with traditional values was loose. Their action was comparable to that of the *santri* of the *Pesantren Darul Ulum* who conducted a demonstration, protesting their *kiai's* policy.

In Jombang there were at least two groups of Muslims, each of which was led by *kiai* who showed opposing attitudes towards *penggembosan*. Although the supporting group was a minority in terms of number, its political voice in conducting this politics in Jombang was heard and gained national acceptance, making this movement succesful. In Jombang some *kiai* and their *pesantren* were also active in supporting this movement. Three out of the four larger *pesantren*, *Pesantren Tebuireng, Pesantren Denanyar* and *Pesantren Bahrul Ulum*[22], supported the *penggembosan*. The heads of *Pesantren Tebuireng* and *Pesantren Denanyar*, Hajj Yusuf Hasyim and Kiai Shohib Bisri respectively, actively promoted this political movement. The leader of *Pesantren Bahrul Ulum*, however, only gave tacit support. According to one source (see Fathoni and Zen, 1992), both Hajj Yusuf Hasyim and Kiai Shohib Bisri were included in the big four *penggembos* (persons who carried out the *penggembosan*) in East Java. Hajj Yusuf Hasyim was a national political figure, while Kiai Shobib Bisri was an NU political figure at the provincial level. Kiai Shohib Bisri was the formal president of the local NU leadership in Jombang at that time.

However, it needs to be noted that despite the formal involvement of the top leaders of these *pesantren* in the *penggembosan*, few *kiai* who taught in and had a familial connection with the founders of these *pesantren*, agreed with this political manoeuvre. The same held true of some *santri*. The point is that only a few of these *kiai* and their *santri* showed enough disagreement to confront the leaders. This situation made the impact of *penggembosan* on the PPP share of the vote vary.

Although the involvement of the *kiai* who supported the *penggembosan* contributed to the general decrease in the PPP share of the vote in Jombang, the evidence indicate that this does not necessarily mean that PPP in the *kecamatan* in which their *kiai* were active in this political manoeuvre suffered the worst decline. Table 6.4 indicates that the greatest decline in PPP's share of the vote in the 1987 general election occurred in Perak and Kesamben (more than 50 percent). PPP's share of the vote in Kecamatan Diwek and Jombang, where Hajj Yusuf Hasyim and Kiai Shohib Bisri lived, declined by about 28.2 and 42.9 percent respectively. Of all *kecamatan*, PPP experienced the greatest decline (about 70.4 percent) in Wonosalam, a *kecamatan* where there was no local *kiai* involved in *penggembosan*.

As these politics were a retaliatory movement which aimed to show that NU had a powerful political influence at the grassroots level (due to the fact that the majority of PPP supporters were derived from this organisation) after it was

---

[22] Although the leaders of the *Pesantren Darul Ulum* had joined Golkar a decade before, which had given rise to a conflict with other *kiai* in Jombang, they were not involved in this political manoeuvre. Their conflict with NU *kiai* a decade previously kept them from involvement in NU politics (see my discussion in Chapter V).

disadvantaged by Naro, the leader of PPP, the *penggembosan* was only a temporary political manoeuvre. These politics were not based on particular principles in regard to the *kiai* politics. It is not surprising that the political attitude of the *kiai* and other NU activists changed in the next general election. No similar political manoeuvre was conducted in the 1992 general election. According to an observer[23], Kiai Shohib Bisri concerned himself with PPP's share of the vote in the 1992 general election in East Java. This *kiai* monitored all developments of PPP during the election. His assistants gave him a daily report on the position of PPP in various regions in East Java. In addition, there was also a request from a PPP leader in Jombang that Kiai Shohib Bisri not ask Muslims to leave PPP, even though this *kiai* was disappointed with this party.

Although the *penggembosan* movement succeeded in causing the defection of many NU members from PPP, because some *kiai* gave their support to this political manoeuvre, it is interesting that the majority of respondents in my study regarded such a movement as inappropriate. Of the 182 respondents interviewed, 64.8 percent noted their disagreement (see Table 6.5). Their reasons varied from a perception that such a movement could split the *umma* to disapproval of the individual political interests of those who pursued such a political manoeuvre. Only 5.5 percent of respondents agreed with such actions. Nevertheless, I found that 14.3 percent of respondents regarded the *penggembosan* as the political right of an individual, indicating that these respondents were not disturbed by this political manouvre. For various reasons, only 1 respondent agreed that it was for the sake of NU.

Table 6.5. Muslim Respondents' Standpoint on Political Manoeuvres of *Penggembosan*

Didn't Agree	All Right	Agree	No answer
118	26	10	28
(64.8)	(14.3)	(5.5)	(15.3)

n = 182

(Source: questionnaire)

The tacit disagreement of these Muslim respondents with *penggembosan* is understandable since in regions where NU's position in the PPP was very strong, like Jombang, the movement was disadvantageous to NU itself. The strength of the NU position can be seen by the fact that of eleven PPP seats in the local parliament in Jombang in 1992, nine were occupied by members of the NU component. Only two being occupied by members of the MI component. Other PPP components, SI and Perti, did not receive any seats in the local parliament. The *penggembosan*, especially in Jombang, was hence a retaliatory movement which was not based on solid reasoning. The exponents of the *penggembosan*

---

[23] Greg Fealy, a Ph.D student, stayed at Kiai Shohib Bisri's house during the 1992 general election; personal communication.

movement did not listen to the political aspirations of their community, which strongly remained supportive of PPP. They did not understand the existing political ethos held by Muslims, and their political actions generally gave rise to internal conflict among NU members in Jombang.

Although the actual politics of the majority of NU members at the grassroots level were not moved by *penggembosan*, the exponents of *penggembosan* won the battle initially because of their hold on NU leadership. Accordingly, the process of withdrawing NU members from PPP in Jombang was significant. NU supporters in PPP came under psychological pressure during and after the *penggembosan* movement[24]. They were accused of not being loyal to NU, a situation which created an unfavourable situation for PPP. The perception that "PPP bukan tempat yang bagus buat warga NU" (PPP is not a good place for NU members) was quite strong, at least temporarily. Accordingly, people felt ashamed to support the party. This resulted in a decrease in the popularity of PPP among some Muslims in Jombang. The decline in popularity of PPP in Jombang therefore was not simply because it changed its ideological base (in fact, as I have shown, many people were unaware of this), but also because of the *kiai's* political direction. The *kiais'* decision to encourage Muslims to support the government party, Golkar, was made prior to the 1987 general election in the *Pesantren Denanyar*, located in the western part of Jombang. It should be noted, however, that this decision was made after long discussion. A young *kiai*, for example, told me that he initially did not agree with the decision of "encouraging NU members to vote for the government's party". After being convinced by senior *kiai*, who suggested that everything was changing in politics, however, he surrendered. He was then asked to encourage Muslims in his district to support Golkar in the 1987 general election[25].

The political manoeuvre of *penggembosan* left an unconducive situation for the former Islamic party. It has resulted in a long standing conflict among NU members and the *kiai*. Although a few *kiai* who conducted *penggembosan* in the 1987 general election tacitly resupported PPP in the 1992 general election, the *penggembosan* gave rise to division among NU members. This division was more

---

[24] As noted previously, the *penggembosan* political manoeuvre carried out by NU politicians aimed to weaken PPP politically. PPP had been dominated nationally by the former Parmusi (now MI: Muslimin Indonesia) component since Naro led the party in 1984. Such domination also occurred in many branches of PPP leadership at the regency level. In Jombang, however, NU still dominated the leadership of the party. Because of this situation, *penggembosan* created conflict among the NU activists themselves.

[25] To this end, the district government, especially during the nights of the campaign season, provided the *kiai* with a police guard, a situation which he had never experienced before. The *kiai* were pleased by the accommodating attitude of NU towards the government which resulted in positive efforts in regard to *da'wa* (preaching) activities. By close communication with the lower level government, *da'wa* activities could be performed smoothly, including those among government officers. The *kiai*, for example, recommended that the 'camat' (district head) and his officers conduct '*id prayer* at the district office. The prayer was attended by all government officers from the district to village level in Ngoro district. Such a situation had never happened before.

obvious in the political arena, and was also felt in the social relationships between various groups. I will return to this matter later in this chapter.

6.4 New Social Groupings

The enthusiasm of devout Muslim society to articulate their political aspirations through PPP is still high. This is especially true among the people in the villages, where PPP is still regarded as the Islamic political party. For Muslim villagers it is difficult to know about the current status of the party, since they do not have sufficient access to knowledge about political manoeuvring. This derives from their lack of active involvement in politics[26]. In addition, the NU community in the villages, especially in Jombang, still think that PPP is identical with NU, since NU was the major force which nursed the birth of the party in 1973. At the time, PPP was the only party through which NU members could appropriately articulate their political aspirations. This perspective still exists, not only among those NU members who have insufficient access to politics, but also among those educated in Jombang. However, a change in attitude also occurred among Muslim villagers. External factors, especially the changing attitudes of their *kiai*, who since 1987 supported Golkar, have contributed to a change in the outlook of some devout Muslims.

It can be said that among the NU members in Jombang, two kinds of political perspectives developed after NU launched its "back to khittah" policy which influenced Muslims at the grassroots level. Firstly, there are NU *kiai* and members who contend that 'back to khittah' is an inappropriate policy. According to them, NU should continue to involve itself in politics. This view is held by a minority of *kiai* and their followers. It is shared by an insignificant number of members of the *Tarekat Cukir*. One *kiai* suggested that politics is like a vehicle to pursue what Muslims are struggling for. As there is no formal Islamic party in Indonesia, this group continues to articulate its political aspirations through PPP. Secondly, there are those who are satisfied with NU's return to being a socio-religious organisation as it was conceptualised by the 'back to khittah' policy. This group includes those NU *kiai* and members who perceive themselves to be active proponents of the policy. Members of this group hold different viewpoints about the implementation of the 'back to khittah' policy. In terms of their political affiliation, two tendencies have emerged. The first consists of those NU *kiai* and members who continue to support PPP. Their continued support for the party is due to the fact that NU in essence did not prohibit its members from affiliating with this party. According to them, what NU did with

---

[26] This situation marks the success of the process of mass depolitisation launched by the Indonesian government. The 'Floating Mass' policy introduced in 1975 by the government confined villager participation in national politics to just once in every five years, i.e. during the general election. In addition, political pressure exerted by some government officers during the general elections has made some people reluctant to participate in politics.

its policy was to dissociate formally from PPP. But it allowed its members to affiliate with any political party, including PPP. The second group are those NU *kiai* and members who changed their support from PPP to Golkar. This group insists that support for Golkar is a necessity. This was indicated by their support of the *penggembosan* movement, a political manoeuvre to weaken PPP. In addition, they also made a decision, preceding the 1987 general election, to encourage NU members to support the government party[27]. This group is supported by a few *pesantren kiai* and those *kiai* who hold formal local NU leadership. They usually refer to themselves as the 'kelompok khittah'[28].

In Jombang, the majority of the *kiai* who own *pesantren* follow the 'back to khittah' line. There are several reasons why they adopted this attitude. The most important one is the affiliation of the *pesantren* with NU which makes its *kiai* follow decisions made by NU[29]. For these *kiai*, therefore, the application of the 'back to khittah' policy, which allows society (the NU's members and sympathisers) to affiliate themselves with any political party, is an important duty. They believe they should make their *santri* and NU members in general understand that NU is no longer formally part of PPP. This is a very difficult task because of the long established link with PPP.

Since there are two poles of interpretation of 'back to khittah' in terms of its implementation, this policy has produced a wider conflict in society. The attitude of most formal NU leaders in Jombang disappointed many *kiai* and NU members in general who still continued to support PPP. These NU leaders, supported by various local *kiai*, tried to weaken PPP by their politics of *penggembosan*. A *pesantren kiai* with wide influence in Jombang, Kiai Shohib Bisri, together with the head of *Pesantren Tebuireng*, Hajj Yusuf Hasyim, were among the four exponents well known as *penggembos*. Three of the four large *pesantren* in Jombang gave public support to the *penggembosan* and encouraged Muslims in Jombang to leave PPP in the 1987 general election. Another great *pesantren* in Jombang, the *Pesantren Darul Ulum*, had been supporting Golkar publicly since 1977 when Kiai Musta'in defected to this party. Although the *kiai* of the three *pesantren, Pesantren Tebuireng, Pesantren Denanyar* and *Pesantren Bahrul Ulum*, publicly discouraged Muslims from supporting PPP in the 1987 general election, this did not mean that all their *kiai* adopted the same line. Kiai Syamsuri Badawi of the *Pesantren Tebuireng*, for example, was a PPP national candidate for parliament. Also among the *kiai* family in the *Pesantren Bahrul Ulum*, there was

---

[27] This decision was made in the *Pesantren Denanyar* (Interview with Kiai Ismail, 2 September 1993).
[28] 'Kelompok' literally means a group of people. 'Kelompok Khittah' refers to the NU faction which considers itself to be a group which supports the application of the 'back to khittah' policy.
[29] It is therefore very difficult for the *kiai* who have a different standpoint to openly oppose the NU decision. As I mentioned in Chapter II, NU has been used by *pesantren kiai* as a network through which problems of their *pesantren* are discussed. In addition, the *pesantren kiai* established *Rabitah Ma'ahid al-Islami*, an organisation under the NU umbrella which coordinates *pesantren*. Through this organisation the *pesantren kiai* maintain a kind of solidarity which directs them to follow the NU's decisions.

a PPP candidate for local parliament. Kiai Syamsuri Badawi's candidacy produced a reaction from the head of *Pesantren Tebuireng*, Yusuf Hasyim. But in this case Syamsuri Badawi was supported by his *santri* who had articulated their interests through PPP. The same held true of *kiai* in the *Pesantren Darul Ulum*. Different political affiliations among *kiai* families produced hidden internal conflicts following the 1987 general election.

Figure 6.3. A Tendency of Social Grouping and Support for a Certain Political Organisation among NU Members (Former PPP Supporters) in Jombang

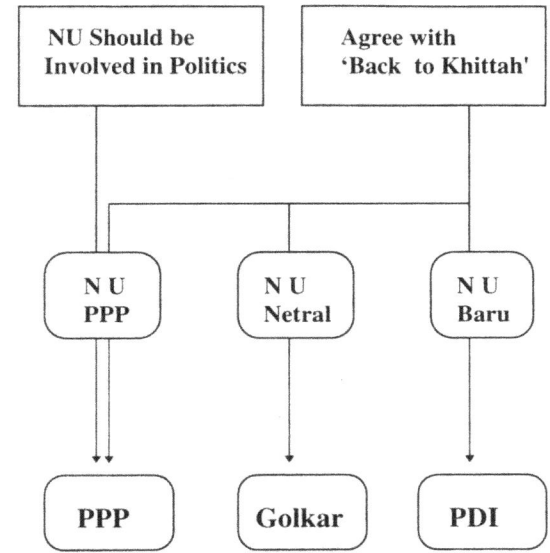

NU PPP :
- *Kiai* of the *Tarekat Cukir*
- Some *Pesantren Kiai*
- Members of the *Tarekat Cukir*

NU Baru :
- Formal NU leaders
- Some *Pesantren Kiai*
- Few NU members (with public servant background)

NU Netral :
- Few *Kiai* of *Tarekat Cukir*
- Few *Pesantren Kiai*
- Few Members of *Tarekat Cukir*

Although the effort to discourage Muslims from supporting PPP was successful, as shown by the fact that PPP lost four seats in the 1987, a large number of former PPP supporters continued to support the party. In the 1992 general election, PPP even regained a half of the seats it lost in the 1987 general election.

The *penggembosan* thus did not destroy the Muslim community's attachment to PPP. The question is why do a large number of the Muslim community in Jombang continue to support PPP, despite the views of some great *pesantren kiai* and of NU leaders? The answer to this question has two aspects. The first relates to the view of *kiai* and NU activists who see themselves as the conveyors of the 'back to khittah' policy. The second relates to the pattern of political awareness of the *umma*, or at least of its leaders. The first can be seen through people's actual political practice, while the second can be understood from the political goal that underlies such awareness.

From the first aspect, it seems that there is ambiguity in the attitude of some *kiai*, which not only confuses the *umma*, but also makes them suspicious of the *kiai's* encouragement to leave PPP. The action suggested by the 'back to khittah' policy has been blurred by these *kiai's* request that the *umma* support Golkar. At the same time, Muslim society's perspective on the difference between PPP and Golkar did not change significantly. The encouragement of some *pesantren kiai* to leave PPP thus did not receive a good response, since anti-PPP sentiment was interpreted as pro-Golkar. This impression derives from the fact that most efforts to weaken PPP were accompanied by encouragement to support Golkar; and those NU leaders who left PPP became Golkar supporters. This encouragement was seen by Muslims as political deviation from what was envisaged by the 'back to khittah'. Muslims therefore used the phrase 'NU-Golkar' to refer cynically to those who claimed to be practising the 'back to khittah' policy, but in fact deviated from it, since they asked people to support Golkar.

A second aspect relates to the identification of PPP with Islam[30]. For the devout Muslim community which has been articulating its aspirations through the Islamic party for some time, PPP remains the first choice. The change in the basics of this party, from Islam to Pancasila, did not influence their perception of the party. PPP is hence still popular among Muslim society in Jombang because it is still regarded as the Islamic political party. The arguments provided by those who have remained loyal to PPP seem more rational than those offered by members encouraging them to leave the party, even though the latter include some *kiai* and NU leaders. For the *kiai* who are still inclined to support PPP, the party is still composed entirely of Muslims, even though the party is no longer Islamic. In an informant's opinion, the party, in terms of its history, has always strived for the interests of Muslim society. He maintained that "such effort is not performed by other political parties". For these reasons, it is logical that people deeply concerned with the interests of Islam would support PPP, since

---

[30] From the survey I conducted in Jombang, a large number of the respondents (68 percent) stated that there had been no change in PPP in terms of its ideology. The findings, therefore, indicate the limited nature of the respondents' knowledge in regard to the current political situation, where PPP is ideologically no longer the Islamic party. I will discuss this matter in detail in the next section.

it constitutes a medium to realise Islamic ideas. An activist in *Muslimat* (an independent organisation of NU members' wives) who frankly stated her support for PPP told me that Muslims who are eager to struggle for the sake of their religion are unlikely to articulate their interests or give their support to a party other than PPP, since other parties, historically, not only have non-Muslim components as their members, but also have never shown any desire to struggle for Muslim society. Hence it would be very hard for Muslims who join them to articulate their ideas or interests. The informant suggested further that to be political, or in her words "to struggle through politics", is the most important ways to struggle for religion, since there is no other better way.

Despite some threats made by government officers that disadvantaged PPP, the support of Muslim members in some villages and their desire to articulate their aspirations through the ex-Islamic party, PPP, were impressive. The encouragement of some *kiai* to leave PPP did not prevent them from voting for this party. The invitation of an NU charismatic leader who came to villages in Jombang, suggesting that villagers leave PPP and condemning those who did not, did not get a significant response[31].

For Masrurah, a member of *Muslimat* in a district of Ngoro, PPP now is not different from PPP before the government introduced the 1985 act which forced all organisations to use only the Pancasila as their ideological base. In her opinion, despite this secular base, PPP is still similar to an Islamic political party, since the goal pursued by this organisation is still the same. According to this activist, the ends are more important than the *azas* (stated formal ideological base) because they are the core of the struggle. Since those who hold the leadership of PPP are still Muslims, it is evident that one should still support this party. As a *wadah* (lit. container) or institution, she further explained, PPP is Islamic. A Muhammadiyah member I met in a large mosque in Jombang held the same opinion. He told me that he had been a PPP supporter for a long time and felt surprised when Muslims in Jombang changed their support to Golkar. In his opinion, Indonesian Muslims have to support PPP. He felt it would be sinful to vote for another party. When I asked him whether there is any difference between PPP now and before 1985, he replied 'no'. In his opinion PPP is currently the only Islamic political party in Indonesia.

The standpoint of the *Muslimat* and Muhammadiyah members seems to represent the common view of the *umma* at the grassroots level. Their piety has helped them maintain their ideals in regard to Islam and they articulate these through PPP. However, the view that PPP is the Islamic party because its leaders are

---

[31] According to a Muslimat activist, Abdurrahman Wahid, the NU national leader, in his speech in Ngoro, southern district of Jombang, condemned those NU local leaders who still occupied a leadership position in PPP. She further suggested that he told people that those who were *mogol* (persistent in administering PPP) would go to hell (interview with H. Maslahah, 4 Mei 1993).

Muslims raises a problem since few PPP leaders[32] at the national level base their actions on Islamic ideals. The activist I interviewed was very aware of this problem, but suggested that such misconduct is only found with a small number of leaders. The majority of the leadership in PPP is still Islamic, which means also that the *wadah*, that is PPP, is Islamic. Since the *wadah* remains Islamic, it is still necessity to support and vote for this party. The existence of some bad leaders, as shown by their opportunistic attitudes, does not necessarily mean that the party as a whole is bad. "It is like a rice field damaged by pests", Masrurah said, "We do not need to abandon the ricefield but to kill the pests".

Masrurah is one among other *Muslimat* members who continue to support PPP. However, she is one of the few who can frankly express this attitude. Most activists or leaders feel reluctant to show their support for the party, since the level of encouragement to leave the party from the main stream of the *Muslimat* is also so great. They are afraid of being humiliated, since activists joining PPP are condemned widely by those NU leaders supporting the *penggembosan*. Only highly influential *kiai*, such as Kiai Khoerul Anwar, the leader of *Tarekat Cukir*, dared to express their outright support for PPP. One may ask why they should feel reluctant if in daily social life PPP is still popular. The reluctance among some *Muslimat* activists to express their support openly for PPP derives from the formal authority of the *Muslimat* leadership, which largely opposed PPP. The formal *Muslimat* leadership is dominated by the power of those oriented towards the mainstream of the NU leadership in Jombang and Indonesia in general who favoured leaving PPP. This situation was related to the organisational structure of NU and its well known leaders, who by that time were inclined to support Golkar and oppose PPP. Some top NU leaders, from the national level down to the district level, encouraged NU members to leave PPP and accused those activists who did not of being hypocritical. This indicates that those NU activists opposing PPP took an offensive position, since NU was structurally or organisationally outside PPP. There emerged a feeling of discomfort among NU activists who expressed their support for PPP since the PPP opponents in NU were dominant and controlled its political discourse, so that PPP supporters did not have a chance to defend their position.

The initial disappointment of Muslims in Jombang with PPP resulted from the standing of the NU representatives in the PPP national leadership[33]. They were either organisationally or individually disadvantaged by other PPP members from the MI component. Some active NU members who executed the

---

[32] A respondent gave as an example that what Naro did in regard to his conflict with the NU component was *tidak dilandasi* (not based) on Islamic interests but his own.
[33] The local PPP leadership has been dominated by members from NU. This means that at the local level NU did not have problem in relation to other components of PPP. The NU conflict with the MI component actually occurred in PPP's national leadership. Among those disadvantaged by PPP national leadership was Hajj Yusuf Hasyim, the leader of the *Pesantren Tebuireng*. He therefore promoted the *penggembosan* to weaken PPP in Jombang.

penggembosan program were thus included in what is called *barisan sakit hati* (the sick heart brigade). The 'back to khittah' policy was used by this group as a medium of revenge, provoking an unpopular situation for PPP. This revenge was not confined to those activists of PPP from organisations other than NU, but also applied to supporters of NU itself. The variation in political orientation in the post-*khittah* era has thus had a negative effect on the unity of NU. Not only do some NU members differ in their political aspirations, but these differences are characterised by open conflict.

Figure 6.4. Muslim Political Orientation in Jombang

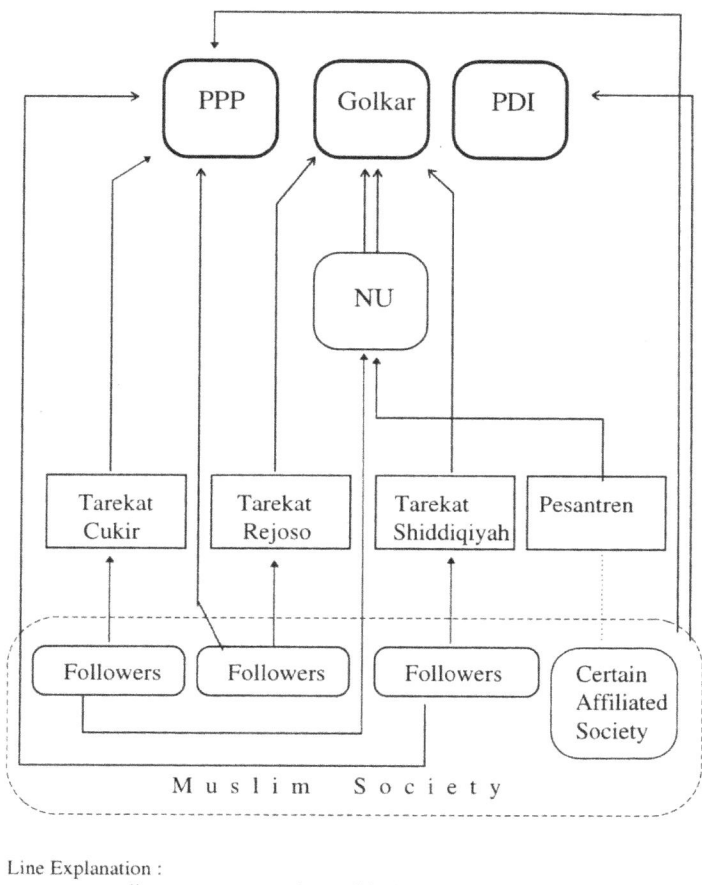

Line Explanation :
⎯⎯⎯ = direct support towards a political party, and a direct affiliation with a certain *tarekat*.
·········· = indirect affiliation

The conflict in some villages in Jombang is creating new types of social groupings in the NU society there. There are groups of *NU-PPP* who continue to support PPP, of *NU-Baru* or *NU-Golkar*, inclined mostly to support the government party, and of *NU-Neutral*, that is those NU members who do not care about other people's political affiliation. It needs to be emphasised here that all groups nominally accepted the introduction of 'back to khittah' policy. However, there is a different emphasis in regard to their political preference. The members of *NU-PPP* realise that their affiliation and support for PPP is in line with the 'back to khittah' policy, while members of *NU-Baru*, especially its leaders who mostly hold positions in the NU local leadership, not only regard their support for Golkar in line with the policy but also regard other groups as deviating from it. They feel that they are the only conveyor of the 'back to khittah' policy. The conflict which occurred between them and members of *NU-PPP* originated from this *NU-Baru* perspective. The third group is more modest in its performance. They do not show an emotional affiliation with any political party. They are not involved in the conflict.

These groupings have established new social patterns, as can be seen in the pattern of their religious activities. While it is evident that the divisions are not so absolute that a member of an NU family supporting Golkar is not allowed to form a social relationship with an NU family supporting PPP, it is important to note that there is an awareness in the minds of these people of the differences between them due to their respective political orientations. For this reason, it is common for a member of *NU-Baru* to be uncomfortable in attending a *pengajian* (religious gathering) held by an NU member who supports PPP, and vice versa. In some villages in Jombang there exist different *pengajian*, since they are administered by groups of NU's activists with different political orientations. Those NU members supporting PPP have a 'Seloso Wage'[34] gathering, while those of *NU-Baru*, favourably disposed toward Golkar, hold *pengajian* on 'Seloso Pon'. In addition, there are other *pengajian* held by NU members, who are openly affiliated to Golkar. This kind of *pengajian*, however, falls outside formal NU activities, since it is organised by Golkar, and people call it *pengajian-Golkar*[35].

Of the various *pengajian* groups that mark the three different political orientations, only the first two are worth discussing. Not only are they characterised by open conflicts, but they also derive from the same source, that is NU. On the historical side, the 'Seloso-Pon' gathering is older and held in almost all districts of Jombang. It was originally formed when PPP was still an Islamic political party. This gathering was used by NU members in PPP to communicate with NU members at the grassroots level. Since NU constituted the main component of this political party, this religious activity was thought

---

[34] 'Seloso Wage' sounds very Javanese, and means Tuesday Wage. In the traditional Javanese calendar, each day has five different characters symbolised by Javanese names. They are pon, kliwon, wage, legi and pahing. So the same symbol of a day, say Seloso-pon, will reappear after 35 days. The same holds true with *Jum'at-Kliwon*.

[35] The various existing *pengajian* in Jombang seem to be highly politicised. These *pengajian* used to be the NU's medium to present and discuss Islam in a more public way. They serve the same purpose as speeches do.

of as the *pengajian* of PPP. After the 'back to khittah' policy was launched in 1984, the *pengajian* was taken over by *NU-Baru* activists. These *NU-Baru* supporters, who constitute the main stream in NU, and, in practice, are sympathetic to Golkar, feel justified in having such *pengajian*, since they were originally established by NU. This situation has resulted in some conflict in those villages in Jombang, where most of the Muslim population are supporters of PPP.

The efforts of this *NU-Baru* group to take over the *pengajian* forum was usually achieved by holding another *pengajian* at the same place and time as the *NU-PPP's*. Armed with this pretended effort to coordinate and strengthen the unity of the NU's members, this group was successful in taking over the forum of the 'Seloso-Pon' gathering. But due to the strong feelings of discomfort among PPP supporters at the grassroots level in sitting together with *NU-Baru* supporters, the former established another *pengajian* forum which is held at 'Seloso Wage'.

It seems that the aversion of the PPP supporters derives from their view that *NU-Baru* do not practise Islam in their political lives. The former deem the latter to be *kurang berprinsip* (do not have strong principles), especially in relation to their actions to weaken the party. A *kiai*, who was a former leader of PPP in Jombang, is critical of the *NU-Baru* group's active collaboration with the government. In his opinion, no basic religious principles sustain their political attitudes. While the NU members supporting PPP have established another *pengajian* forum, the more aggressive group in this conflict is the *NU-Baru* group. It was the latter that usually tried to disturb the former, thinking they had the right to disturb the religious activities of the former[36].

In brief, it is evident that the 'back to khittah' policy has intensified internal conflict in NU. Although the existing conflict in villages in Jombang does not often come to the surface, its vibrations are felt by all members of society. It seems that NU members at the grassroots level, or even those NU activists from the regency down to the village level, are not ready to accept the reality of the differences in political orientation that exist in their midst. The most visible expression of these differences is the *pengajian* forum. In addition, we can see the division through the existing patterns of relationships between *kiai* of these different groups. NU in Jombang, which happens to be administered by the *NU-Baru* supporter group, never invites *kiai*, let alone NU activists, who support

---

[36] This conflict occurred not only in Jombang but also in other regions of East Java. It is said that the *Jam'iyah Ahli Thoriqoh Al-Mu'tabaroh An-Nahdliyah* held a great ritual in another city in East Java. Kiai Makki, the *murshid*, had hoped to be one of the main speakers. A similar *NU-Baru* group in the city indicated their willingness to cooperate in this ritual, because they also had a religious ritual, the rituals were then organised together. The *NU-Baru* group organised the program of the ritual in such a way that Kiai Makki was not given a chance to give his speech. He was, instead, asked to give a closing prayer (membaca do'a penutup). This situation disappointed many followers of the *Tarekat An-Nahdliyah* and their cynical attitude towards *NU-Baru* increased.

PPP. Hence, the NU's activities in Jombang, according to an informant, constitute the activities of what is called *NU-Baru*. On the other hand, the activists and the *kiai*, who support PPP have other activities, including religious ones, conducted by the *tarekat*, which they do not want the former to be involved in. The activities of *tarekat* in Jombang may be a good example of how religious activities previously provided for all NU members are now conducted by a limited number of people from a particular group.

In addition, the internal conflicts occurring within NU are also brought into the realm of the family. An NU PPP supporter, whom I interviewed, for example, asked me to lower my voice when I was discussing the conflicts within PPP with her in her house due to her anxiety about being heard by her brother who happens to be a member of the *NU-Baru*. The possibility of such intra-familial conflict is a new phenomenon within NU. Nevertheless, different from what occurred in the 1950s. In the 1950s the family determined the ideological orientation of its members, so that it was very rare for a conflict to emerge in a family (see Geertz, 1960)[37]. What usually occurred was a conflict between families. This situation was sustained by the fact that the ideological demarcation lines between Islamic and non-Islamic groups or between sub-groups within Islam itself, such as the difference between NU and Muhammadiyah, were very clear-cut. Once the head of a family joined an organisation, all members of the family[38] would adopt the same ideological orientation. A conflict between a member of one family and a member of another family would bring all members of both families into it because each family was united in its ideological orientation. What I found in present day Jombang, however, is very different. The boundaries of ideological orientation of the Javanese are not as sharp as in the past, since NU itself has given religious legitimacy for its members to join or affiliate with any political organisation. This openness has allowed NU members to struggle for Islam through a better organisation[39]. In the past, the correct 'better organisation' in a worldly sense was not necessarily the preferred option. Any organisation also had to be religiously legitimate. Accordingly, in present day Jombang it is not rare for different ideological orientations to give

---

[37] The current political orientation of NU society is different from the social situation as depicted by Geertz (1960), who suggests that ideological orientation of the Mojokuto society had certain social patterns in its socio-economic relations and other relations, such as marriage. A devout member of the Muslim society would only have relations or do business with his own group (and in a more specific situation, as happened in my village in West Java, a Muhammadiyah family will only marry his son or daughter to a son or daughter of another Muhammadiyah family). Today, however, ideological orientation does not reflect a pattern of networks which directs social relations in such an inclusive pattern. It is common for an NU member to marry a Muhammadiyah. It is also not uncommon for a devout member of Muslim society to have a business relationship with an *abangan*.

[38] It should be emphasised here that what I mean by family is not only the nuclear family, but might also be the extended family.

[39] Organisationally, of the three political organisations which exist in Indonesia, Golkar appears the best. It is well managed and financially strong. Golkar also has better cadres than the other two political organisations, PPP and PDI.

rise to conflict among family members. Unlike the situation in the past when the political orientation of the head of a family would be adopted by the whole family, the political orientation of the head of the family may now be challenged by family members with different political affiliations or opinions.

6.5 Islam and Electoral Behaviour

There is no doubt that the influence of Islam on the political attitudes of some Muslims in Jombang has remained strong. It was understandable that parties other than PPP also used Islamic symbols to attract support from Muslims. Although PPP seemed to be the party which was eligible to use Islamic symbols because of its Islamic credentials, other parties also tried a more practical approach towards Muslims in an attempt to gain their support. Golkar had such an approach for a long time. Golkar, for example, established GUPPI, a joint effort in promoting *pesantren* education. Although GUPPI was supported by some *'ulama*, Golkar's intention in the formation of GUPPI was to use it as a means to encourage Muslims to give their support. A more recent institution established by Golkar for political purposes in Jombang is *pengajian al-hidayah* [40]. *Al-hidayah* is a more grounded *pengajian* activity in the sense that it has a wide audience, although not comparable to *pengajian* organised by PPP and NU. It has been established in all *kecamatan*, and in some villages. In contrast to other *pengajian, al-hidayah* is structurally under the management of the *kecamatan* office. PDI also tried to use Islamic symbols in its attempt to attract support from Muslim society, although in Jombang it did not have any method similar to Golkar to approach Muslims.

The influence of Islam on the electoral behaviour of Muslims in Jombang can be seen, for example, in the reasons given by Muslims for their support of PPP. In an interview, of 105 respondents who voted for PPP in the 1977 general election, 72.3 percent said that they did so because it was an Islamic party, and 21.0 percent said that they were affected by the *lingkungan* (social environment)[41]. Only 1 respondent supported PPP because NU was a component of the party (see Table 6.6). In the following general elections, the same reasons held true for respondents. The data I obtained reveal that there was little variation in regard to respondents' voting behaviour in a number of elections.

---

[40] *Al-hidayah* draws its constituency from *pegawai negeri* (public servant) families and other government affiliated members. Recently *al-hidayah* in various districts in Jombang has drawn its audience and sympathisers from NU members. These members are those who changed their political affiliation from PPP to Golkar after NU launched its 'back to khittah' policy.

[41] I should mention here that this answer is a formulation of various responses. The question about the reason of voting for a certain political party was open-ended. Three types of answers were given by the respondents, i.e. 'followed my family', and 'followed a friend'.

Table 6.6. Percentage of Muslim Respondents' Reasons for their Support for PPP

General Election	As the Islamic Party	Social Environment	NU (PPP Component)	No Reason
1977	76 (72.3)	22 (21.0)	1 (1.0)	6 (5.7)
1982	70 (71.4)	21 (21.4)	1 (1.1)	6 (6.2)
1987	65 (70.0)	21 (22.6)	1 (1.0)	6 (6.4)
1992	64 (69.6)	21 (22.8)	1 (1.0)	6 (6.5)

(Source: questionnaire)

There was no difference in the situation before and after NU left PPP. The respondents seemed to decide which party to vote for long before the campaign was held. This applied especially to PPP supporters, who seemed to be more ideological and not influenced by the offers made by competing political parties. Despite the change in respondents' support for PPP from 105 respondents in the 1977 general election to 98 respondents in the 1982 general election, followed by another decrease in their number to 93 and to 92 respondents in 1987 and 1992 general election respectively (see Table 6.6 and 6.7), the percentage of respondents' reasons for voting for PPP varied slightly in these four general elections. PPP supporters who voted for this party because it was or was deemed to be an Islamic party accounted for 72.3 percent, 71.4 percent, 70.0 percent and 69.6 percent in the 1977, 1982, 1987 and 1992 general elections respectively.

Table 6.7. Percentage of Voting Pattern of Muslim Respondents in the 1977, 1982, 1987 and 1992 General Elections

	1977	1982	1987	1992
PPP	105 (57.7)	98 (53.8)	93 (51.1)	92 (50.5)
Golkar	63 (34.6)	75 (41.2)	81 (44.5)	81 (44.5)
PDI	1 (0.6)	2 (1.1)	4 (2.2)	4 (2.2)
No Answer	13 (7.1)	7 (3.8)	4 (2.2)	4 (2.2)
Vote for All Parties	—	—	—	1 (0.5)

n = 182

(Source: questionnaire)

It is interesting to note that the change in the respondents support for PPP was indicated by their support for Golkar. It was commonly held by some Muslim leaders in Jombang that former PPP supporters would support Golkar because Golkar was more acceptable to them than PDI. Golkar constitutes a mixed party of various groups, while PDI was a merger of nationalist and other religious parties, Catholic and Christian. Muslims feel uncomfortable supporting a party established by other religions. According to these leaders, there have been some Muslim figures in Golkar, such as those *kiai* from *Pesantren Darul Ulum*. However, the current political situation in Jombang is more complex. Some respondents whom I surveyed, for example, voted PDI in the 1992 general election although they previously voted PPP.

Islam and Politics: Implications in Electoral Behaviour

There were some factors which influenced few former PPP supporters to vote PDI in the 1987 and 1992 general elections. In the 1987 general election in Jombang, Muslims who were disappointed with the national PPP leadership under Naro changed their support to Golkar. These Golkar supporters who found no satisfaction with this party, but still disappointed with PPP, gave their support to PDI in the 1992 general election. The situation in Jombang indicated that this dissatisfaction spread among former PPP supporters. In Cukir, for example, a big poster to support PDI was hung at the market by a *santri* from *Pesantren Tebuireng*. It was also reported that a *kiai* from Brodot, western Jombang, supported PDI publicly.

The disappointment of PPP supporters actually followed the recent conflict between some *kiai*. To give an example, in *Pesantren Tebuireng* there were two opposing groups of Muslim supporters preceding the 1987 general election. The first tried to continue their support of PPP, while the others were inclined to support Golkar. The first was led by Kiai Syamsuri Badawi, who by that time taught in this *pesantren*, while the second group was led by Hajj Yusuf Hasyim, the leader of this *pesantren*. The action of the *Pesantren Tebuireng santri* who put up the poster in the 1992 general election not only reflected his disappointment but also a wider disappointment among the *santri* over the conflict between Islamic leaders in the previous election[42].

---

[42] I was told, for example, that a *santri* of the *Pesantren Darul Ulum* organised a large group of people in his city (not Jombang) to attend a campaign held by PDI (whereas it was common that supporters of a political party did not attend a campaign carried out by other political organisations). As in other cities, in Jombang, especially in the 1992 general election, the campaign meetings held by PDI were largely attended by a huge number of the younger generation. This means that the increase in PDI's share of the vote in Jombang may also have derived from younger voters who voted for the first time in the 1992 general election.

Table 6.7a. Changing Voting Pattern of PPP Respondents

Reasons for Voting in the 1977 General Election	Voting for a Political Party in the 1987 General Election		
	PPP	Golkar	PDI
1. As an Islamic Party	61	12	2
2. Social Environment	20	2	—
3. NU as PPP Component	1	—	—
4. No Reason	6	—	—

n = 104.
(Source: questionnaire).

Table 6.7a shows that of 16 respondents supporting PPP in the 1977 general election, two supported PDI in the 1987 general election and the rest changed their support to Golkar. The two respondents who supported PDI derived from the group of those supporting PPP because it was an Islamic party, while those supporting Golkar, 12 were derived partially from those who supported PPP because it was an Islamic party and partially from those who supported this party because many people in their village supported it (social environment). These respondents voted for the same party in the 1992 general election. This tendency is in line with the fact that PDI in Jombang increased its share of the votes in the 1982, 1987 and 1992 general election.

Despite the decrease in the PPP share of the vote, some Muslims continued to support this party. There is an interesting point to highlight in regard to this continuing support for PPP. A majority of respondents supporting PPP in the 1992 general election still regarded this party as an Islamic party. This is because Muslims at the grassroots level either did not know that PPP had changed its Islamic base to Pancasila in 1985, or were unconcerned about it. Among its supporters, PPP was still regarded as representing the interests of Islamic society, regardless of whether it was still officially an Islamic party. This situation was sustained by some *kiai* in Jombang who continued to support PPP, despite the fact that NU had formally left the party.

Muslims' view of PPP seems to be enduring, a factor which accounts for society's continuing support for the party. This is because some Muslims did not know that PPP had changed its Islamic base to Pancasila[43] in 1985. My findings in Jombang indicate that only 26.4 percent of the respondents mentioned that the present day PPP is different from the political organisation prior to 1985 (see Table 6.8). Among those who mentioned this difference, 18.7 percent attributed it to the change in the party's base; and 31.2 percent referred to the dissociation of NU from PPP. The majority of the respondents (68.1 percent), however, did not consider that there had been any great change in the nature of PPP. It is thus understandable that they continued to support the party. For the few people who knew of PPP's change in ideological basis, their continuing support for the party is due to religious reasons. In their opinion, PPP is the only party in which all the leaders are Muslims. Moreover, this perspective derives from a *wasiat* (lit. last will and testament) of a great *kiai* in Jombang, Adlan Ali, who called PPP 'the house of Muslims'[44]. This *wasiat* was supported by a *fatwa* of Kiai Syamsuri Badawi suggesting that "umat Islam wajib mendukung PPP" (Muslim society is obliged religiously to support PPP). Such a *wasiat* and *fatwa*[45] are socially important, since they were spoken of at a time when Muslim society in Jombang, especially NU members, were bewildered by the political situation marked by conflict between leading NU figures in the second half of the 1980s. These *wasiat* and *fatwa* have become symbols to reunify a large part of NU

---

[43] The question I asked was whether there was any difference between the existence or character of PPP now compared with before 1985 when the 'Azas Tunggal', Pancasila, policy was applied. I used an indirect question to avoid biasing the respondents' answers. I wanted to know whether the respondents knew that PPP had changed its ideological base from Islam to Pancasila. If the respondents answered yes, I posed a further question 'in which field or area'. Only a few respondents referred to the difference in PPP as being concerned with its ideological base.

[44] Interview with Hafidh Ma'shum, Jombang, 9 September 1993. The *wasiat* was spoken of during the 1987 general election campaign in which PPP was threatened by the politics of *penggembosan*. As I mentioned previously, some NU activists aimed to weaken PPP by *penggembosan*.

[45] A decade before, that is in the 1977 general election, Kiai Bisri Syansuri delivered the same *fatwa* which obliged Muslims to support PPP. If Kiai Bisri Syansuri's *fatwa* was intended to increase PPP's share of the vote, Kiai Syamsuri Badawi's *fatwa* was aimed to prevent PPP's votes from decreasing since the *fatwa* was spoken in the context of the decrease in NU *kiai* support for PPP (see TEMPO, 15 February 1986).

society in Jombang, especially the *tarekat* followers, and remind them of the moral necessity to return to their house (that is, to support PPP).

Table 6.8. Percentage of the Muslim Respondents' Perspective on the Difference in PPP after 1985, and the Area in which such a Difference Occurs

Reasons	There are Differences	No Differences	No Answer
1. Change in the ideological Base	9(18.7)	—	—
2. NU dissociated from the party	15(31.2)	—	—
3. Change in Direction	4(8.3)	—	—
4. Internal Conflict	7(14.6)	—	—
5. Less Cohesion	2(4.2)	—	—
6. No Reason	11(22.9)	124(100.0)	10(100.0)
Total	48(26.4)	124(68.1)	10(5.5)

n = 182

(Source: questionnaire)

Society's support for PPP as an Islamic political party is closely related to the 'Islamic' political ethos which had and still has a strong influence on the attitude of Javanese Muslims. This ethos has placed Islam as the dominant ideas which continuously remind Muslims to behave according to their values. It has become a driving force which engenders a feeling of discomfort among those who ignore it. Some examples can be found among those who continued to support PPP regardless of the pressure or even threats from other people. Although this ethos as a variable is not the sole factor, it greatly influenced Muslims' political behaviour. A young man of twenty told me that he felt that he had to support PPP because all his family and friends, as well as other people in his village, supported the party. Although he had no ideological reason to support PPP — he did not mention its relation with Islam and he did not come from a devout family — he felt ashamed to support another party. His attitude was manifested by his voting for PPP in the election[46]. This case is one of few examples which indicate that the 'Islamic' political ethos continues to be strongly embedded and influences Muslims' political behaviour. Earlier supporting PPP was usually accompanied by a feeling of religious obligation, but in the 1987 and 1992 general elections it had no religious sanction, since NU allowed its members to vote for any political organisation (which meant there was no religious legitimacy behind the feeling of obligation). However, as the Islamic political ethos is embedded in the consciousness of devout Muslims, it still exerted moral pressure to remain in support of PPP. It was this Islamic ethos which propelled young Javanese to support PPP.

---

[46] This young Javanese Muslim realised in advance that his decision to vote for PPP would disadvantage him since the village head had decided not to give him an ID card if he did. However, he still voted for PPP, which resulted in the cancellation of his move to Kalimantan to get a job (because without an ID card he could not go).

As the significance of Muslim's shared experience in Jombang has constantly been informed by Islamic values and norms, Islam has therefore predisposed its members to hold certain political attitudes. A respondent suggested, for example, that the religious necessity to support PPP, especially when it was an Islamic party, was explicitly expected of all Muslims. Not only did the Islamic political party clearly constitute the vehicle that could realise Islamic ideals, but support for the party also had religious consequences.

Nevertheless, looking at the performance of PPP during the general election under the New Order (see Figure 6.1), we actually see a continuous change in regard to its gains. The change is more significant when we compare its share of the vote with that of the Islamic parties in the 1955 election[47], although a significant number of Muslims continued to support the party even after the party changed its ideology to Pancasila. There were some factors which contributed to the change in the PPP's share of the vote. The first was the continuous political pressure put upon devout Muslims in Jombang preceding the general election. The second was the extensive bureaucratisation by which an increasing number of Muslims were absorbed into the government offices, making them unable to refuse the government's encouragement to support Golkar. Finally there was the change in the PPP's ideological base from Islam to Pancasila, a situation which placed PPP in the same position as the other political parties.

---

[47] As I mentioned in footnote 1, in the 1955 general election NU obtained 14 out of 35 seats available in the local parliament in Jombang.

Chapter 7: The Kiai in the Context of Socio-Political Change

This chapter discusses the influence of the *kiai* in politics. It highlights the emerging changes in Muslim political perspective at the grassroots level in Jombang. Such changes constitute their response to the existing and continuous changes in the socio-political realm at the national level. This change in perspective on the part of both *kiai* and Muslims in general actually marks the failure of their politics.

The failure of Islamic politics has pushed the *kiai*, through NU, to free Muslim society from the necessity of adhering to a certain political orientation, so that the religious affiliations which formerly directed the political steps of society has become blurred. The moral (religious) obligations which were often attached to politics have been loosened. The *kiai's* views of the government, for example, have changed significantly. This has resulted in a general reformulation of the Islamic ideals that they must pursue.

The chapter also highlights the political influence of the *kiai* after they deformalised Islam in the Indonesian politics. It is argued that the *kiai's* political influence in present day Jombang is less strong compared to that when Islam characterised a political party. Many followers of the *kiai* did not follow their *kiai* political lead. This means that in general the *kiai* are less charismatic.

7.1 Changing Kiai's Islamic Politics

The debate about Islamic politics has not yet given the final picture of the form of such politics. This is so since there is no explicit text either from the Qur'an or the hadith which mentions a certain format of politics. Nevertheless, from the experience of some countries claiming to be Islamic and of Indonesia itself, the concept and the form of an idealised Islamic state has been promoted by Muslim thinkers and leaders several times. Nasir of the Masjumi and Wahab Chasbullah of NU clearly conceptualised the ideal form of an 'Islamic' state. The former once suggested that:

> Islam is a philosophy of life, an ideology, a system of living for the victory of man now and in the hereafter ..... Because of this, we as Muslims, cannot detach ourselves from our ideology, namely Islam. For us, to construct Islam cannot be separated from constructing society, constructing the state, constructing freedom ...... Concerning the relationship of man with his fellow man, the function of religion is to defend that connection in all aspects of life. Here we should notice the function of politics in defending the relationship. Does politics cover one aspect of life or all aspects? Politics only includes one aspect of the

relationship between man with his fellow man, while the function of religion is to defend this relationship in all aspects of life. So how is it possible that religion, which is inclusive of all aspects, can be separated from politics, which only includes one aspect?[1]

How such a conceptualisation was applied can be seen through the struggle of Islamic political parties on the Indonesian political scene and by the way Islamic leaders pursued what they idealised[2]. The formation of Islamic political parties was indeed aimed at articulating the political interests of the *umma*. Islamic objectives were hence stated clearly, either by Masjumi or NU[3], as their primary ends which sustained their political struggles. It is important to note that what was done by Islamic political parties after Indonesian independence was a continuation of what Indonesian Muslims had done during Dutch colonialisation. The difference between Dutch colonialism and Indonesia independence in relation to the situation of Indonesian Muslims changed only the method of their struggle. The essence of their objective remained the same, that is *'izzu al-Islam wa'l-Muslimin* (for the sake of Islam and Muslim society). During the exploitative Dutch colonialism, the political struggle of Indonesian Muslims was aimed at confronting the Dutch[4] who distorted Islam and its culture, while after Indonesian independence, Islamic politics was focused on realising Islamic ideals as they were conceptualised.

However, the long struggle of Muslims against the Dutch was not resolved by the application of Islamic politics during the time of Indonesian Independence, since the political situation was not conducive to the realisation of such ideals. It was rather marked by the decline of Islamic politics itself[5]. The political

---

[1] See Samson (1978:214)

[2] In practice, the ideal form of politics which the Islamic leaders conceptualised depended on their interpretation of Islam generally. Differences between Nasir and Wahab Chasbullah, for example, were apparently differences in applying or pursuing what they idealised. Nasir, with his Masjumi was more strict and unwilling to compromise, while Wahab Chasbullah, with his NU was more accommodating to the existing situation. For a description of NU's political aspirations and how they applied what they understood from Islam in regard to politics, see Fealy, G (forthcoming), *Entrenching Traditional Islam: A Political History of Nahdlatul Ulama, 1952–1968* (thesis, Monash University). See also Haidar, M Ali (1994), *Nahdatul Ulama dan Islam di Indonesia: Pendekatan Fikih dalam Politik*. Jakarta: Gramedia Pustaka Utama.

[3] As I mentioned, NU was a political party from 1952 to 1973. It was formed in 1926 as a socio-religious organisation. Masjumi was another Islamic political party which was banned by the Soekarno government in 1960. Masjumi was a coalition of various Islamic organisations and, until 1951, NU was one of its components. In 1973, NU was one of the PPP components; and in 1984 it became a socio-religious organisation again, formally leaving politics.

[4] The Muslims' efforts to oppose the Dutch have been widely discussed by scholars. See, for example, Kartodirdjo, S (1973), *Protest Movement in Rural Java: a Study of Agrarian Unrest in the Nineteenth and early Twentieth Century*. Kuala Lumpur: Oxford University Press. Also his *Ratu Adil*, published by Sinar Harapan in 1984.

[5] The emergence of the nationalists, preceding Indonesia's independence, contributed to this. The emergence of a nationalistic independent Indonesia was a decisive point which positioned Islamic politics. The nationalists, like Soekarno, seemed to have a more strategic position because their politics

situation during the Soekarno government gave the impression that Islam had not received a reasonable share of Indonesian politics[6]. The same held true during the New Order government in which Islam was even further weakened. This was so not only because the New Order government claimed to be non-ideologically oriented and tried to prevent any ideological conflict, but also because of the recurrent internal conflicts among Muslim groups in PPP. The Islamic political party, PPP, was therefore pushed into a very weak position. The government's efforts to weaken Islamic politics culminated in the introduction of the 'Asas Tunggal' (sole ideology) in 1985, which ordered all socio-political organisations to use Pancasila as their ideological base.

Following the decrease of Islamic politics, the early 1990s was marked by a change in the government's standpoint on Islam in general. The government tended to be more accommodating towards Indonesian Muslims and its strict policy changed dramatically. The government, for example, promoted or gave full support to the formation of *Ikatan Cendekiawan Muslim Se-Indonesia* (ICMI, All Indonesian Muslim Intellectuals). It is interesting to note that a few Ministers of the Suharto government are also ICMI members; and the top leader of ICMI is the Minister for Research and Technology, Prof. B.J. Habibi.

On the Muslim side, the change has been more significant. Muslim society, which up to the early 1980s had been marked by an attitude of what was called by Western observers, opposition, gave increasing support to the government in the third decade of its reign. Islam, which was political, is now more cultural (Ali, 1994). This change is not only shown by ICMI, which received full support from the government, but also by various other Islamic organisations, like NU and Muhammadiyah. The change in Muslims' politics has hence been quite obvious. The participants in the change are drawn from two levels, that is the level of the Muslim intellectuals or middle class and the grassroot Muslims in general. The change at the intellectual or middle class level actually occurred in the early period of the New Order government. It was marked by the slogan "Islam Yes, Politics No" echoed by Nurkholis Madjid[7]. The change at the grassroots level clearly occurred after the government's promotion of de-Islamisation[8] of politics had prevailed. Since the *kiai* is the socio-political

---

were more acceptable to various groups of Indonesian society. Their idea of a nationalistic state, therefore, prevailed.

[6] The impression was indicated by the reaction of some Muslims who established separatist movements. The first reaction was expressed by the establishment of the *Darul Islam* movement led by Kartosuwirjo. Another reaction was a PRRI movement which involved some members of an Islamic political party, Masjumi.

[7] See Aly, F (1994b), *Keharusan Demokratisasi dalam Islam di Indonesia, a* paper presented at a seminar held in LIPI by Majelis Sinergi Kalam, ICMI.

[8] Some Muslim intellectuals see the introduction of the 'sole ideology' (Azas Tunggal) by the government, urging all socio-political organisations to use Pancasila as their base, as de-islamisation of politics. A few of them use the term 'deformalisation of Islam'. To understand their reaction to this government's policy of de-islamisation of politics, see *Panji Masyarakat* (21 January 1995).

interpreter whose informal leadership is deeply embedded in Muslim society, the change at the grassroots level was attributed to a change in the *kiai's* standpoint on politics[9]. The change really occurred after the *kiai* introduced the concept of free political affiliation for Muslims and accepted the Pancasila, in place of Islam, as their organisation's ideological base.

As Indonesian *kiai* have secularised politics, the political ethos of Indonesian Muslims, which used to be 'Islamic'[10], has been undermined. The significance of the change in *kiai* politics is the concomitant change in the ethos of Indonesian Muslim society. This change of ethos is marked by the breaking of the formal link between Islam and politics. As politics in this sense is no longer intertwined with Islam, there is no longer any moral obligation for a Muslim to affiliate with a certain political party. As a result, there is an increasing number of Muslims in Indonesia who now do not hesitate to support or affiliate with Golkar or PDI, actions which some years ago would have been deemed as having religious consequences. Some *kiai* have now even become supporters of the government and its political party[11].

Since the change in the Muslims' perspective on politics is marked by a change at the grassroots level, it is socially significant. The adoption of the Pancasila by NU's *kiai* for their ideological base, replacing Islam, and their encouragement of free political affiliation for Muslims have replaced the traditionalist Muslim perspective on politics. The Muslim efforts to promote the politics of Islam, which have long been pursued, have been replaced by a wider perspective which is more nationalistic in character. I mean by this that most Muslim leaders are now inclined to consider politics in a wider context[12].

---

[9] Geertz (1959a) mentions the *kiai* as a cultural broker. See also Horikoshi (1976), *A Traditional Leader in a Time of Change: the Kyai and Ulama in West Java*. Thesis for the degree of Doctor of Philosophy, University of Illinois.

[10] If an ethos is conceptually formed through a set of historical events which force society to interpret the existing order in a certain way, the historical evidence of the long established Islam in Indonesia are factors which have contributed to the formation of the Indonesian political ethos. The *kiai's* acceptance of Pancasila as their ideological base has not just distorted the existing ethos but it has also secularised politics itself.

[11] In the past, almost all *kiai* in Jombang and other regions of East Java were affiliated with PPP. Those who joined Golkar were humiliated by their colleagues (see my discussion in the last section of this chapter. See also my discussion in Chapter V). The change in Muslim politics, nevertheless, is advantageous for the development of Islam for the near future in Indonesia. Not only does Islam get support from the government but also its *da'wa* (preaching) can reach all segments of Indonesian society. In other words, the political change in Indonesia, which is especially marked by the accommodating attitude of the government towards Islam, has given Muslims a chance to pursue their former political goals in another way.

[12] The actor behind this change was Kiai Ahmad Shiddiq. Long before the 'back to khittah' policy was launched, Kiai Ahmad Shiddiq had conceptualised the idealised politics which must be pursued by NU (see Bruinessen, Martin "Tradition for the Future: the Reconstruction of Traditionalist Discourse within NU". In Greg Barton and Greg Fealy [1996, forthcoming]. *Nahdlatul Ulama, Traditional Islam and Modernity in Indonesia*. Centre of Southeast Asian Studies, Monash University).

The Kiai in the Context of Socio-Political Change

According to this framework, the *kiai* no longer see politics as the only avenue through which Islamic messages can be conveyed or its ideals pursued. The Islamic leaders, therefore, do not necessarily involve themselves in the formal structure of Indonesian politics as they did according to the former perspective. So, rather than thinking of Islam as a source of political ideas, the Islamic leaders now tend to consider and focus their thinking more on the prosperity of Muslim society. They concentrate on creating a favourable situation for the benefit of society, rather than imposing 'Islamic politics' on the Indonesian political scene. The way to spread and develop Islam, in the opinion of an educated Muslim, should not be restricted to politics. Rather, it must be emphasised through what is theoretically called the institutionalisation of Islam into people's daily lives. The politics of Islam does not necessarily mean the politics by which Islam is strictly applied to all aspects of their life, as would be the situation in the formation of an Islamic state or the application of Islamic law to the society. The politics of Islam, instead, should be directed toward the creation of a favourable situation for Muslims in their everyday lives. Muslims at the grassroots level, in the view of a young Muslim intellectual interviewed, must be lifted from poverty. They should be provided with facilities that can help solve their economic problems. Also they have to be provided with a secure political situation, since politics in Indonesia has often disturbed their lives. Such a situation is needed for the development of Islam itself, since in such a situation Islamic preaching can take place smoothly.

The question is how could the *kiai* who formerly introduced the religious necessity for Muslims to affilate with an Islamic political party now free themselves to affiliate with any political party? As I mentioned, Kiai Bisri Syansuri, preceding the 1977 general election, maintained that it was compulsory for Muslims (*wajb*) to support and vote for the Islamic party, PPP. Although this political message did not explicitly prohibit Muslims from voting for another party, it implied such a meaning. The concept of *wajb* in *fiqh* (lit. Islamic jurisprudence) means that those performing the *wajb* would receive a reward, while those not performing it would be sinful. Although the interpretation of the religious necessity (*wajb*) to support the Islamic party varied among NU's *kiai*[13], this political message was formal in the sense that it was delivered by the *kiai* representing NU in PPP. The question is: how could the *kiai* have aspirations that at one time were different from those at a later time. How could a position previously prohibited now become encouraged? There is no single answer to this *kiai* 'religious justification'. What is certain is that the *kiai's* change in attitude was based on the Islamic norms or precepts which they

---

[13] A younger *kiai* whom I interviewed questioned the meaning of *wajb* suggested by his senior colleague. If the *wajb* in giving support for PPP was like that conceptualised in *fiqh*, a large number of Indonesian Muslims were sinful since they were affiliated with and gave support to political parties other than PPP.

understood. At least we need to understand how the *kiai* see politics and what the general framework sustaining this perspective is. A good example of the change in the *kiai's* politics was provided by a younger *kiai* whom I interviewed. This *kiai* asked his senior colleague about his political stand of supporting the government party especially in the 1987 general election. The senior *kiai* answered that he was 'isis', a Javanese term to express 'feeling hot'. Because of so many stressful situations, this *kiai* felt as though he was in a very hot summer. So he needed to get a cooler and more comfortable situation by moving into another party. Such a statement of course related to the situation of the former Islamic political party, PPP, which was coloured by an internal conflict between its constituent groups so that such a situation was unfavourable. So it was better for this *kiai* to join another party since the spirit of Islam underlying PPP was discarded by the partial interests of its factions. The perception of this senior *kiai* on politics can be understood by recourse to his perception about life, the framework through which the *kiai* see wordly activities such as politics. Wordly life in the *kiai's* perception is less important compared to religious life[14]. It exists to strengthen religious life. He did not need to take it as serious as his spiritual life. As politics was a worldly matter, there was therefore no difficulty for him to shift from one political orientation or affiliation to another, as expressed by his joining the government party when he felt that the situation in PPP was not favourable.

In addition, the change in *kiai* politics was also contextual. Thus it did not occur without the influence of the political situation surrounding it. The most important factor was the lack of an Islamic political party. According to one *kiai*, the change in the *kiai* politics was possible because one of the important prerequisites was removed. The religious obligation to support PPP therefore ceased after the party ceased to be Islamic. In their opinion *al-hukmu yaduru ma'a 'illatihi*, which means that from the Islamic perspective, the legitimacy of the law concerned with certain things or behaviour is dependent on its cause. If the cause has changed, the legitimacy of such law also changes. This perspective is basically a guidance for *kiai* in deciding things under the domain of *fiqh*. One example is that the prohibition of eating something in a normal situation is waived in an emergency. The change in anything from *fiqh* perspective is very possible, and very much dependent on the situation. In practice, this principle has become a perspective for the understanding of socio-political problems as well. The inconsistency in attitude, or, in more appropriate words, the fluctuation of the politics of the *kiai* should therefore be understood by reference to this principle. Especially in relation to politics, which is often seen to be filled with opportunistic situations, the change in the *kiai's* attitude should therefore be understood as more

---

[14] The senior *kiai* referred to a widely known verse of the Qur'an which states that "verily life in the world is just a play".

paradigmatic, not merely opportunistic[15]. From the fact that *fiqh* provides the *kiai* with a general framework by which they can move from one paradigm to another in politics, the world of *kiai* must be dynamic.

This evidence indicates that despite being regarded opportunistically by some critics, the *kiai's* change in politics was based on certain norms conceptualised by Islam and on their understanding of these norms. Because the *kiai* are the guardian of Islam, they always base their politics on an Islamic perspective. The *kiai* often use Islamic concepts[16] as the guide and the framework in their thinking. Therefore, the *kiai* can be hard and uncompromising when they are faced with things contradictory to Islam. But they can be most accommodating when things are acceptable to the Islamic point of view. As the Muslims in Jombang are devout enough to use Islam in their politics, the political change brought about by the *kiai* was acceptable since it was sustained by religious arguments.

7.2 Kiai's Political Influence: Post-'Back to Khittah'

The political aspect of the *kiai's* leadership needs attention since it reveals the pattern of patronage in his relation with society, and how his power is clearly discernible. The centrality of the *kiai's* authority and power in society (discussed in Chapter IV) raises the assumption that his influence is not confined to social relations but is also applicable in the field of politics. This assumption is evidenced by the fact that during a general election, for example, the contesting parties tried to use the *kiai* to increase their share of the vote. The influence of the *kiai* was indeed obvious among devout Muslims who often follow their political lead. But Muslims' submission is not without reservation, since they also have basic principles which they use to examine whether or not the political steps of the *kiai* are religiously legitimate.

Looking at the research findings of other researchers (Geertz, 1965 and 1959; Horikoshi, 1976 and Mansurnoor, 1990) it is evident that the *kiai's* role in moulding society and in inducing the socio-political action of its members is critical, since the *kiai* is a leading figure in Islamic society in Java. Deference to the *kiai* is actually reinforced by the culture of Indonesian society. There is an unequal relationship between the *kiai*, as patron, and his followers as subordinates or clients. The patron is seen as a source who can fulfil the material and spiritual needs of his followers and, in turn, command their respect. In his research in West Java, Jackson (1973) understood this pattern of relationships

---

[15] For a detailed discussion of the *'ulama's* approach of *fiqh*, see Haidar, M Ali (1994), *Nahdatul Ulama dan Islam di Indonesia: Pendekatan Fikih dalam Politik*. Jakarta: Gramedia Pustaka Utama.

[16] The practice of religious politics by Indonesian *kiai* is transparent in the sense that anyone can easily recognise it. The *kiai's* political tradition of "seeking revelation" through *istikhara* is easily known because the *kiai* themselves often publicise such prayers. The *istikhara* is a prayer undertaken by a Muslim to obtain a "divine hint" regarding important matters that become his concern. By praying the Muslim asks Allah to give a hint, for example whether a marriage will be good or bad. *Istikhara* is usually conducted when the *kiai* face crucial issues concerned with the life of the nation.

to be sustained by what he called 'traditional authority'. This authority is the authority of the patron[17] who influences and arouses emotion from his followers. They will do their utmost to retain the esteem of the patron. This pattern of relationships is loosely entrenched among some village people in Indonesia and is often utilised to serve political interests since society can easily be mobilised just by mobilising the higher echelon of the patrons. The political affiliation of the patron is commonly adopted by his client. In addition, any change in political attitude made by the former will result in a similar change in the political attitude of the latter. One would expect from this pattern that obedient followers would comply with any request for support from their *kiai*, even if this was for the government party. Some followers would do this without question because they believe that the *kiai* can foresee what ordinary Muslims cannot.

In Jombang, the case of Kiai Musta'in's joining Golkar preceding the 1977 general election showed how a *kiai's* political example was followed by some followers, and at the same time it indicated how he was powerless in encouraging other followers to follow his lead. In most cases, the *kiai* who left the Islamic party and then joined another party (non-Islamic one) was not followed by his followers. Kiai Musta'in's case showed that a large number of his followers established another *tarekat* organisation and remained supporters of PPP rather than following his political example.

As the *kiai* is a charismatic leader, whose words have traditionally been followed by Muslim villagers, it should be recognised that the increase in the number of devout Muslims who did support Golkar could be attributed to the *kiai's* support for this party. In Jombang, despite the increase in PDI's votes in the 1992 general election, the number of *kiai* supporting Golkar is actually increasing. This is a result of NU's policy of 'back to khittah'. In the 1977 general election, only Kiai Musta'in and his close fellows voted for Golkar[18] in Jombang. Even other *kiai* of the *Pesantren Darul Ulum* led by Kiai Musta'in persisted in supporting PPP until NU launched its 'back to khittah' policy in 1984. The *kiai* of the three major *pesantren* (*Tebuireng, Darul Ulum* and *Denanyar*) openly gave their support to Golkar in the 1987 general election. It should be acknowledged that this situation

---

[17] Jackson's findings, however, hold for a more general relationship between two different people. It is not restricted just to figures such as the *kiai* and his followers. The character of 'traditional authority', which can incur emotional response on the part of the client derives from the client's feeling of indebtedness. A client might borrow some money from someone else, who then becomes his patron. The client would feel morally obliged to do a favour (rather than give money) to guard his patron's integrity. This is only one way among many to repay his moral debt (berhutang budi).

[18] It is a truism that during a general election campaign, *kiai* who supported a certain political party tried to religiously justify the appropriateness of the party. Under the cloak of religion, moreover, they attacked their fellow *kiai* who supported another party. In so doing, some *kiai* used Islamic verses. The situation was commonly known as 'perang ayat' (lit. war of verses). Such a situation occurred especially during the 1971 and 1977 general elections. The government then encouraged the *kiai* not to use Qur'anic verses for political ends during political campaigns.

contributed to the change in the electoral pattern of Muslims in Jombang and to the decrease in PPP's votes in the 1987 general election. The increase in Muslim support for Golkar[19] in present day Jombang was due to the influence of a number of *kiai* who increasingly supported this party. Ibu Hindun, for example, was a former *Muslimat* (NU's Woman organisation) leader in Ngoro district and a former fanatical supporter of PPP. She transferred her support from PPP to Golkar in the 1987 general election when a few leading *kiai* in Jombang encouraged Muslims to leave PPP and support Golkar[20]. Ibu Hindun has continued to be a Golkar supporter ever since. Although in previous elections it was impossible for her to vote for Golkar for religious reasons, she now feels comfortable with her decision to support Golkar in the last two general elections (1987 and 1992).

In brief, the application of the 'back to khittah' policy and the adoption of the Pancasila by PPP have resulted in a change in Muslim electoral behaviour in Jombang. This situation has made the pattern of Muslims electoral behaviour more complex in terms of kiai influence. As the kiai mainly reinforce the religious commitment of the electoral behaviour of Muslims, the 1987 general election marked the diminution of the kiai's (as an institution) influence in general. Some Muslims were hesitant to accept the encouragement of certain kiai to support Golkar. This is so because there were some other kiai who continued to encourage Muslims in Jombang to persist in supporting PPP. A significant number of Muslims in Jombang therefore continued to support PPP in the 1987 elections, disregarding their kiai (penggembosan supporters) who asked them to support Golkar. But it should be noted that most of those who changed their support by voting for Golkar in the 1987 and 1992 general elections were following their kiai, while a few were affected by their disappointment with PPP leadership under Naro. The latter's decision was sustained by the encouragement of some kiai to support Golkar. This gave their decision legitimacy.

After the introduction of the 'back to khittah' policy, the political steps of a *kiai* would only be followed by those Muslims who are very close to him and shared his political perspective. But it should be noted that there are also followers who are very close to the *kiai* but have a different political standpoint. Therefore the *kiai* support for Golkar does not necessarily mean that all their followers will support this party. In the same way, when *kiai* support PPP, some of their followers may support Golkar or PDI. In the past there was a more direct correlation between the followers' intentions to vote for an Islamic party and their *kiai's* encouragement to vote this party. In present day Jombang it is not rare for followers to have different political standpoints from their *kiai*. Some followers continued to support PPP in the 1987 general election although their *kiai* urged

---

[19] See also my discussion on Muslim electoral behaviour in Chapter VI.
[20] See also my discussion in Chapter VI.

them to leave the party. On the other hand, a few followers of a *kiai* supported Golkar in the 1987 general election leaving their *kiai* who persisted in supporting the former Islamic party, PPP. In the first case the followers based their persistent support for PPP on the assumption that this party still represented the politics of the *umma*. They kept to a religious commitment to support the former Islamic party. In the second case the followers based their preference on the fact that there was no Islamic political party which obliged them (morally) to support it. It can be said that, in general, a large number of Muslims in Jombang based their support for either PPP or Golkar in the 1987 and 1992 general elections on their own preference and not because they were following their *kiai's* footsteps.

Nevertheless, it should be recognised that the *kiai* still played a role in Muslim electoral behaviour although its role was confined to 'triggering' a Muslim's decision to vote for a particular political party. According to one respondent, "saya puas kalau pilihan saya cocok dengan apa yang dianjurkan kiai saya" (I am satisfied if my choice of a party is compatible with what is recommended by my *kiai*). The continued presence of charismatic *kiai* with widespread influence throughout the villages in Jombang is a contributing factor to the influence of the *kiai* as a group on Muslim electoral behaviour. There were a few cases in which both a Muslim's preference which was based on both religious commitment and the *kiai's* influence strongly affected political behaviour in present day Jombang. When some Muslims were asked by their local *kiai* to support a certain political party which did not fit with their choice, they tried to get guidance from more senior *kiai*. The *kiai* as an institution was still seen as important in deciding electoral behaviour. In this case, a senior *kiai's* influence would be greater than that of a junior *kiai* in affecting and giving emotional satisfaction in regard to politics.

One example of this from my research was that of a devout Muslim respondent who went to another *kiai* in Magelang of Central Java, around 400 km from Jombang because he was dissatisfied with the local *kiai's* encouragement to support the government party in the 1992 general election. The respondent greatly respected his local *kiai* because he had been one of his obedient followers. On this occasion, however, his *kiai's* advice 'tidak pas di hati' (did not fit with his heart), since his moral intuition consistently urged him to support PPP. Because of this dilemma he tried to get advice from a more senior *kiai* who had higher religious authority than his local *kiai*. This senior *kiai* recommended that he support the party which had a symbol that would not break down until the 'hari kiamat' (the apocalypse day). The symbol alluded to by this *kiai* was the star, the symbol of PPP. Compared to the banyan tree (the symbol for the government party) and the head of the wild buffalo (the symbol of PDI), the star would continue to exist for much longer. The *kiai's* metaphor was thus interpreted as recommending him to support PPP. The respondent was satisfied with the advice of this senior *kiai*. Not only did it follow his moral intuition (in supporting PPP) but it was also religiously legitimised by the more senior *kiai* [21]. For this respondent the legitimacy of the *kiai* was very important in regard to difficult political matters, including his desire to support the former Islamic party. What is evident from this case is that the *kiai's* advice was needed by his follower to sanction his political actions, since there was no difference between political organisations after PPP adopted secular ideology, the Pancasila.

From my examination of the existing political situation in Jombang, I assume that no *kiai* has a very wide influence there. This is because the political standpoint of some *kiai* and the formal NU leadership are in opposition to devout society at the grassroots level. A large number of devout Muslims still hoped that their *kiai* would remain affiliated with PPP. Although the party is no longer Islamic, they still have a psychological attachment to it, not only because it was the party which they supported for a long time but also because it was very close to their aspirations (almost all PPP leaders in Jombang were NU members). Some followers thus felt the need to reformulate their relationship to their *kiai*, since the latter were sometimes regarded as deviating from 'Islamic politics', as conventionally conceptualised. Thus it is common for a follower to have a different political orientation from his *kiai*, though in other ways their relationship remains as before. The follower still gives his allegiance as he should. The same situation holds true for the relationship between those *kiai* who were inclined to support PPP and their followers who were NU members disappointed with PPP leadership. This situation has resulted in the development of a degree of political liberation or of maturation, since the political choice of the society during the election, for example, was based more on individual choices than their *kiai's* influence. The political standpoint and attitude of society towards certain political parties was not dominated by the politics of the *kiai*, since no one *kiai* has overarching influence in Jombang.

Despite this fact, the existing political situation has led to uncertainty for a few Muslims. They were hesitant about which party they should vote for since the *kiai* gave different advice. One result of this is that a few members of the *umma* became *Golpis* [22] (Golongan Pilih Semua, the group which voted for all political

---

[21] As I have mentioned previously, the need to follow the *kiai* is absolute for some Muslims. An example of this is provided by the fact that some followers of Kiai Musta'in supported the government party because the *kiai* joined this party. This occurred despite the national *fatwa* at the time which maintained the religious necessity of supporting PPP as the Islamic party. The respondent discussed above in the text would have supported the government party if the senior *kiai* had asked him to do that. In Jombang there are two main blocks of Muslim supporters, both of which are legitimised by the *kiai*. The first comprises the supporters of the government party and is represented by the mainstream of NU in Jombang. The second block supports PPP (I have discussed this matter at length in Chapter VI). My respondent was hesitant to support PPP because his own *kiai* asked him to support Golkar. This situation indicated the close relationship between Muslims in Jombang and their own *kiai*.

[22] I had this term from a *Muslimat* activist who discussed with me the new tendency among a few NU members in Ngoro to vote for no party in the 1992 general election. But I think this tendency also occurred in the 1987 general election when the conflict between *kiai*, as I discussed in Chapter VI, was more obvious.

parties). They chose all three contestant parties, which means that their votes were not valid. Another result was a variation among individual voters in regard to their support at the three different levels of election[23]. In contrast to the first group, whose votes were not valid, the second group could vote for PPP at the national level, for Golkar at the provincial level and for PDI at the regency level. This tendency will be clearer when we relate it to the assumed reality that people in Indonesia commonly vote for the same party at these three levels of parliament.

Although the encouragement of some *kiai* to support the government party was not followed by a large number of members of society, since it contradicted their ideas about politics, one still needs to consider the *kiai's* political role in regard to the *tarekat* followers. This is necessary since the *kiai*, the *murshid* and his *khalifa*[24], have a special place in the lives of *tarekat* followers. Obedience to the master, especially the *murshid*, in the *tarekat* is strongly stressed. Since the *murshid* is the person who can bestow *baraka*, a situation sought by every Muslim, one might assume that his political example would be copied by his followers. But I found that such obedience is not absolute. Some followers accept that it is not possible to follow all the *murshid's* advice. "We just perform what we can in regard to the *murshid* steps or his encouragement", a *tarekat* follower told me.

Some *tarekat* followers even tried not to relate their political behaviour to their obedience to the *murshid*. In their opinion, the question of obedience to the *murshid* is separate from following his politics. In addition, their *murshid* never asked them to support or affiliate with a certain political party. The *murshid* gave them free choice in regard to political action. Such statements, however, seem to contradict the facts, since the leader of the *Tarekat Rejoso*, in his speech in 1991, tried to guide his followers, and even asked them to support Golkar in the 1992 general election[25]. The same held true with the leaders of the *Tarekat Cukir* in Jombang. Although they did not publicly ask members of this *tarekat*, they encouraged them strongly in all social encounters to vote for PPP in the 1987 and 1992 general elections. Nevertheless, not all members would be influenced by such a political message. Those who were reached by such a message might not act as they were asked because they maintained that there was no relation between obedience to the *murshid* and individual political choice.

In addition, the *tarekat* as an institution should be differentiated from those who lead it, on the one hand, and their followers, on the other. The *tarekat* as an institution is different from the elites who manage it; and both are different from the followers. The majority of its followers know little about politics and do not

---

[23] In a general election, people in Indonesia choose representatives at three levels of parliament, that is national, province, and regency. People also vote for the party, not the personalities of the candidates.
[24] Both the *murshid* and his *khalifa* are *kiai*. In the *tarekat* they are highly respected (see my discussion in Chapter III and IV).
[25] Interview with Hafidh Ma'shum, 9 September 1993.

have much political interest, although they would be aware of their obligation as Muslims in politics. It is thus very likely that *murshid* encouragement to support a certain political party would not be accepted by his followers if the latter felt unprepared to give support. However, I am sure that if the particular *murshid* had asked his followers to support PPP as happened among followers of the *Tarekat Cukir*, such a request would have been accepted without question, since of the three contesting parties PPP was the only Islamic party and, although since 1985 it was no longer an Islamic party, all of its leaders were Muslims.

In Jombang, there are two streams of *tarekat*, which have a large number of followers, that is the *Tarekat Qadiriyah Wa Naqsyabandiyah* which is coordinated by *Jam'iyah Ahli Thoriqoh Al-Mu'tabaroh Indonesia* and the *Tarekat Qadiriyah Wa Naqsyabandiyah* coordinated by the *Jam'iyah Ahli Thoriqoh Al-Mu'tabaroh An-Nahdliyah* [26]. The discussion above relates to the followers of the former who did not follow their *murshid's* support for Golkar. They did not agree with the political views of their *murshid*, and it is very likely that they[27] voted for PPP in the elections. Despite their political standpoint, they continued to give their allegiance to their *murshid*. In their opinion, there is no need for absolute obedience in matters relating to an individual's basic rights, as in politics. This means that, although the *murshid* encouraged the followers to support the government party, the final decision lay with the followers. Since the sympathies of a large number of *kiai* in this *tarekat* were with the government party, those followers who supported Golkar in the 1977 and 1982 general elections (when PPP was the Islamic party) probably based their decision to do so on the perceived need to follow the *kiai's* advice. In this case, their political attitudes were based on the notion that one's political action did not have any relation with being a Muslim. In other words, voting for Golkar or PDI was not sinful as some other Muslims felt it to be. This tendency is similar to that among *kiai* followers outside the *tarekat*.

In brief, the recent change in the pattern of support for political organisations contributes to a decrease in the *kiai's* influence in relation to politics. In addition, it also led to variations in voting pattern among Muslims in Jombang. Some followers did not need to follow their *kiai* who supported Golkar. Other followers could not help being in opposition to their *kiai* when they continued to support PPP. This tendency occurred especially during the last two general elections. It needs to be noted, however, that this deviation from the *kiai's* political lead was

---

[26] There is a third *tarekat* in Jombang called *Shiddiqiyah*, but this *tarekat* has fewer followers compared to those I mentioned above (see my discussion in Chapter III).
[27] A younger member refused to answer my question when I asked him about his support for a political party in the general election. His explanation about the difference between obedience to the *murshid* and following the *murshid's* political example, nevertheless, gave me enough understanding that he had a different political standpoint from his *murshid*. His unwillingness to answer my question, I think, was because of this different political standpoint. He did not want to show that he really had such difference from his *murshid's*. It seemed that he felt uncomfortable with this situation.

greater among followers whose *kiai* supported Golkar. This was because devout Muslims commonly felt more comfortable to affiliate with PPP rather than Golkar. They continued to do so even after PPP ceased to be an Islamic party. On the other hand, followers who deviated from their *kiai* who continued to support PPP in the 1987 and 1992 general elections were mostly disappointed with PPP national leadership.

Based on these findings it seems that the changing influence of the *kiai* in politics must be attributable to other factors. The influence of the *kiai* relates to society's ideological understanding which is formed by society's interpretation of the necessity to pursue religious ideals. In the past, this understanding obligated a Muslim to behave politically in a certain way, that is to support the Islamic political party. Ideological understanding can constitute an interpretation, especially by the *kiai*, of the existing ideals conceptualised in the Qur'an. It is hence normative and actualised in a set of moral concepts which affect the behaviour of Muslim society. The moral impulse is stronger when an Islamic political party exists. It nonetheless needs to be noted that the unavailability of an Islamic party does not necessarily cause the moral impulse to cease. This is because it is the Muslims' interpretation of Islam, rather than the Islamic party, which gives rise to the moral impulse. However, since an Islamic party is a means by which Muslims can pursue their ideals, its very establishment can be said to result from a moral impulse. The change in the *kiai's* interpretation of politics has affected Muslims' interpretation of the existing political understanding. This change provided an opportunity for individuals to interpret the existing order, rather than being influenced by structural factors, such as the *kiai's* influence[28]. Muslims were given the freedom of political choice, and it is therefore understandable that they then decided which party to vote for by themselves, not by following their *kiai*.

If this change can lead to political maturation, variations in voting pattern of individual Muslims, especially among a few who voted different political parties at the three levels of election also led to situation that was not conducive to the development of politics itself. Looking at the political culture of Indonesia, which can largely be subsumed under the term 'parochial' (see Almond, 1978) this variation in voting seems unusual. In addition, the system of elections in Indonesia is based on party voting, rather than voting for a particular candidate, so that voting preference is based on loyalty to a party. Voting preference reflects the ideological orientation of the party. Since the pattern of voting is grounded on ideological preference (allegiance), it is therefore very probable that society would vote for the same party at all three levels of parliament. The fact that this sometimes does not occur indicates that there has been a revolt by a few people

---

[28] Like a person who digs his own grave, the *kiai* changed their interpretation of politics which then resulted in a decrease in their political influence.

who were dissatisfied with the existing political situation of the Muslims in Indonesia. Such a revolt is also expressed by those followers who hold different political attitudes from their *kiai*.

7.3 The Charisma factor

The decrease in the *kiai* political influence is attributable to the general change in the socio-political situation among Jombang's population. Variation in *kiai's* politics, as expressed by their support of various political organisations and the disassociation of Islam from politics is the decisive factor which has contributed to the decrease in the *kiai's* political influence. This decrease was also the result of the lack of charismatic *kiai* in Jombang comparable to Kiai Hasyim Asy'ari, Kiai Wahab Chasbullah and Kiai Bisri Syansuri[29]. The availability of a very charismatic *kiai* not only contributed to the unity of the *kiai* as a group but was also influential on the electoral behaviour of all Muslims in Jombang. Every Muslim in present day Jombang relies on his own local *kiai*. When his political standpoint is different from that of the *kiai*, he will follow his own common sense rather than following the *kiai*. He dares to be different from his *kiai* partly because the *kiai* does not have a very strong charismatic influence. Muslims in Jombang have no influential figures other than their local *kiai* nor is there a charismatic *kiai* with sufficient influence to make all Muslims respect and listen to him.

The survey I conducted in four districts of Jombang shows that no *kiai* is known well by all respondents. When I asked the respondents to mention five *kiai* well known to them, most named very local *kiai*. By local I mean that most respondents did not mention *kiai* living outside their own districts. In addition, not all respondents could name five *kiai*. Some mentioned only four, and a few respondents only mentioned three. The survey of 182 respondents revealed only eight *kiai* who were widely known, being mentioned by more than ten respondents across at least three villages where I conducted the survey. These *kiai* are Syamsuri Badawi, Rifai Romly, As'ad Umar, Yusuf Hasyim, Muchtar Mu'thi, Shohib Bisri, Mahfudz Anwar and Makki Ma'shum (see Table 7.1).

---

[29] However, the present situation in regard to *kiaiship* in Jombang does not necessarily mean that no *kiai* has extensive Islamic knowledge comparable to the former three great *kiai*.

Table 7.1. Number of Respondents in the Four Villages of Three Districts of Jombang to whom Jombang Kiai are Known (The Kiai are Listed in Alphabetical Order)

	Rejo Agung	Peterongan	Cukir	Puton	Total
A. Latif	—	—	—	10	10
A. Muhajir	—	—	—	7	7
A. Rahman	—	—	—	19	19
A. Rohim	—	—	—	14	14
Arwani	—	2	1	—	3
As'ad	5	53	3	1	62
Aziz M	1	—	—	—	1
Dimyati	2	7	—	—	9
Fatih	—	4	—	—	4
Hanan	15	—	—	—	15
Hisyam	1	—	—	—	1
Jamaluddin	23	—	—	—	23
Khoerul	1	—	1	2	4
Khudori	17	—	—	—	17
Mahfudz	1	2	11	1	15
Makki	—	4	6	1	11
Ma'shum	—	1	—	2	3
Muchtar	26	3	1	—	30
Muhdlor	—	1	—	—	1
Nasrullah	4	—	1	—	5
Ridwan	—	—	3	—	3
Rifai	2	10	52	2	66
Shohib	5	10	—	2	17
Sholihin	—	1	—	—	1
Sholeh	—	—	1	—	1
Sulthon	3	2	—	1	6
Syamsuri	4	—	41	11	66
Yusuf	8	15	31	3	57

(Source: questionnaire)

Table 7.1 shows that, in general, most *kiai* were best known by respondents from the same district. Kiai Syamsuri Badawi from Cukir, for example, was mentioned as a well known *kiai* by 41 respondents who in fact came from the same village as he did. The eight *kiai* named above, however, are different in that they are also known by some Muslims in other districts of Jombang. They are, with the exception to Kiai Mahfudz Anwar, the *kiai* who have supra village influence, Muslim figures with either provincial or national reputations. Syamsuri Badawi, for example, is a national member of parliament from PPP, while As'ad Umar is a member of parliament from Golkar at provincial level.

In addition to the fact that no *kiai* is mentioned by all Muslim respondents, there are some interesting points to note from the data I collected. First, there is an exception to the general tendency that a *kiai* is especially well known to Muslim society in his own village or district. This exception is Kiai Rifai, who was the only one of the eight *kiai* well known to more respondents in other villages than in his own village. In Table 7.1 we can see that Kiai Rifai was mentioned by 52 respondents from Cukir, while in his own district (Peterongan) he was mentioned by only ten respondents. Secondly, some NU top figures were less mentioned in certain villages, and in many respects were even not mentioned at all. Kiai Sholeh is a senior *kiai* among NU *kiai* in Jombang, but he was only mentioned by one respondent. In addition, it is interesting that Kiai Sulthon, the President of NU in Jombang, for example, was only mentioned by six respondents from three villages. His position as the NU president might imply his familiarity to all Muslims in Jombang. The same holds true of local NU chairman, Kiai Abdurrahman Usman. This *kiai*, who assumed local NU leadership in 1993, around four months before my survey was conducted, was not even mentioned by one respondent, although he had been teaching at *Pesantren Tebuireng*, and before assuming local NU leadership had been a young active *kiai*.

It seems that there is another factor which contributes to a *kiai's* familiarity to Muslims in Jombang. Holding a formal position in NU therefore does not guarantee that a *kiai* will be known to all Muslims. The same happens in the *tarekat*. Kiai Makki, for example, was only mentioned by six respondents from Cukir, yet as a *murshid* of the *Jam'iyah Ahli Thoriqoh Al-Mu'tabaroh An-Nahdliyah* centred in Cukir village (District of Diwek) he should at least be well known to most respondents from Cukir, although he himself comes from another district. Two other *murshid* of this *tarekat*, Kiai Hisyam and Kiai Sholihin, were each mentioned by only one respondent.

Despite the popularity of the eight *kiai* mentioned above compared to other *kiai* in Jombang, no one *kiai* is really well known by all Muslims in Jombang. The majority of the *kiai* are only well known to Muslims in their own district. Although the lack of a very charismatic *kiai* has contributed to the decline in the *kiai's* political influence on inducing Muslims' political action, the *kiai* as an institution is still generally regarded as important. The pattern of the *kiai's* relationship with his society remains strong. The process of modernisation, which has introduced secular values and produced anxiety in regard to Muslim religious lives, has raised the hope of the Muslim population that the *kiai* will become more active in their religious lives. In addition, as Muslims still base their actions on the Qur'anic norms, their attachment to the *kiai* persists, since the *kiai* is the person who best understands the Qur'an. *Kiai* leadership hence continues to be expected by Indonesian Muslims.

The data in Table 7.2 indicates that the Muslim population's continued trust in the *kiai*, despite the decrease in his political influence. Of the 182 respondents whom I interviewed, for example, 71.4 percent suggested that the *kiai* is the most suitable person to lead an Islamic organisation. Only 3.8 percent of respondents recommended that an Islamic organisation be led by an intellectual. The remaining respondents, accounting for about 13.2 percent, said that anybody was acceptable to lead an Islamic organisation as long as he was a capable Muslim. Nevertheless, these findings do not mean that *kiai* and *'ulama* in general are not vulnerable to the development of society. In an increasingly modernising society, their leadership needs continually to adjust to the current situation to remain relevant.

Table 7.2. The Respondents' Views on the Idealised Person to Lead an Islamic Organisation

I	II	III	IV	V	VI	VII
NU	114	5	16	5	6	146
	(78.1)	(3.4)	(11.0)	(3.4)	(4.1)	(100.0)
Others	16	2	8	3	7	36
	(44.4)	(5.6)	(22.2)	(8.3)	(19.4)	(100.0)
Total	130	7	24	8	13	182
	(71.4)	(3.8)	(13.2)	(4.4)	(7.2)	(100.0)

n = 182
(Source: questionnaire)

Explanation of Symbols:

I. Organisational Affiliation

II. Ulama

III. Intellectual

IV. Anybody

V. A Person who Follow the Prophet

VI. Do not Know

VII. Total

[29a] There are 4 organisations through which the respondents affiliate with. These are NU, Muhammadiyah, LDII and Pangestu. 'Others' means other than those organisations mentioned in the Table. This meaning holds for the same "Others" in Table 8.1, 8.3 and 8.5.

7.4 The Kiai's New Relationship with Authority

Despite being less significant in their role in Muslim electoral behaviour, the *kiai* generally have an important role in Indonesian politics. This role has been performed since the period of Dutch colonialism in Indonesia. The importance of their role lies in their being the religious leaders of Indonesian Muslims, so that their influence is embedded in society. The Indonesian *kiai* used to be grouped into an Islamic political party, which on some occasions challenged government authority since their basic concern was "...to preserve a comprehensive Islamic community in contrast to the secular outside world of the national system" (Horikoshi, 1976:375).

The *kiai* and the government both have power in relation to society, and they use this to bargain and profit from each other. From the government perspective, the *kiai's* power is strong enough to influence society's socio-political actions.

This is because they occupy the position of religious legitimator; and a Muslim society, such as in Indonesia, needs the legitimacy of the *kiai* to conduct their worldly affairs. The different perspectives of the *kiai* and the government in looking at various problems of society often provoke a situation where their relationship is marked by disharmony or even tension. In Indonesia, this tension commonly occurred because the government needed the *kiai*, and *'ulama* in general, to obtain political support from the Muslim society. It also sought the legitimacy of the *kiai* for its worldly policies that impinged on the religious domain.

The Indonesian *kiai* have held a leading position in the society since the coming of Islam to Indonesia. Since the formation of the Islamic kingdom in early Indonesia, some prominent *kiai* have been involved in governmental matters. However, the relationship between the *kiai* and the Indonesian government has fluctuated. In essence, the existing views of this relationship derive mostly from the *salaf 'ulama* (lit. earlier *'ulama*). For most of the time, association with the government has been viewed pessimistically. There exists a common perception that becoming part of the government is not good, since once it occurs one will be exposed to things less religiously acceptable. The line between 'acceptable' and 'not acceptable' is nonetheless clearly defined. Any *kiai* who actually approached the government would become a target of gossip and be humiliated as *kiai keceng*[30].

The closeness of the *kiai* to the government can be identified through certain actions, such as involvement in the GUPPI (Joint Effort for the Development of Islamic Education), or membership in Golkar. The reaction of *kiai* and Muslim society in general against those *kiai* who are regarded as a part of the "government's machine" remains negative. This can be seen from the reaction of Jombang society and Muslims in East Java in general to Kiai Musta'in[31], former

---

[30] I had this term from an informant who described Muslim reaction in Jombang against the *kiai* joining Golkar. "Keceng" is a Javanese word, which means unprincipled or opportunistic. This word was also used for those *kiai* who were more accommodating to the government because of the NU's 'back to khittah' policy.

[31] An informant told me that Kiai Muafi Zain, the leader of *Pesantren Najja Al-Tullab* in Madura, was also abandoned by his *santri* soon after he announced that he had joined Golkar. He was a loyal *santri* of Kiai Musta'in. Of the approximately 800 *santri* studying in his *pesantren*, only eight remained. A religious teacher whom I know well in a village in West Java was a very famous and respected *kiai* before he gave support to the government political party. Not only was he a wealthy Muslim, but he was also a good orator, whose speeches were pleasant to hear (He did not have any students or a traditional Islamic school; he was a stage *kiai*). His popularity declined drastically soon after he gave tacit support for the government political party of Golkar in 1977. This *kiai* felt obliged to give such support since his son was a village head who campaigned for Golkar. The *kiai* thus showed behaviour contradictory to that of his other colleagues. Although he himself did not campaign for Golkar or visibly support the party, his son's political action gave the surrounding community and many of his followers sufficient reason to leave him. The popularity which he had established simultaneously faded. The community stopped asking him to give religious speeches and no longer invited him to even lead a religious ceremony. He was unlucky as a religious leader, since even when NU allowed its member to

leader of the *Pesantren Darul Ulum*. When he supported the government, he was not only left by a large part of his followers, but also by his fellow *kiai*. Kiai Musta'in was accused of being *kafir*[32] (an infidel) because of his cooperation with the government. He was hence judged unsuitable, for example, to lead (be an *imam* in) prayer. Even Kiai As'ad, the current head of the *Pesantren Darul Ulum*, and a colleague and member of Kiai Musta'in's close family, was humiliated by his *santri* when he led the prayer, since the students were disappointed with As'ad's joining Golkar. In an evening prayer, the *santri* said 'Golkaaaaaar' loudly, instead of 'Amiiiin' when As'ad finished reciting *al-fatiha*[33]. The same experience held true for other *kiai* who joined Golkar.

As the relationship between the *kiai* and society has long been institutionalised through patron-client norms, the Indonesian government is aware of the decisive position of the *kiai* in influencing people's socio-political actions, and in guiding them to adopt certain ways. The government has been trying to incorporate the *kiai* into its machinery by establishing a formal institution called the *Majlis Ulama Indonesia* or MUI (Council for the Indonesian 'Ulama) from the national level down to the district level. The original objective of this institution was to bridge the gap between the government on the one hand and Muslim society on the other. In a more practical way, however, the institution is often criticised for being a government tool to legitimise its programs. However, only a small number of *kiai* have accepted recruitment into this government corporate body. The majority of them remain independent.

It is the *kiai* in MUI who usually deliver national *fatwa* related to the dilemmas posed by a Muslim society. MUI, for example, was the first group of the *'ulama* to suggest that 'family planning' was religiously permitted, when most of the *'ulama* in Indonesia encouraged Muslims not to participate in the program. In spite of MUI closeness to government, however, the 'religious advice' delivered by them is not simply on behalf of the government. Their 'religious advice' is based on decisions made for the sake of the Muslim society itself. The 'religious advice' concerned with family planning, for example, was not only given because the program is a government program but also because Islamic rationale recommends that the Muslims participate in this important program for the prosperity of 'Islamic society'. The fact that family planning is a government program is just a coincidence.

---

affiliate with other political organisations in 1984, he was unable to regain his respected position in his community.

[32] The situation was terrible. According to a *kiai*, some *kiai* who opposed and supported Kiai Musta'in called each other *kafir* (saling mengkafirkan).

[33] Reciting *al-fatiha* is one of necessities in a prayer. When an *imam* finishes reading it, Muslims who follow his prayer will say 'amiiin'. In As'ad's case, his *santri*, instead, said 'Golkaaar' just to show their disappointment with his political actions.

In addition, it is also important to note that MUI often produced 'religious advice' which is opposed to government programs. One example is 'Porkas', a fund raising program for sports in Indonesia administered by the Ministry of Social Affairs. Under this program, donors received a ticket for a lucky number in return for their donation. MUI declared this program as religiously prohibited, even though their 'religious advice' was delivered after the 'Porkas' had been in operation for a couple of months. MUI suggested that the government ban 'Porkas'.

Nevertheless, many educated Muslims do not have a completely favourable impression of MUI. MUI is still suspected of being a tool of the government to legitimise its policies. Such suspicion is understandable, since the formation of MUI at all levels was marked by the recruitment of *kiai* more favourably disposed towards the government, and constitutes a part of the corporate structure of the government. A large number of *kiai* who are not involved in MUI are cynical about MUI; and some people looked down on those recruited as tools of the government. Recent critics mocked MUI by called it as 'Majlis Ular Indonesia' (the Council for Indonesian Snake).

The relationship between the *kiai* and the government in Java has been marked by tension. Since the government is the party with the most power, it keeps trying to use various means not just to defeat the *kiai* but also to recruit them onto its side in supporting its political policies. MUI is especially important for establishing the legitimacy of government politics and the validity of its administration. One way that it tried to counter the *kiai's* politics was to impose some restrictions on *da'wa*[34] activities conducted by the *kiai*. The government at the district level often delayed giving permission, and sometimes did not give any permission for such ativities. The government's restrictions on these religious activities seem to derive from the fact that in the past these religious sessions (*da'wa*) were often used by anti-government *kiai* to give sharp criticism of and to provoke an unpopular situation for the government. This provided the government with a pretext not only to restrict preaching activities but also on some occasions to ban them. A purely religious ritual that I observed in a village, conducted by members of *Sholawat Wahidiyah*, was almost cancelled just because permission had not been given by the provincial police office. This sufi order is actually included among those that support the government. Nevertheless, it still needed to get formal permission from the government for its ritual.

In addition to such restrictions, other stricter steps taken by the government are concerned with pressuring the *kiai* to give their support to the government

---

[34] *Da'wa* is one of the most important religious activities held by Muslims in Indonesia. The *kiai* in his *da'wa* gives religious advice. In addition, through the medium of *da'wa* he bridges the information gap, so that people can get a variety of important information when they attend a *da'wa* session. The importance of *da'wa* increased during critical situations, since it was used by some *kiai* as a medium to criticise the government.

political party during general elections. Even though the pressure was imposed on the *kiai* at village or district level, it was done with the permission of the government at the regency level. In the 1971 and 1977 general elections, such pressure was evident. As reported by some mass media, the *kiai* living in less 'devout-villages' received serious physical threats[35]. As the government officials had to win the election by any means at their disposal, despite the fact that the Muslim society did not generally support the government party, the support for Golkar from such an important figure as a *kiai* becomes a necessity since the *kiai's* role in the general election would be critical. Some *camat* (district head) in Jombang therefore encouraged the village heads under their authority to recruit the local *kiai* into the village administration. A *camat* in the southern region of Jombang, Bareng, for example, proudly mentioned that he had no serious problems in terms of popular support for the government during the election because he had appointed some local *kiai* to the administration of critical villages[36].

It would be inappropriate, however, to analyse the relationship between the *kiai* and the government only through the difference in the institutions in which they play a part. The difference in their institutions or in the roles which they play are not the main factor that gives rise to the non-harmonious relations that often occur between them. The relationship, instead, can be seen in the context of the existing socio-political situation. We have seen, for example, the difference in the *kiai* attitude towards the government between the years when they were struggling through an Islamic political party and their attitude after the elimination of the Islamic political party. In the former, the relationship between the *kiai* and the government was marked by tension. The *kiai* not only had a different perspective from the government's, but they were also grouped into a political party. This demonstrated their disagreement with the government and they were, therefore, accused of opposing the government. The persistence of the *kiai* in defending Islamic principles as far as they were articulated through PPP gave the impression that they were a radical group that could not easily be defeated by the government. For example, they had even staged a 'walk out' from the parliamentary assembly, an action uncharacteristic of Indonesian political culture.

Today, however, the *kiai's* relationship with the government seems to be harmonious. Many *kiai* seem to show their sympathy for the government. They give full support to the leadership of Suharto[37]. Several reasons sustain these

---

[35] A younger *kiai* told me a story about an NU *kiai* in a district in Central Java during the 1971 general election, who was taken by the district security officers. He was forced to wear a necklace of fireworks, which were then burned.

[36] Interview with the *Camat* of Bareng, 11 November 1992.

[37] Such a view seemed to result from NU national congress in 1984. In this congress, however, there was actually no decision recommending that the *kiai* and their followers support the government. Rather

attitudes of the *kiai*. Firstly, the government is a leader just as are the *kiai*, and the former's legitimate authority needs to be supported as long as it does not represent a corrupt power. Secondly, the government in the most often stated view by the *kiai* has done a lot for Indonesian society. Since the majority of Indonesians are Muslims, the government has therefore actually benefited Muslim society.

This sympathetic attitude of the *kiai* has been balanced in return by the changed attitude of the government itself. The most salient change for the Indonesian Muslims resulting from the current government's attitude is a lack of strict monitoring of *da'wa* activities. Currently in Java, seeking government permission for a *da'wa* activity no longer involves a long process, especially if the project officers of the activity hold government party membership cards. This change in government attitude is felt by Muslims at the grassroots level, whose religious activities were often disturbed in the past by security officers[38].

In brief, what is interesting about this relationship is the major change in attitude on the part of the *kiai* with respect to the government. While in the past it very often happened that the government's offer of support was refused by the *kiai*, currently in Java such a situation would rarely occur[39]. Some *kiai* might be ready to accept any government offer of particular non-bureaucratic formal positions. Looking at the two reasons underlying the change in attitude of the *kiai*, we are faced with further questions since the reasons seem to have been taken for granted. If the government is deemed to be doing a lot for Muslims in Indonesia, the question is: why have these reasons only lately come to the surface? Is it not the case that such responses are, from a more modern perspective, concerned with the function of the state and the government? To answer this, it is necessary to look at the socio-political context underlying the change in the *kiai's* attitude. It should be noted that this change seems to have another dimension, indicating that the *kiai* are actually open to change and are responding to the current state of affairs. The change in attitude did not take place in a vacuum but rather was shaped by the socio-political situation.

---

it was suggested that their followers could be affiliated with any political organisation (not only the former Islamic party of PPP). Secondly, the congress came to a very important decision which suggested that the *kiai* organisation accept the secular ideology of Pancasila as its base. NU was the first organisation which accepted Pancasila as its ideological base

[38] It is interesting to note that a significant number of the respondents I interviewed suggested that the good relationship between the *'ulama* and the *umara* (government) should be maintained, since it advantages such religious activities as *da'wa*.

[39] In 1990, a *kiai* from Jombang received a number of bottles of milk sent by the government. This *kiai* returned the milk. The main reason underlying his attitude was that the milk was sent by the government. Although this case was in fact a matter of incorrect delivery, since the government did not intend to send the milk to this *kiai* but to another *kiai*, this *kiai's* attitude showed the persistent un-accommodating perspective among some *kiai* toward the government. This *kiai* also did not know that the government delivered the milk wrongly. This *kiai* steadfastly refused the government's offer of funds for his *pesantren* and university.

The *kiai* have actually been pursuing certain strategies to reach their ideal for some time. The formation of the Islamic political party, PPP or NU (by the *'ulama*), were an indication that they had held ideas or plans which differed from the government's. However, the on-going government mistrust or suspicion of the behaviour of Islamic leaders, including the *kiai*, led to the former discouraging any idea of an Islamic state. The *kiai's* struggle through politics had thus come to a dead end. The government's policy of 'Azas Tunggal' held a significant consequence for the pattern of the *kiai* struggle for Islam, since it provided the conditions for the de-institutionalisation of Islamic political parties.

The *kiai* were aware of this consequence, but because there was no alternative, they could do nothing to prevent it. From this one might deduce that the change in attitude shown by the *kiai* stemmed from the fact that the avenue of Islamic politics was no longer open to them. The change was compensated by the fact that the government "has done a lot for Muslims in Indonesia". The government in their opinion is no longer the other faction that needs to be suspected, but rather is a counterpart that must be supported. This helps explain why in the second half of the 1980s, there was no fissure marking the conflict between the *kiai* and the government. Hence, some *kiai* gave public support to the government. In 1992, a few months before the general election, a great number of the *kiai* in East Java publicly supported Suharto, proposing that he be elected for the next presidency. The same holds true in the current situation. Many *kiai* came to see Suharto in his palace just to give him implicit support. In June 1995, several *kiai* from Jombang and East Java, led by Kiai As'ad Umar from the *Pesantren Darul Ulum*, gave political support to President Suharto's candidacy for another term in office (1998).

However, the current situation marks a change in position of the *kiai* in the eyes of the government. My informant gave me a cynical description. "In the past", he said, "the government pursued the *kiai*. But in present day Jombang, the *kiai* pursue the government". He suggested further, "If you go to a great *kiai* after you perform your *'idu'l-fitr* prayer, I am sure you will not meet him, because the *kiai* must see the bupati (the regent) in his house. In the past, the bupati came to see the *kiai* after the former performed *'idu'l-fitr* prayer"[40].

Although only a few such cases have happened, it becomes clear that there is a change in the social structure in relation to the *'ulama*-government relationship. Some *santri* suggested, therefore, that although some cooperation with the

---

[40] Another case was described by another informant. In commencing his term of office in Jombang, a bupati held a party. Kiai Shohib Bisri, a former local NU president and the head of the *Pesantren Denanyar*, and other *kiai* in Jombang were invited to the party. Without considering the *kiai's* presence, the bupati provided entertainment in the form of local Javanese dance. As he was sitting in the front row, Kiai Shohib Bisri was asked by a lady dancer to dance together. Although Kiai Shohib refused, this accident disappointed some Muslim leaders. They viewed the government officers as ignorant of the *kiai* tradition and conceived the incident as humiliating.

government is valuable, it is too risky to be too close to it. The *kiai* had better to be more preoccupied with their *pesantren*, and leave the politics to other NU activists.

Chapter 8: The Kiai's Effort in Remoulding Relationships with Other Muslim Groups

Islam in Indonesia is not homogeneous in terms of its religious practice. There are what are commonly called the traditionalist and the modernist groups. The traditionalist in Jombang is represented by NU[1] while the modernist by Muhammadiyah. The traditionalists are those who usually acknowledge themselves as following one of the four *madhhab* (school of law) in Islam, while the modernists base their practice of Islam on their reasoning. The traditionalists often relate their practice of Islam to Syafi'i, Hambali, Maliki or Hanafi, while the modernists relate to no one. In addition, the traditionalists always refer to the Qur'an, the hadith, the *ijma'* (consensus) of the *'ulama* and *qiyas* (analogy) as their sources in practising Islam, while the modernists only refer to the Qur'an and hadith. The NU tradition of referring to one of the four *madhhab* and its use of the *ijma'* make its members constantly refer to the work of *salaf* (earlier) *'ulama* for any interpretation which they make, while Muhammadiyah members try to use only the Qur'an and the hadith to come to the correct interpretation of any problem, without having to refer to the work of *salaf* or *kholaf* (later) *'ulama* to justify their current interpretation.

In addition, there is also another group which, compared to the above groups, is more syncretic in their Islamic practice. This group consists of those Muslims considered less devout from the Islamic perspective compared to the above mentioned groups. Members of this group derive from former *abangan* and their younger generation. The process of Islamic reassertion which is taking place among the *abangan* makes their younger generation's practices of Islam closer to that of devout Muslims.

This chapter highlights the nature of the relationship between the three groups. These groups are also the social base that gave rise to larger various socio-political groupings in Jombang. In the past, the political orientation of each group is defined by its ideological practice of Islam. As the relationship in the past was generally marked by conflict, it is worth seeing it in present day Jombang. Although this change is attributed to the modernisation process in general, it became more evident after Muslims changed their politics at the end of the 1980s. In present day Jombang some changes accordingly have impinged on the ideological lines of demarcation between various Muslim groups. This chapter aims to illuminate the social context in which the socio-political leadership of the *kiai* takes place.

---

[1] See also my description about NU in Chapter II.

8.1 Differences and Locality

In general, Muslim society in Jombang is divided into two groups in terms of orientation. The first one is the devout group, and the other is the less devout group or the *abangan*. These groupings express the existing social reality of the Jombang population. By the devout I mean those Jombang population who practise Islam in a more orthodox way, while the less devout are members of society who, due to their ignorance of Islam, tend to practise syncretic Islam (cf. Fox and Dirjosanjoto, 1989). The devout group is represented by NU (the traditionalist) and Muhammadiyah[2] (the modernist).

I nonetheless recognise that such a grouping is not adequate. Not only does it not cover all various existing groups in Muslim society in Jombang, but it also lacks the specificity and detail of the variety of characteristics of each group. In addition, what is important to emphasise is that the characteristic commonly ascribed to NU and Muhammadiyah, as the orthodox Muslims, are not necessarily applicable to the current situation. The development of NU, as described by Bruinessen[3], exhibits the same dynamics as that of a modern Islamic organisation. At least, the idea of adapting to the changing socio-political situation warrants the attention of its leaders. In addition, the general characteristics of these Islamic organisations are obscured by local characteristics.

Nevertheless, there are a general characteristics which differentiates the devout Muslims from the *abangan*. The same holds true with the characteristic of the traditionalist and the modernist. In the following discussion I will focus on the different characteristics of these two Islamic groups. The sociological bases underlying the existence of these two Islamic groups are different. The modernist group is generally more preoccupied with idealised efforts and is trying to change the social reality of Muslim society in regard to its religious practice. Current practice, in the modernist's perspective, is neither ideal nor religiously correct. There must be a socio-political movement to alter it. On the other hand, the traditionalist[4] group has been trying to coordinate, nurture and even develop existing religious beliefs, practice and culture in general. This attitude is based on a religious formula: *al-muhafaza bi'l-qadim al-salih wa'l-akhdhu bi'l-jadid al-aslah* (lit. preserving the good existing order and adopting the new one which is better). The former is trying to develop toward an idealised situation, while the latter is working within the real social situation.

---

[2] Muhammadiyah is only one among several modernist Muslim organisations.
[3] See Bruinessen's "Traditions for the Future: the Reconstruction of Traditionalist Discourse within NU". In Barton, Greg and Greg Fealy, ed. (1996, forthcoming). *Nahdlatul Ulama, Traditional Islam and Modernity in Indonesia*. Centre of Southeast Asian Studies, Monash University.
[4] Some scientists suggest that the emergence of NU in 1926 was a reaction to what was being done by Muhammadiyah. This suggestion derives from the fact that NU was established after Muhammadiyah had been in existence for about 15 years.

For the purpose of analysis of these differences in religious practice, I will try to focus on the doctrinal and social dimensions of these two Islamic groups. The doctrinal dimension which differentiates them derives from their difference in interpreting the precepts of the Qur'an. Their differences do not actually impinge on the basics of Islam, like theology, but rather they touch only on parts commonly called *furu'* (lit. branches). Although the differences between NU and Muhammadiyah occur only in the domain of *furu'* which touches only on aspects of the application of their interpretation of *fiqh* matters, such differences are expressed through their praxis of Islamic rituals in everyday life and influence the world view and social behaviour of their members.

The different interpretation of the available doctrine by the modernists has provoked an unfavourable and latent situation of conflict with the traditionalists since the modernist has been trying to purify traditional practices of Islam such as those practised by NU society. This situation has been heightened by differences in political orientation[5], and each group disparages the other due to its feeling of superiority in regard to its own culture and practice of religion. A member of Muhammadiyah considers his Islamic practice purer and better because he discards anything less Islamic. On the other hand, an NU member regards Muhammadiyah's practice of Islam as too rigid because of its tendency to be puritanical, and its avoidance, in many respects, of the existing socio-cultural environment. Since these differences occur in the more practical domain of daily religious life, they have been more salient. This situation marked a general tendency among Muslims in Java, especially during the 1950s and 1960s, although in Jombang it has been less pronounced.

There is one important Islamic concept which became the basis of their cultural and religious practice but was interpreted differently by both groups. This concept is related to the perception of religious practices which were not performed by the Prophet Muhammad and the earlier generation of his *sahaba* (companions). These practices are conceptualised in what is commonly called *bid'a* (heretical practice). The interpretation of the concept of *bid'a* at the grassroots level occurs in a rather haphazard manner (salah kaprah). Members of Muhammadiyah conceptualise what they call *bid'a* in terms of black and white. Everything not practised by the Prophet Muhammad is deemed to be *bid'a* by lay followers of the modernist stream. This understanding derives from the Islamic doctrine according to which "each heresy is going astray, and those going astray would go to hell" ("qullu bid'a zolala, wa qullu zolala fi al-nar"). On the other hand, NU society, which grounds its perspective in a less black-white format, classifies *bid'a* into two kinds, that is *bid'a hasana* and *bid'a*

---

[5] In the 1950s, these two groups became affiliated with different political organisations. Muhammadiyah affiliated with the Masjumi and NU stood as another Islamic political party. NU established itself as a political party in 1952 after being in the Masjumi for about 6 years.

sayyi'a (bad and good *bid'a*). This difference in interpretation derives from the different sources which they use or from the way they understand the norms which must be established in Islam.

The underlying difference in understanding the concept of *bid'a* which marks the Muhammadiyah and NU practice of religion in Jombang is limited to what is called *'ibada* (Islamic ritual). However, this has occurred not only at the level of interpretation of Islamic precepts but also at the level of worldview. Based on their understanding of the concept of *bid'a* and their adaptation to the existing order, the members of NU society have always grounded their understandings of Islamic social relations on the concept of 'harmony'. On the other hand, Muhammadiyah society is inclined to attribute such social reality to what they call 'diperintahkan' (divinely ordered).

The characteristic of Muhammadiyah, which bases its standpoint on strictness as it is conceptualised by the Qur'an has made its lay members rigid in their understanding of socio-cultural development. Thus Muhammadiyah only does what is religiously ordered (written in the Qur'an and the hadith), while NU always tries to work on what is not definitely prohibited[6] in its practice of Islam. Thus Muhammadiyah members are trying to discard any heretical Islamic practice which may be alive among Javanese since it is not religiously ordered or written. These practices include such activities as *tahlil*[7] and *slametan*, the latter of which is deemed to have Hinduistic elements. They strictly suggests that all *bid'a* is 'zolala' (going astray). NU, on the other hand, does not always consider the *bid'a* to be bad. In their opinion, it is only the bad *bid'a* that can bring its doer to hell. Thus such *'ibada* as *tahlil* is of significance, since it is not only classified as good Islamic practice but can also accrue to what is religiously expected of all Muslims. Such practice could therefore be subsumed under what is commonly called *sunna* (recommended)[8]. By performing such thing, a Muslim hopes to add to the other *'ibada* (observance required by the Islamic faith) to his religious obligations, which he might have carried out imperfectly.

Local socio-environmental factors, however, have affected Muhammadiyah and NU. But compared to Muhammadiyah, variation in NU practices of Islam may be lower. This is because NU tries to accommodate to the existing practices, while Muhammadiyah tries to transform them to the idealised. It is therefore not surprising that various local Muhammadiyah organisations might differ in

---

[6] I am indebted to Dr. Taufik Abdullah for this understanding (informal talk with him, 29 November 1994).

[7] *Tahlil* is a ritual following one's death. The family performs such ritual to pray for the dead. The essence of this ritual is to stress the oneness of Allah. *Tahlil* is performed from the first to the seventh day after a death.

[8] There are five qualifications of behaviour which the Islamic law and ethics have traditionally categorised (Netton, 1992:22). These are *wajb* (obligatory), *sunna* (recommended), *mubah* (morally neutral), *makruh* (reprehensible) and *haram* (forbidden). The obligatory *'ibada*, like prayer five times a day, is clearly written. The recommended *'ibada*, like *tahlil*, is a matter of interpretation.

their religious practice from the mainstream since the process of change in different regions does not happen in the same pattern or direction because of different local conditions.

Muhammadiyah in Jombang is indeed different from that in other regions in terms of its culture and a few of their Islamic practices. Although it is essentially anti-tradition, its practice of Islam is very much influenced by local culture so that its characteristics are culturally close to that of NU. Abdurrahman, for example, is a Muhammadiyah member living in the district of Ploso. He is a rich man who grew up in a very Muhammadiyah environment, but he is also the leader of a group performing regular *tahlil* in his district. When he was asked why he was involved in a *tahlil* activity, a religious practice commonly performed by NU society but deemed *bid'a* by Muhammadiyah, he rejoindered that he did not discard all religious practices which do not sound Muhammadiyah, but rather he also performs practices such as *tahlil*, since it is religiously good.

Abdurrahman's practice of Islam constitutes a 'culture representation' which marks the difference between Muhammadiyah in Jombang from that in other cities. His practice is influenced by the existing culture of traditional Muslims in his surroundings, which strongly emphasises the need to carry out good Islamic practices classified as *'ibada*. The attitude of Abdurrahman in terms of his religious practice is affected by NU culture in Jombang[9].

In brief, different interpretations of the existing doctrine which result in the emergence of ideological groupings is affected by local culture. There is no stereotype or model which absolutely delineates the special character of a group of Muslims, like NU, from another. As shown in the case of Abdurrahman, a religious practice which is commonly attributed to traditionalist Muslims can also be conducted by modernist followers. This situation occurs because the doctrinal interpretation of modernist members at the grassroots level varies. In addition, the Muhammadiyah practice of Islam in Jombang seems to be more accommodating to local culture. The members' efforts to purify society's practice of Islam is not as strict as in other areas. This is not only because Muhammadiyah

---

[9] The emergence of Muhammadiyah in 1912 in Yogyakarta with its modernisation or purification efforts cannot be separated from the situation of Islamic politics at that time either in Indonesia or in the Middle East. In an interview, Dr. Taufik Abdullah suggested that the process of orthodoxisation or modernisation carried out by religious movements throughout the history of Islam in Indonesia is very much affected by the changes in the Middle East. These regions in Indonesian Islamic history constituted either the sources or the medium through which Islam has been transported, interpreted and disseminated. The *Padri* movement in West Sumatra, for example, which tried to modernise Islam, was affected by the *Wahhabis* movement in Saudi Arabia. This was possible because communication with Saudi Arabia had been taking place long before Muhammadiyah was established in Java. Also some movements which inclined towards 'traditionalism' in West Sumatra emerged after the popularity of *Wahhabis* in Saudi Arabia declined. It is evident that religious movements in Indonesia seem not to derive from the independent thoughts of Indonesian Muslims, but rather they were the result of identification with the Arabic world. Both modernism and traditionalism in Indonesia in their early stages were prompted by what transpired in the Middle East.

members in Jombang have changed their methods of *da'wa* but also because many of the elite originally come from an NU family background. Also, some of them were educated in NU *pesantren*. This is very important to illuminate the accommodating nature of Muhammadiyah in Jombang, since at the level where primary socialisation took place, some Muhammadiyah leaders were introduced to traditionalist cultural values which influenced their practice of Islam.

Shiddiq Abbas, a prominent leader of Muhammadiyah in Jombang, for example, was educated in the *Pesantren Bahrul Ulum*, the oldest NU *pesantren*. Azhar, a leader of Muhammadiyah in Ngoro, is the son of an NU member who had family ties with the founder of NU, Kiai Hasyim Asy'ari. These two Muhammadiyah leaders are familiar with the NU's tradition through their primary socialisation and religious education. Their joining Muhammadiyah was inspired by consciousness and an understanding of what it means to purify Islamic practice and what should be done by Muhammadiyah in accordance with its mission. To be a member of Muhammadiyah in their view is not merely to be different from being an NU member in terms of religious practice. This is why Shiddiq Abbas and Azhar differ from other Muhammadiyah leaders in Jombang and in other cities. They have more knowledge of the religious practice of the Jombang Muslim population in general. Their purification movements through Muhammadiyah do not start from a position of ignorance and indifference to the existing local culture, as others do who may be unfamiliar with the actual religious practices and thoughts of the traditionalists. These two leaders ground their actions on a tradition which they know well. It is this situation which gives rise to the general similarity in the religious practice of both Muhammadiyah and NU in Jombang.

Despite the efforts of Muhammadiyah leaders, such as Shiddiq Abbas and Azhar, some Muhammadiyah members tend to maintain a different religious interpretation or practice from NU members just for the sake of being different. Some Muhammadiyah members in Jombang, for example, argued about certain parts of prayer practices performed by their colleagues which they considered not to be Muhammadiyah style. They recommended that their colleagues change such practices. These recommended prayer practices, however, actually resemble those of NU members in another city in East Java.

However, it can be argued that in general the debate between modernist and traditionalist followers at the grassroots level has actually been trivial, with no religious significance. In the 1950s and 1960s, when social tension between the traditionalist and modernist Muslims was great, this tension in villages in Jombang and Java revolved around insignificant matters, such as two *azan* in Friday prayer or using a *bedug*[10] in a mosque, which were not essential parts of

---

[10] *Adhan* is the call (in Arabic) by a Muslim in a mosque which is commonly used to indicate that the prayer time has come; while the *bedug* is a wooden drum which is beaten preceding the *adhan*. Two

the religious ritual. The *bedug* for the lay modernist is indeed *bid'a*, in the sense of being novel because it was not found during the Prophet's life. For the traditionalists, however, the use of *bedug* is not a primary part of the religious ritual. It is merely used to give a signal to Muslims that the time for prayer has come. It is therefore evident that much of the conflict derived from their tendency to underestimate and humiliate each other. Each group felt its standpoint and interpretation of Islam was the right one.

From a few cases which I observed, my impression is that the different interpretation of both lay members of Muhammadiyah and NU does not derive from solid religious reasoning. On some occasions, they arose just from the intention to be different. The essence of the logic sustaining lay modernist arguments about *bid'a*, for example, is actually blurred, as is shown when comparisons are made with their colleagues in other cities, since in many respects it is based on unfounded generalisations. So their concept of *bid'a* can be misleading.

This point is important in order to illuminate the reasoning underlying the modernist understanding of Islam, and how such an understanding is interpreted by lay Muslims at the grassroots level. It is evident that there is inconsistency in the lay modernists' arguments concerning the concept of *bid'a*. Not only do their interpretations vary but, in some cases, they were paradoxical. The idea that a *bedug* is *bid'a* is interesting when compared it with other modern innovations, such as loud speakers, which are used as tools in all Islamic ritual. Nakamura (1979:259– 263) found in his research in Yogyakarta that when Muhammadiyah members were going to mosque for the *'idu'l-fitri* prayer they were accompanied by a drum band, instead of a *bedug*.

These observations invite questions in regard to the essence or the underlying reasoning of what is classified as *bid'a* and what is not. Why is the *bedug* classified as *bid'a*, because it is an unsuitable religious tool for use in a mosque, while a drum band is judged as suitable to accompany Muslims reciting *takbir* (saying 'Allahu Akbar': Allah is the Great) along their way to the mosque? Is the *bedug* seen as *bid'a* because it is a cultural product of the traditional Javanese? How does it differ from a loud speaker or a drum band? All are novel or modern additions which function just to complement a religious activity. These questions are the most frequently asked by the traditionalists.

adhan usually occur during the Friday prayer of traditionalist Muslims. The difference between the traditionalist and the modernist in these matters is that the former does *adhan* when the Friday prayer time has come and when the *khatib* (sermon giver) is going to start delivering his Friday sermon. For the modernist, the *adhan* in Friday prayer is done once only, that is when the *khatib* is going to deliver his Friday sermon. The *bedug* is a common tool available in any mosque of the traditionalists, which is used to give an indication to society that prayer time has come. Both *bedug* and the second *adhan* during Friday prayer are deemed as *bid'a* by the modernists since both are novel in the sense of not being available during the Prophet's life.

Such questions seem to undermine the arguments used by people who acknowledge themselves as part of the modernist movement. Their generalisation about what is and what is not *bid'a* derives from inconsistent principles, particularly at the level of lay Muslims. At the elite level, the arguments are grounded on a deeper understanding of Qur'anic precepts, so that it is unlikely that such *salah kaprah* (misunderstanding) could occur. Hence, the problem here relates to the uneven diffusion of information. The views of the elite of the modernist at the centre might not reach their fellow members at the grassroots level. The distance from the centre has resulted in distortion in regard to the formal interpretations made by the elites.

The possibility of misunderstanding by lay followers is great in the early stage of the development of Islamic organisation in Indonesia. With just a few qualified thinkers, this misunderstanding is very possible since the political situation which surrounded Muslims in Indonesia encouraged each group to defend its position. This is a side effect which appears when a competing situation exists between religious movements. Such a situation has pushed each group to be persistently different from the other. This misunderstanding[11] nonetheless allows us to see how these religious groups perceive their worldly and religious situation.

8.2 The Conflict Reduced

The conflict between the various groups of Muslims in Indonesia started when contact with the Middle East intensified in the early 20th century. The conflict was more pronounced after various Islamic groups emerged during the second and third decades of 20th century. The emergence of modern Islamic groups such as Muhammadiyah and NU has made manifest the conflict among Muslims at the grassroots level. This conflict was intensified when political competition between the Islamic *aliran* (streams) reached their peak during the liberal democracy period.

The groups' various standpoints in terms of Islamic practice have resulted in continuous hidden conflict since each group feels its own interpretation and practice of Islam is better. In addition, each group has tried to extend its own particular practice to groups where other practices of Islam are performed. In

---

[11] Some figures of both Muhammadiyah and NU in Jombang realised the side effects resulting from their competition in promoting their particular practices of Islam. Shiddiq Abbas, a leading figure of Muhammadiyah in Jombang, therefore felt the need to restate his program of purification. In a *halal bihalal* (a religious ceremony following '*idu'l-fitri*), he stressed that "in a religious realm, the introduction of novel things is not allowed" (so in his opinion the line is clear). This emphasis was made by reference to a certain group of religious organisations which he deemed to have crossed that line. He emphasised that purification is confined to what is called 'masalah-masalah ibadah' (matters relating to religious practices). He suggests that basic reasoning should be more textually Qur'anic or attentive to hadith. It is not allowed therefore to introduce additional practices which are not written in the Qur'an and hadith.

the past, conflict in Javanese villages was commonly expressed in the struggle to manage a mosque or in the struggle to lead the village. As a mosque was not only a symbol of Muslim existence in society but also a representation of a particular practice of Islam, a group which owned or managed a mosque could expand the influence of the group and its Islamic parties. An NU mosque would represent traditionalist beliefs and practices, while a Muhammadiyah mosque would promote 'more purified Islamic beliefs and practices'. A mosque was a very important medium through which religious beliefs and practices were disseminated since Muslims gathered there five times daily to perform their practice of Islam. Since most of the mosques in Javanese villages were erected by member of the wider society rather than by certain Islamic groups, they constituted a place where the conflict between Islamic groups, especially between NU and Muhammadiyah, was manifest.

The problem of *bid'a* in certain aspects of Islamic rituals, such as *tahlil* or *ziyara* [12], has been deemed by Muhammadiyah as amounting to *shirk*. Muhammadiyah members consider that much of NU's practice of Islam is mixed with that of other religions, so that NU has been called syncretic. For NU members, however, their practice of Islam can not only enriched the culture of Islam itself due to its adoption of the existing local culture, but can also be backed by strong arguments. In the opinion of one NU member, Islam not only comprises pure ritual practices as described by the Qur'an or the hadith, but also pays attention to understanding the psychological aspect of its adherents' lives. By this he means that any effort to understand the social life of an Islamic society should not neglect the psychological aspect. He suggested further that "the application of a certain interpretation in regard to such *'ibada* (devotional action) as *tahlil*, should take into consideration the psychological dimension of the local people's lives". The ritual practices conducted by NU, in his opinion, have been more *'ibada* in character rather than deviating from the 'real' Islam itself. "Tahlil, for example, which is regarded by Muhammadiyah members as heretical, is actually very Islamic since all the *tahlil* rituals are *dhikr* (stating the oneness of Allah)", he emphasised. So the *tahlil* itself is Islamic in essence. "What is wrong with doing a lot of such *'ibada* as reciting *tahlil* or *tahmid*[13]?", this NU member asked.

The different Islamic practices have also been emphasised by their proponents' different political orientations, especially during the liberal democracy period. Throughout Java, the ideological conflict between the traditionalists and the modernists at the grassroots level has been tremendous. The unwillingness of NU and Muhammadiyah members to assimilate or cooperate has been sustained

---

[12] *Ziyara* is visiting the grave. It aims to pray for the dead. Similar to *tahlil, ziyara* practice is embedded in NU tradition but rejected by Muhammadiyah.
[13] *Tahmid* is to praise Allah. It is usually performed inherently in any religious ritual. So, *tahlil* and *tahmid* are two terms used by the traditionalists interchangeably.

by the political situation. Relations between the groups have also deteriorated because of their views which encourage them to be continuously different[14]. As indicated by their unwillingness to marry, few NU members in villages in Java, and especially in Madura, have a negative perception of Muhammadiyah. Such a perception is still alive even today, and can be extreme in regions where NU's embeddedness has been particularly strong, and the Muhammadiyah is less known.

As the culture or religious practice of the Javanese is essentially traditional and syncretic, and hence very close to that of NU society, the Muhammadiyah's efforts to change the existing practice represent a threat to most Javanese Muslim villagers. The conflicts which flourished among Muslim groups in Indonesia during the 1950s has given rise to another situation where every group feels that it has done the correct thing in terms of its practice of religion. This ideological conflict resulted in a situation where each group humiliated the others. Among Javanese villagers there even emerged a subtle accusation that the conduct of Muhammadiyah members was less Islamic or outside Islam itself. A simple but significant case illustrates this problem in the relationship between the modernist and traditionalist (orthodox) Muslims in Java. Due to its simplicity, this case has become a joke in any conversation or social encounter between Islamic intellectuals. I will quote an extract written by an NU intellectual and published in an NU magazine of East Java. This intellectual was disappointed with the fact that among members of NU society there still exist such naive perceptions of other Islamic organisations. He wrote and I translate and paraphrase:

> One night I was visited by a guest (I was told that he had come to my house five times but had not found me available). I thought he must have very important things to discuss. But when I asked him, I realised that his problem concerned his daughter. He mentioned that a young man from Banyuwangi (East Java) had asked to marry his youngest daughter, my student at the Islamic University of Malang in Semester VII. He had not responded to this request because the young man came from a different religious background. The guest realised that this young man was indeed a student of the Islamic University of Malang, but objected because the latter's religion was Muhammadiyah. My guest thus regarded Muhammadiyah as a religion. So, what is the problem? My guest's problem was that his daughter loved the young man very much (they could not be separated). His question was whether it was religiously legitimate to marry his daughter to this young Muhammadiyah man.

---

[14] There is a hadith which suggests that: "difference (in standpoint) between my *umma* could be a blessing". This hadith may establish a positive situation where Islam actually allows its people to have different standpoints in understanding a particular problem or a different ideological orientation as a means to pursue Islamic goals. Islam could actually instill a freedom of thinking among its *umma*.

It is evident that some NU members at the grassroots level have a very negative view of Muhammadiyah. This is expressed not only in their unwillingness to allow inter-marriage, but also in their perception that Muhammadiyah is not Islamic. I need also to give a description of how the conflict still continues to the present time. The following quote from a report in the monthly magazine, AULA, concerns the battle between NU and Muhammadiyah for ownership of an Islamic educational institution in a regency in East Java:

NU VS MUHAMMADIYAH IN BOJONEGORO

There are some NU properties which have changed to other ownership. The causes are 'left unmanaged', greed and ignorance. Today we found that a madrasa (Islamic educational Institution of NU) has been taken illegally.

...In Bojonegoro there is a land case that involves NU and Muhammadiyah. The case is concerned with ownership of the land and building of the 'Madrasah Islahiyah' in Panjuna village, Kalitidu district, Bojonegoro.

...The land was *waqf* (endowment) land from H. Nurhasim, a local NU member. On this land was built 'Madrasah Islahiyah' under the legal act No. 240/87 signed by Yatiman Hadisuparjo (and then renewed by the legal act No.750/1991). The legal document concerning this *waqf* mentions that the 'Madrasah Islahiyah' is given as a *waqf* property to NU.

In 1990, another *waqf* document about this 'Madrasah Alislahiyah' was made by the KUA (the office of Ministry of Religion at the district level) of Kalitidu district suggesting Muhammadiyah as the *nazir* (recipient of the *waqf*). The village head of Panjuna asked that the latter *waqf* document be withdrawn. The NU branch at Kalitidu gave authority to the local 'Private Office for Legal Aid', which then reminded the KUA of the facts and accused the office and the local branch of Muhammadiyah of procuring a false *waqf* document.

—(Translated from AULA, August 1991)

The Muhammadiyah tendency in Jombang to try to increase its influence in society, in addition to its efforts of purification, has not only provoked internal conflict in Islamic society, but has also resulted in confusion among members of society who are mainly NU members or sympathisers. For lay Javanese, who have no appropriate basic knowledge in regard to their Islamic understanding, the competition between Muhammadiyah and NU has made them unsure about the essence of Islam itself.

What happened in Puton, a village in Jombang where the majority of the population were less devout Muslims, can illustrate this phenomenon. In the beginning of the New Order government, Muslims in Puton were trying to practise Islam in a more correct way. Their reassertion of Islam pushed them to be more active Muslims in terms of Islamic practice (not just nominal Muslims as before). Their practice of Islam was traditionalist, since in this village NU had long been the sole representative of Islamic organisations. In a *tarawih* [15], however, a Muhammadiyah member tried to introduce a practice commonly performed by modernists. As this practice differed from that of NU members, many people were confused, since they were new in their practice of *tarawih* and in their acquisition of Islamic knowledge. The people in Puton and in many other villages in Jombang have not been inclined to accept Muhammadiyah practice. Not only have most people in these areas been oriented to NU for a long time but also the practice of Islam offered by Muhammadiyah is culturally alien to them[16].

This conflict between the two dominant Muslim groups in Jombang, which basically derives from their different interpretation of Islamic precepts as applied in their daily Islamic practice, has extended to other areas. It has impinged on the social and political domain of Jombangese lives. *'Asabiya* or group fanaticism[17] is the driving force that affects the relationship between Muslims in Jombang. Such *'asabiya*, according to a Muslim intellectual in Jombang, has even weakened the pillars of unity which had been established for a long time.

The change in the bureaucratic structure brought about by the Suharto government at the beginning of the 1970s had a big impact on the relationship between various Muslim groups in Jombang. The promotion of a Muhammadiyah intellectual, Mukti Ali, to the position of Minister in the Ministry of Religion, not only constituted government social engineering that aimed to curtail the influence of NU in this department, which it had dominated for a long time, but it also changed the constellation of the social structure in the bureaucracy of the

---

[15] *Tarawih* is a prayer performed by Muslims during Ramadan (one of the months in the Muslim calendar). It is carried out after Muslims conduct *'isha* prayer in the evening. This prayer is *sunna* (recommended). The different between *tarawih* practised by NU and Muhammadiyah is that NU performed it in 20 *raka'at* (lit. bowing, unit of prayer), while Muhammadiyah 8. Both NU and Muhammadiyah base their practices of *tarawih* on the hadith. This difference was an issue of debate during the 1950s in various villages in Java.

[16] As I mentioned in a previous section, Muhammadiyah has been trying to purify the existing religious practice of local people, which in its view is syncretic. NU, on the other hand, has been accommodating to such practice by absorbing and colouring it with Islam. Hence, NU society has a similar practice of *slametan* to that of *abangan*. The difference is that in the former the *slametan* is transformed into a more Islamic situation, while in the latter it is syncretic. All the prayers in the former are recited in Arabic, while in the latter Hindu elements are still dominant.

[17] *'Asabiya*, or group fanaticism, is a sociologically common phenomenon that can occur in any society. From the Islamic perspective, *'asabiya* is condemned, since it can not only disadvantage the Muslim community, but can also disrupt the promoted unity between Muslim groups. Islam actually introduced a concept of brotherhood, which has been deliberately misinterpreted by various groups which are driven by political interest. *'Asabiya* is obvious in the Indonesian Muslims' lives. It is interesting to look at how the promotion process for the office of Ministry of Religion at the regency or district level in Jombang and other regions is affected by a tendency towards *'asabiya*.

Ministry of Religion. The change in the political map by the promotion of Mukti Ali was followed by the restructuring of all personnel in the Ministry of Religion throughout Indonesia from the central office down to the district level. NU's domination of this department was replaced by Muhammadiyah's even in cities like Jombang where the number of NU members constitutes an absolute majority.

The change in the pattern of bureaucratic leadership through politics is impressive, ignoring as it does the objective condition of the local society. It is likely that a gap has emerged which characterises the relationship between local society and these bureaucrats. The character of the bureaucratic machine is impersonal, and this condition can be attributed or applied to the existing bureaucracy from the central government to the regency level. At the district level in Java, however, the bureaucracy had been better staffed by personnel well known to local society. At the district level individual members of society know each other. Furthermore, their understanding of Islamic precepts and norms is applied more directly in their daily lives. The fact that a Muhammadiyah officer of the Ministry of Religion at the district level (Kantor Urusan Agama=KUA) has a different understanding of these precepts from the surrounding NU society can lead to problems.

An important conflict also occurred between these organisations and the LDII (the preaching institution of Islam). LDII was formerly called *Islam Jamaah* (lit. the group of Muslims). This group is more responsive to the existing condition of Muslim society. Socially, however, it is more exclusive since what it conceptualises as "the real Islam" is restricted to the group's own practices. Accordingly, they regard both Muhammadiyah and NU as outside Islam. The group's first move when it emerged in Ngoro, was to burn *kitab*[18] (books) which had been used by traditionalist *kiai* as their references. In the opinion of members of this movement, these books would lead to stagnancy among Muslims in Java. They could divert Islam from its true course. This very exclusive and extreme conceptualisation of Islam estranged the followers of this organisation from the rest of the Islamic community. The feeling that they are the only Islamic group provoked a negative relationship with other Muslim groups since such an attitude is offensive. Due to its exclusivism, other Islamic groups cannot help but be suspicious of LDII.

The members' relations with the rest of society are not established and maintained with reference to the existing social order. The concepts of purity and impurity, derived from their self acknowledgement as the only pure Muslim group, have guided the development of such a relationship. I was told by people that a member of Ngoro society, Muhadi (my next door neighbour during my research; not his real name), has maintained very rigid relations with other members of

---

[18] Interview with Azhar, 12 December 1992.

society. He is a small trader in Ngoro, selling such daily needs as rice. Being a member of LDII, he looked down on other Muslims who did business with him. In his shop, Muhadi tried to avoid any hand contact with his customers just because the latter were deemed impure.

Societal suspicion of this Islamic group pushed the government to ban it. The group changed its name twice following the government's ban. In spite of *kiai* pressure, the government is reluctant to ban it again. The tendency of the group to emphasise the importance of *zakat* (alms giving) has made it self-sufficient in terms of financial support. Members are urged to allocate some of their income to support their organisation, since *zakat* is an important task they have to perform on the path of Allah. The former Minister of Home Affair, Rudini[19], suggested that this group is potentially very strong, since it is economically independent.

Despite these facts that characterise the life of Muslim groups in Jombang and their relations, the degree of tension between them, especially between NU and Muhammadiyah, in present day Jombang has decreased significantly. The tendency to reconcile and reach mutual understanding about their differences is also growing. The NU *kiai* are occasionally invited to Muhammadiyah *pengajian*, and vice versa. Also the domination of Muhammadiyah in the management of a mosque as big as *Mesjid Jami'* (the great mosque) of Jombang is much reduced. The *imam* (the person who leads the prayer) and the sermon giver at Friday Prayer in this mosque, for example, may come from Muhammadiyah or NU. If the *imam* is of Muhammadiyah background, the Friday Prayer will follow the Muhammadiyah style. If the *imam* is an NU member, it will be carried out in the NU style.

From several interviews with NU members in Jombang, I did not find a negative perception of Muhammadiyah, such as I have described above, since Muslims here are more open to the modern situation. NU society now rarely tries to humiliate Muhammadiyah. The term 'Kamandulah'[20], which was popularly used among NU society of East Java to humiliate Muhammadiyah adherents, is not known among the younger generation in present day Jombang. Several factors sustain this situation in Jombang. Firstly, Jombang is strategically located and connects many cities in East Java. This made the flow of information concerned with either Islamic development or its politics easier to reach the Muslim society in Jombang. This was because Muslims in Jombang were more sensitive to their problems, including their internal conflicts. Secondly, Jombang has produced some well known national Islamic figures, such as Kiai Hasyim Asy'ari or the

---

[19] Interview with Kiai Aziz Masyhuri, 19 April 1993.
[20] *Kamandullah* is taken from Muhammadiyah. Altering a word in this way was intended to disparage. Muhammadiyah members also called NU 'Wanao', from the word NO (In the past NU was spelled as Nahdlatul Oelama).

current Muslim intellectuals, Dr. Nurkholis Madjid and Abdurrahman Wahid, the NU national chairman. The emergence of national leading figures in Jombang has made its Muslim population proud. This has reduced differences[21] among groups, since these figures derive not only from NU but also from Muhammadiyah. Thirdly, around one third of the devout Muslims in Jombang are involved in the *tarekat* movement. The existence of the various *tarekat* movements in Jombang has not only resulted in the clear delineation of Muslim groupings but can also broaden their members' perspectives. Despite the divisions between the various groups due to different political orientations, they are sociologically still bound together, since these *tarekat* groups have the same cultural roots. NU members' affiliation with various *tarekat* groups has laid down the basic principles of unity. The consciousness of the members has been raised and they can see that similarity in membership (in NU) can be complemented by different affiliations (with the *tarekat* movements). Their grouping as members of NU does not prevent them from acknowledging the existence of other Islamic groups, such as Muhammadiyah which tends to be anti-*tarekat*. In practical Islam, the practices of other Islamic groups must be acknowledged as real a practice of Islam as their own. Finally, Muhammadiyah in Jombang is relatively small in size and poses little threat to the established culture of traditional Muslims. In addition, most Muhammadiyah leading figures in Jombang come from families with NU background.

In brief, it is evident that the socio-political situation that surrounds the life of Muslim society in Jombang has not provoked extreme antagonism between Muslim groups. There has been no significant conflict between the traditionalist and modernist Islamic groups in present day Jombang. This situation is supported by the fact that the number of followers on both sides is not comparable. The traditionalist followers constitute half of the Muslim population in Jombang, while the modernists only exist in a few districts as a minority. The rest are *abangan* and others.

The discordant situation based on different ideological understandings has declined significantly, although each Islamic group retains a cynical attitude deriving from such differences which are expressed in everyday life. The *pengajian* (religious teaching) is a common forum used by Islamic groups to criticise or even humiliate others. In one *pengajian* session, for example, I noticed that a Muhammadiyah leader in his speech criticised a certain group of Islam for persisting in doing what he called a blind *taqlid*, that is following a *madhhab*

---

[21] In the past the different background of Islamic groups could mean everything. Those who come from an NU background do not like any achievement of Muhammadiyah figures, and vice versa. Such a feeling has declined significantly among Muslims in Jombang, especially if such an achievement happens at the national level. Accordingly, NU members would be proud if a person from Jombang became a national figure, no matter which organisation he or she comes from. Muslim groupings in present day Jombang therefore seem to raise no problem, since they have been replaced by a more general categorisation.

(school of Islamic thoughts) without being critical. He suggested that among a certain group of Muslims all texts spoken or written in Arabic are deemed as sacred, whereas the content or meaning of these words might not have any relation to Islam or could even be classified as 'bahasa cinta' (words of love). The failure to understand correctly what comes from religion and what is added to it, in his opinion, is due to people's ignorance (kebodohan, literally stupidity). This criticism was actually made and directed to those Muslims, that is NU members, who due to their tendency to be more religiously minded, are inclined to be uncritical of everything that sounds Arabic.

8.3 Reformulation of Ukhuwa Islamiya

NU's effort to return to being *Jam'iya Islamiya* (lit. an Islamic organisation), a move which marked the defeat of Islamic politics[22], has produced a favourable situation for the emergence of a new consciousness among members of the necessity to work on Islamic development generally rather than becoming involved in politics. The consciousness has also pushed them to reevaluate the nature of their relationship with other Muslim groups. They try to have recourse to the source which they usually used, that is Islam itself, by revaluing the concept of *ukhuwa Islamiya* (Muslim Brotherhood). This new consciousness has brought them to the notion that the ideological differences between various Islamic groups should be put aside.

Previously in Jombang, as I have noted, the conflict between various Islamic groups was not as sharp as in other cities. Nevertheless, it was a common phenomenon, especially during the 1950s and the 1960s. In the opinion of a Muhammadiyah leader in Ngoro, Azhar, it was rare and almost impossible for NU members previously to sit together with Muhammadiyah members in a *pengajian*. This was due to the negative attitude of NU members towards Muhammadiyah. He further said that a few NU members even regarded Muhammadiyah as *kafir*. During the period of communist killing, according to Azhar[23], one *kiai* suggested that "setelah menyembelih PKI, ya menyembelih Muhammadiyah" (lit. after killing communists, the second step is to kill Muhammadiyah). Azhar nevertheless realised that the attitude of NU members towards his organisation is changing. When I asked some Muslim villagers about their perception of a group other than their own, for example, the response was always the same: "mereka sama-sama Islam" (they are all Muslims). This change in consciousness in respect of the relationship between various groups is significant.

Most Muslim figures in Jombang realise that group fanaticism previously marked the relationship between various Muslim groups. According to them, the political

---
[22] See the discussion in Chapter VII.
[23] Interview with Azhar, 20 January 1993.

situation made the relationship between Muslim groups deviate from what is conceptualised by Islam, and politics made the differences between these groups an issue which estranged one group from another. Islam actually provides guidelines on how the relationship between Muslims should be. A precept of the Qur'an states that "verily Muslims are brothers". In a well known hadith it is suggested that "a Muslim relationship's to another is like a building in which all parts are meant to support each other". The relationship between Muslims is conceptualised in what is called *ukhuwa Islamiya*. Each Muslim should treat another Muslim as a brother or sister. The concept of *ukhuwa Islamiya* hence tries to bind Muslims together. As Islam is the underlying factor in this relationship, the emotional factor, arising from being similar in faith, has actually provided Muslims with a large house, that is the *umma* (Muslim society).

The essence of the concept of Muslim brotherhood, according to Kiai Arwani[24], is actually inherent in the acknowledgement of the oneness of Allah. This acknowledgement can juxtapose one Muslim to another, since everything is owned by Allah. Everything done by a Muslim will essentially return to Allah, not to the individual's group or for his own benefit. In practice, the essence of this concept is applied in the life of some Muslims. For example, the concept of *hadiya* (offering prayers for the dead) in the *tarekat* world, according to Arwani, is an expression of such brotherhood, since Muslims in this sense are praying for other Muslims. The application of this concept is thus not limited to living Muslims but can also extend to relations between them and dead Muslims. It is very common for a *tarekat* member to offer a *hadiya* for his brother or another Muslim who has died.

The re-evaluation and application of *ukhuwa Islamiya* in a more appropriate way represents a self critique by Muslims of themselves after they experienced and acknowledged their misconduct in regard to their relationships with each other. One may then ask: what is the attitude of Muslims towards the existence of a number of Islamic organisations, which were in fact the source that gave rise to internal conflict between them. As the *umma* or *ukhuwa Islamiya* would lead to the unification of all Muslim interests for the sake of Islam, the availability of so many Islamic organisations may hinder efforts to reach such a feeling of unity. There is no single answer to this question, since there are a number of variables which should be taken into consideration. One thing that is clear, however, is that the effort to apply the concept of *umma* does not necessarily mean putting Muslims into one big institution. Not only would this be impossible, but it also contradicts the nature of Islam, which acknowledges a variety of Muslim groups either in terms of ethnic differences or differences of interests.

---

[24] Interview with Kiai Arwani, 14 December 1995.

From the interviews which I conducted, it is interesting to note that the majority of respondents disagreed with any effort to merge the various existing Islamic organisations into one. They suggested (71.4 percent) that Islamic organisations "harus dibiarkan apa adanya" (should be kept as they are). There is no need to reduce their number. Those who advocated the formation of a sole organisation for all Muslims in Indonesia accounted for about 13.7 percent. Only 6.0 percent of respondents recommended that the number of other Islamic organisations be reduced and their members be absorbed into the respondents' own organisation (see Table 8.1).

Table 8.1. Percentage of Respondents' Attitude to the Availability of Many Islamic Organisations

Affilation	I	II	III	IV
Muhammadiyah	—	1 (16.7)	4 (66.7)	1 (16.7)
NU	11 (7.5)	19 (13.0)	108 (74.0)	8 (5.5)
Others	—	5 (16.7)	18 (60.0)	7 (23.3)
Total	11 (6.0)	25 (13.7)	130 (71.4)	16 (8.8)

n = 182.
(Source: questionaire).

Explanation of symbols:

I. Should be grouped into my organisation
II. Should be united into one organisation
III. Should be kept as they are
IV. Do not know

The change in the perception of NU members about other Muslim groups, particularly Muhammadiyah, can be attributed to the change in attitude of NU's *da'i* (preacher). There are two points I would like to highlight here. The first relates to the Muslim idea of Islam. The second relates to the relationship between the various groups, or more specifically, to the Muslims' perception of each other. If NU has changed from being political to being cultural, such a change in village life is marked by the intensification of *da'wa*. In the opinion of one *kiai*, politics is only one among several means to promote or spread Islam. Muslims are now trying to mould society's religiosity not through politics but rather by increasing society's awareness through *da'wa*.

Thus some Muslim leaders and *kiai* who have long seen the process of Islamisation by the state and by society as an inseparable effort, are inclined to choose society as their means of Islamisation rather than the power structure and political authority (Abdullah, 1988:17). It seems that *kiai* within NU now focus on managing education and spreading Islam generally rather than being involved in practical politics. This phenomenon is significant compared to that which existed during the 1950s when the idea of the Islamic state was so prevalent among Muslims. This phenomenon at least indicates that the number of Muslims pursuing the idea of an Islamic state or stressing everything by relating it to Islam, such as the application of Islamic law, has decreased. It is interesting to note that when I asked some respondents what the ideal form of society was, a large number did not refer to the application of Islamic principles. In contrast, they chose other options. From my survey of 182 respondents in four villages of Jombang, only 32.4 percent preferred to have Islamic law applied in society. About 26.9 percent of respondents chose to have a prosperous society, while around 17.0 percent suggested that they wanted their society to live morally (see Table 8.2).

Table 8.2. Percentage of Respondents' Perspective of the Ideal Society

1. Prosperous society	26.9
2. Moralistic society	17.0
3. Society applying Islamic law	32.4
4. Society in which worldly and religious life are in balance	9.9
5. Safe and harmonious society	5.5
6. Do not know	8.2

(Source: questionnaire)

Although the proportion of respondents who wanted to see the application of Islamic law is larger than any other single preference, it still only accounts for one third of all respondents. These findings indicate that the respondents are attempting to find a balance between religious matters and prosperity in their lives. The existence of *pesantren*, which emphasise the need to strengthen religiosity, on the one hand, and the invasion of the inevitable modernisation process on the other, have influenced respondents' perception of what a good society is. In one respondent's view, the ideal society is not only one which is affluent but one which is also religious.

The change in the attitude of Muslims of various organisations in Jombang about their inter-relationships cannot be separated from the change in perspective among the elites of Muhammadiyah and NU at the national level. The national Muhammadiyah and NU leaders, for example, held a joint conference to discuss their problems and to try to reach mutual understanding. Some of the leaders of both Muhammadiyah and NU even proposed that these organisations should provide the same identity cards for their members.

Although this change in attitude among Muslims in Jombang has occurred most importantly at the elite level of each Muslim organisation, it has also led to similar changes at the grassroots level. The effort of reformulating the concept of *ukhuwa* (brotherhood), for example, has not only warranted attention from the general Muslim population in Jombang, but has also affected daily behaviour, including the attitude of NU members towards marrying their children to members of other Muslim groups. I collected data related to marriage because of its widespread importance. Socially, intermarriage between Muslim groups can trigger changes in other aspects of their relations. For example, intermarriage between Muslim groups can reduce feelings of mutual mistrust or prejudice and can lead to better relationships in general. Previously intermarriage was a great issue among Muslims in Jombang.

The data I collected indicate that the unwillingness of NU members to marry with a member of the modernist group, Muhammadiyah, has declined significantly. Although the data only relate to attitudes, it is not rare to find members with an NU family background in Jombang married to members of Muhammadiyah. Only a small number of respondents remained uneasy about intermarriage. A common reason underlying this minority view revolves around the worry of being influenced by Muhammadiyah religious thoughts and practices. From Table 8.3 we can see that only a small percentage of respondents mentioned their dislike of intermarriage between Muslims of various groups (14.3 percent). About 82.9 percent respondents with NU background agreed with intermarriage; while 15.8 percent disapproved of such intermarriage.

Table 8.3. Perception of Intermarriage Between Members of Various Muslim Groups

	All Right	Do not like	No Answer
NU	121 (82.9)	23 (15.8)	2 (1.4)
Others	31 (86.1)	3 (8.3)	2 (5.6)
Total	152 (83.5)	26 (14.3)	4 (2.2)

n = 182

(Source: questionnaire)

This change in attitude, especially among NU members, may create a favourable situation for the development of Islam in Jombang in the future. Most NU respondents in present day Jombang do not see Muhammadiyah as a threat but as a partner in the obligation to develop Islam. Their acceptance of intermarriage indicates that they acknowledge that their difference with other groups is a matter of different Islamic practice and that the interpretation of Islam can vary from one group to another. It is hence feasible for various Islamic practices to be performed in one Muslim family. The wife may follow NU's practice of Islam, while her husband can follow Muhammadiyah practice. Masyhuri, an NU respondent, told me that he had a new member in his big family, who was Muhammadiyah in background. In his opinion, this did not raise any problem since all members of the family, including the new one, had a mutual understanding of their different practice of Islam.

Table 8.4. Reasons to Accept and Refuse Intermarriage

	I	II	III	IV
All Right	135 (88.8)	8 (5.3)	—	9 (5.9)
Don't Like	—	—	23 (88.5)	3 (11.5)

n = 178

(Source: questionnaire)

Explanation of Symbols:

I.   They are Muslims
II. Human right
III. Worried about adverse influence
IV. No reason

Despite this positive tendency, many respondents still prefer to marry their children to people from the same Islamic organisation as themselves. Religious reasons are dominant in sustaining this preference. In the respondents' opinion, other people's religious background, as expressed through their affiliation with certain Islamic groups, is an important factor when considering whether to accept someone as a member of the family. This preference is understandable. Most people still think that their practices of Islam are the best compared to those of other groups, though this no longer necessarily involves disparaging the latter.

Table 8.5. Percentage of Respondents' Preference as Marriage Partner for their Children

Background	Preference of NU background of the partner		
	First choice	The 2nd choice	No answer
1. NU	105 (71.9)	3 (2.1)	38 (26.0)
2. Others	15 (41.7)	5 (13.8)	16 (44.4)

n = 182

(Source: questionnaire)

Of the 120 respondents who chose NU members as their first preference as marriage partners for their children, 105 of them are affiliated with NU. This means that around 71.9 percent of the total number of NU respondents preferred to have their children married to people with NU family background. Only 3 respondents with NU background chose members of another Islamic organisation as their preferred choice of marriage partner for their children. They chose Muhammadiyah. The same pattern holds true of Muhammadiyah respondents. Most preferred people with Muhammadiyah background for their children. Of the various Islamic organisations in Jombang, the majority of respondents with NU background chose Muhammadiyah members as their second choice[25].

8.4 Expanding Da'wa

Since there is no longer any real problem in regard to the relationship between the various Muslim groups in Jombang, as illustrated by their willingness to strengthen the *ukhuwa Islamiya*, the major effort of Muslims in Jombang is hence focused on moulding people's religiosity by extending *da'wa* activities. While the *da'wa* has traditionally been performed among the devout Muslims, in present day Jombang it is also conducted among the less devout. For NU activists, such extensions of *da'wa* are a realisation of the policy of 'back to khittah'. With this policy NU is not only trying to accelerate its program of education and *da'wa* among its members, but also to extend such effort to the less devout.

The pattern of *da'wa* (preaching) carried out by Islamic leaders or *da'i* (preacher) in Jombang has changed. Some *da'wa* are planned by Islamic organisations, but such *da'wa* do not touch on the existing socio-cultural life of the less devout society in any radical way. The *da'wa* is merely a medium to deliver Islamic messages. In Ngepeh village which used to be a communist village in Ngoro district, the *pengajian* movements organised by the *Muslimat* (female NU organisation) and *alhidayah* (a government sponsored institution) are established on a family basis. These *pengajian* move from house to house every fortnight. Similar *pengajian* are found in other districts. They are a breakthrough which not only indicates the increased interest of Muslims in giving *da'wa*, but also a change in the relationship between various Islamic groups[26]. This pattern of *da'wa* will not only prevent open conflict, derived from group exclusivism, but will also introduce new values that are properly pious from an Islamic perspective.

Factors contributing to the success of such *da'wa* include the persuasive nature of the *da'wa* conducted by *kiai* and other *da'i* in Jombang, and the current culture of the *kiai* and their practice of Islam. There is no significant conflict with or refusal of such *da'wa* on the part of the less devout. The adaptive nature of Jombang's NU society has made the *da'wa* of its *kiai* acceptable. The *kiai*, for example, does not prohibit the practice of *slametan*. This is not only because NU has a similar practice but also because there is clearly some Islamic influence

---

[25] The respondents were asked to rank preferred organisational background of people with whom their children would marry. There are five Islamic organisations I asked the respondents to choose, that is NU, Muhammadiyah, SI, MI and LDII.

[26] I was told by an informant that during the 1950s relations between the devout and the less devout or *abangan* in Ngoro were terrible. His mother was always worried any time she had to go to the market. The mother, who was a devout Muslim, had to pass through the *abangan* village when she went to the market. A few *abangan* villagers often disturbed her by pulling down their trousers, and pointing their naked bottoms at her when she passed through their village. The same experience held true with other devout female Muslims.

in the *slametan* practice of the less devout. For the *kiai*, the problem is not how to exclude such a syncretic practice from his *da'wa*, but rather how to incorporate it and colour it with Islam.

It is commonly understood that *da'wa* should be conducted in a very smooth way. *Da'wa* should not confront or criticise other groups. According to one *pesantren* leader[27], such *da'wa* is in line with what is ordered by Islam. In his view, the existence of pluralistic Islamic groupings in Indonesia should be properly understood. Such groupings should be accepted in the context of the different understanding of Islam itself held by various segments of the Islamic community. Islam in Indonesia, he said further, varies in terms of its practice of *'ibada* and of the religious quality of its adherents. The level of devoutness is hence just a nuance or a degree of the quality of belief that can be attained by any Muslim. The difference between the devout and the less devout is therefore a matter of quality; it does not touch on the theological domain. This *kiai* asked his colleagues to delete terms or jargon such as *abangan* which can split the *umma*. He mentioned several misconceptions regarding the concept of *abangan*. Not only is such a concept politically disadvantageous for the unity of the Islamic community, but also the content or meaning of this concept is misleading, since it has been distorted for political ends[28].

The same strategy has been adopted by other Islamic organisations. Muhammadiyah has changed its pattern of *da'wa* among Muslims in Jombang, especially among the less devout. Muhammadiyah, with its idea of purification, has traditionally tried to cut off or cleanse Islam from traditions adopted by the less devout (*abangan*). It typically applies a concept of *bid'a*, which basically rejects religious beliefs such as practised by the *abangan*. But with its efforts to be more accommodating to the existing culture, it has tried to be less radical in its *da'wa* among the *abangan*. Muhammadiyah in Jombang is gradually gaining new members from among former *abangan*. A young Muhammadiyah activist in Ngoro suggested that the change in strategy to be more accommodating to

---

[27] From the opening address by Hajj Yusuf Hasyim, the leader of *Pesantren Tebuireng*, in accordance with NU's *bahsul masa 'il* (discussion on religious problem) held in Tebuireng, 12 January 1993.

[28] Hajj Yusuf Hasyim further suggested that to relate political affiliation to the quality of one's religiosity could be misleading. He here is referring to a categorisation of Javanese political affiliation based on religiosity as conceptualised by Geertz (1965) and Feith (1970). These scholars suggest that those who were affiliated with the PNI (Indonesian National Party) or the communist party were *abangan*, while those who were affiliated with NU or Masjumi were *santri*. Hajj Yusuf Hasyim gave the example about Subandrio, former Minister of Foreign Affairs in the Soekarno government, whom he knows well. In his opinion, Subandrio is a good Muslim. Based on a story which was told by Subandrio himself, Hajj Yusuf Hasyim jokingly stated that not one of NU's *kiai* would as be as devout as Subandrio in regard to *'ibada*. Subandrio at that time was in prison. He was said to perform *tahajjud* (midnight prayer) very often. So Hajj Yusuf Hasyim questioned whether Subandrio could be subsumed among the *abangan* because he was not affiliated with an Islamic party. In his opinion, one's Muslimness, therefore, cannot be reduced to or determined by one's affiliation with any political party. His attitude as expressed here is political. He is eager to promote the same perception that Muslims are not divided due to their various practices of Islam.

the existing socio-cultural situation is a necessity if Muhammadiyah wants to be accepted by Jombang society. He conducted a door-to-door *da'wa* encouraging the people around his neighbourhood (who are mostly *abangan*) to attend *pengajian* and practise Islam in their daily lives without promoting his Muhammadiyah message. He avoided the criticisms commonly made by a few NU *da'i* which impinge on the *abangan's* way of life. He helped the poor and sick *abangan* who could not afford medical treatment by asking Muhammadiyah clinics in his district to give free medical treatment.

The accommodative nature of Muhammadiyah *da'wa* in Ngoro district has resulted in the sympathetic acceptance of the *abangan* who attend its *pengajian*. In a Muhammadiyah *pengajian*, I was initially surprised when I met my young neighbour in Ngoro. I was surprised because I knew that in his daily life this young Javanese was *abangan* in character. He organised cock fights, and on certain occasions, such as the festival for commemorating Indonesian independence, he was assigned to be one of the committee members of the 'Jaran Kepang' performance (a Javanese performing art). When I asked him why he attended Muhammadiyah's *pengajian*, he told me that the Muhammadiyah *da'i* focused more on what Islam is and what Muslims should do to face the future rather than criticising the Javanese way of life. He noted further that some NU *da'i* often made criticisms which impinged on ethical problems of Javanese daily life, such as going to the toilet and other matters. This was offending to him in many respects.

It is clear that the effort of *da'wa* of various Islamic organisations and the change in their attitude towards the less devout has resulted in a change in their religiosity. At least the younger generation of the less devout Muslims in Jombang differ from their parents in their view of Islam and the devout society in general. A number of important factors have contributed to this change. One already discussed is the *da'wa* program carried out effectively by various Islamic organisations. Another relates to changes in the process of primary socialisation among children in general in Jombang. An increasing focus on Islam and a growing identification with it as a social entity has followed the establishment of Islamic schools in a large number of villages in Jombang. In Puton and Bareng, two villages which had no mosque during the 1960s, there are now *madrasa* (Islamic educational institutions) which provide Islamic teaching at primary school level. In villages that are located very close to capital district towns, there are Islamic kindergarden or pre-school programs. This level of Islamic education is called "Taman Pendidikan al-Qur'an" (TPA, Qur'anic Education of Kindergarten) which provides formal lessons in the recitation of the Qur'an[29].

---

[29] I have to differentiate between this kind of formal education and me-*ngaji*. Me-*ngaji* is a traditional system of education in reciting the Qur'an which is conducted informally. Children usually come to a *guru* (teacher) to learn Qur'anic recitation. Me-*ngaji* sessions are usually conducted after *magrib prayer*, around 7 pm. In contrast, Qur'an Education in Kindergarten is held during school hours, usually in the

In Puton and Bareng, such schools are attended by children whose parents are less devout or *abangan* in background. Moreover, the introduction of Islamic norms and values is not restricted to *madrasa* or TPA and *pesantren* in general but also occurs in public school, since in the latter Islam is also taught as a subject. For those children who continue their education to a higher level, their introduction to Islam is more extensive, since in most big cities and campuses in Java, Islam is obviously taught and practised by students in their daily lives. The students who then return to their villages introduce these new ideas and Islamic concepts which they have obtained from their period of living in a more urbanised situation. In Bareng, for example, there is a young man who is studying at Brawijaya University in Malang. He has been organising a *pengajian* group among his friends in Bareng, although his parents are of *abangan* background.

It is therefore not surprising that a change in religiosity is occurring among villagers in Jombang. Even if this cannot be subsumed under 'Islamic reassertion', it certainly marks a decrease of *abangan* practice in general. 'Upacara adat' (traditional ceremony), for example, is only preserved by the older generation of villagers. Only this generation acknowledge the meaning of such ceremonies. The younger generation, who have been socialised into popular culture, are not interested in understanding such religious practices. In Puton, for example, it is difficult to find anyone who can lead an 'adat ceremony', a situation which leads to less qualified people occupying the religious position of *tukang ujub* (local term for an expert to lead the traditional religious ceremony). Formely in Puton, *tukang ujub* consituted a specialist in the various types of expertise in the religious domain. In contrast to a *modin*, a government promoted religious position which functioned to carry out Islamic rituals, *tukang ujub* specialised in leading religious rituals which were more traditional or Javanese in character. When a person in Puton intended to hold a wedding ceremony, he would ask a *modin* to conduct it. However, in the case of a *slametan* ritual, such as 'hajat bumi' (lit. rituals to have good soil), he would invite the *tukang ujub* to conduct the ritual. The shortage of experts in the domain of *adat* (lit. tradition) in present day Puton has resulted in a changed pattern for the *adat* ceremony itself. This situation has also resulted in a former *santri* occupying the *tukang ujub* position. This promotion occurred because this former *santri* was the only person who was expert in ritual practices. It is therefore not surprising to find a ritual such as *slametan*, which was *abangan* in character now furnished with more *santri* symbols.

In brief, there is an expansion and intensification of *da'wa* program promoted by Muslims in Jombang. Various Muslim groups despite their differences carried out this program and expand it to reach what was commonly called the *abangan*

---

morning. *Pengajian*, although it literally has the same meaning as me-*ngaji*, refers to a religious gathering and sermon among older Muslims.

society. Thus there is a process of Islamic reassertion among the *abangan* villages which marks not only the success of the NU program of 'back to khittah' but also the Muslim program in general in introducing Islam. As the *kiai* is the guardian of the Islamic society in villages in Java, the expansion of Islamic influence among the *abangan* means also the expansion of the *kiai* influence. In other words, the *da'wa* program is a means to remould the *kiai* leadership after they experienced a decline in their political influence.

Chapter 9: Conclusion

There are two formal institutions through which the *kiai's* relationship with society is established. These institutions have simultaneously created two different patterns of relationship; and they constitute important avenues which sustain the *kiaiship* in Java. The two institutions are *pesantren* and *tarekat*. Although the *pesantren* and the *tarekat* constitute two important institutions associated with *kiaiship*, each of them has its own character. In addition, there exists variation and nuances that differentiate one *pesantren* or *tarekat* from another.

The *pesantren* in Jombang are not stereotypical. In addition to the traditional *pesantren*, there are some modern *pesantren* as far as their educational system is concerned. The large *pesantren* in Jombang constitute modern educational institutions with little of their traditional character remaining. In the *tarekat*, emerging variation is marked by an increasing number of *aliran* (factions), each of which has different ritual practices. Both the *pesantren* and the *tarekat* are led by *kiai*. The *pesantren* and *tarekat* worlds in Indonesia are associated with NU society. They are, however, not structurally established within the NU organisation. They are culturally recognised as associated with NU because the *kiai* of the *pesantren* and of the *tarekat* are members of NU. Since NU has two (informal) affiliated institutions, the *pesantren* and the *tarekat*, we can infer that within NU there exist various sub-cultures, each of which differs from others in many respects. Although all of these institutions remain under the umbrella of NU, their differences are indicated through the attitudes and behaviour displayed by their followers.

As the roles of the *pesantren* and the *tarekat* are so dominant in the life of some NU members in Jombang, their allegiance is given to the *pesantren* and the *tarekat* rather than to NU itself. This means that NU's strength, in practice, lies in its sub-institutions. To put it another way, the strength of NU leadership has been established and centred on the leadership of the *kiai* in these two institutions. Popular emotional attachment towards NU has for a long time been built through the *pesantren* and *tarekat*. It is the *kiai*, as leaders of *pesantren* or *tarekat* who, due to their closeness to local society, have established an ideological commitment among NU members and related them to NU as an organisation. In other words, it is the *kiai* who run *pesantren* or lead *tarekat*, not NU itself, who have mass followers identified as NU members.

There are several main points which arise from my discussion in regard to *kiai* leadership in Jombang. Firstly the relationship between the *kiai* and his society is extremely strong, marking a special characteristic of Muslim lives in Jombang. The *kiai* occupy a highly respected position in this society. This is because

Muslims in Jombang have a society which has been moulded by the existence of so many *pesantren*. The *kiai's* knowledge of Islam is hence an important factor which makes him a respected person in his society. Compared to that of the *pesantren kiai*, however, the relationship between the *tarekat kiai* and their followers is stronger. The emotional attachment, imbued with religious overtones, is more clearly expressed. The *murshid* in the *tarekat*, who is seen as a spiritual guide who would bring those individuals involved in the *tarekat* closer to Allah, is very decisive in establishing this relationship. That is why the influence of the *murshid* in the *tarekat* is so strong, enabling the *murshid* and his *khalifa* to build a cohesive community held together by the same emotion. Certain members of society hope that they can receive *baraka* by getting in touch with the *kiai*. It is commonly believed that *baraka* flows from the hand of the *kiai*.

However, each *kiai*, as an informal Islamic leader, is independent from another. Thus conflicts which may arise from the *kiai's* different political views can lead to indirect conflict between their followers. This conflict, which does not usually impinge on the ideological domain, actually constitutes an expression of the tension among the *kiai* as leaders of *pesantren* or of *tarekat*. The conflict which emerged in the *Tarekat Qadiriyah Wa Naqsyabandiyah* when its leader joined the government party is a good example. This conflict demonstrated the power of the *kiai* in influencing Muslims in Jombang. Kiai Musta'in, the leader of the *Tarekat Qadiriyah Wa Naqsyabandiyah* and the national leader of the *Jam'iyah Ahli Thoriqoh Al-Mu'tabaroh*, was abandoned by a large number of his followers who left him to follow other *kiai*. This case indicated that the authority of even a greatly admired *kiai* to influence society is limited. The *kiai* who held a different political opinion at that time left their colleague, Kiai Musta'in, and tried to establish another *tarekat* from the one that he led. Followers who left Kiai Musta'in joined the new *tarekat* led by these *kiai*. Another example of the independent authority of a single *kiai* was the conflict which followed the introduction of free political affiliation after NU launched its 'back to khittah' policy. The *kiai* in Jombang split into three groups, followed by their followers or sympathisers. In addition, these conflicts also indicate that NU as an organisation in Jombang does not have a monopoly of power. In certain cases it might be powerless, since the existing power is spread among the *kiai* running the *pesantren* or heading the *tarekat*. Such dispersion of power indicates the fragility of the social structure in NU society. This structure can easily incur social tension, or even lead to conflict, when the different attitudes held by the *kiai* of the various *pesantren*, the *kiai* of the *tarekat*, or differences between the *kiai* of the *pesantren* and the *tarekat*, cannot be reconciled.

Secondly, Islam in Jombang was, and to a certain extent still is, embedded in the life of its society. This is a result of long established *pesantren* there. The *kiai* through their *pesantren* had an important role in inculcating Islamic values and norms into the lives of Muslims in Jombang. This was so, not only because the *kiai* were informal charismatic leaders in Indonesian society, but also because they were committed to the formation of a society characterised by Islam. In other words, the institutionalisation of Islamic values was made possible by the contribution of the *kiai*. Through their informal leadership role, the *kiai* made society more religious, as conceptualised by Islam, in all aspects of life. The *kiai*, as a group, tried to make the existing social order compatible with religious ideals or to nativise these religious ideals to be compatible with the existing order. The religious requirements which the *kiai* believes in have created ideals which he must strive to realise, for, as Geertz (1965) suggests, those who accept religion as their ultimate source of authority are obliged to bring their worldly experiences into harmony with the world symbolised in religious behaviour.

The success of the *kiai* in inculcating Islamic values owes much to the fact that their leadership is different from other formal and informal leaders in Indonesia. With a charismatic pattern of leadership, the *kiai* form good, close relationships with their followers, a situation which cannot be created by other leaders. Especially in the *tarekat*, the relationship can be described as a 'guru-murid' (master-student) relationship, or more theoretically, clientilism, in which subordination of the clients is a necessity.

Finally, Muslims in Jombang have access to the wider socio-political life of the nation, since they have for a long time included figures with a national reputation. Some *kiai* from Jombang have been national leaders of NU and of PPP, which placed them among the national political elite. It is understandable that the vicissitudes of national politics have often been felt by Muslims in Jombang. In addition, any political conflict among Muslim figures or groups at the national level has also been followed by conflict between various related groups in Jombang. The conflict within the NU faction in the PPP national leadership which occurred at the end of the 1980s is the most obvious example. This conflict gave rise to conflict among *kiai* in Jombang. Two leaderships positions appeared in NU, and Muslims at the grassroots level split according to the line taken as a result of their *kiai's* different political attitudes.

There are some interesting points which need to be presented here in relation to the *kiai's* political leadership among Muslims in Jombang. Muslims in Jombang exhibit a strong Islamic attitude in relation to their political performance. The close attachment of Muslims to the Islamic political party was not merely because Islam was embedded in their lives but can also be attributed to and influenced by the *kiai's* continued support for the Islamic party. The *kiai*, as persons who had great concern about Islam, tried to established what was called 'Islamic politics'. The convergence between the Muslim tendency to support the Islamic party and the *kiai's* support for it was an important factor which contributed to the popularity of the Islamic party in the eyes of Muslims in the core *kecamatan* in Jombang. This was evidenced by the fact that in this core the Islamic parties took the lead in the 1971 general election. For example, although it did not represent a majority, the Islamic parties received more that 40 percent of the vote in nine out of 17 *kecamatan* in Jombang. In five *kecamatan*, they received more than 50 percent. This figure continued at nearly the same level in following general elections until the 1987 general election when PPP's share of the vote declined significantly in almost all *kecamatan*.

The *kiai* leadership in Jombang is, however, changing. The change derives particularly from the changing situation in relation to *pesantren* education. The *pesantren* have been transformed by establishing a schooling system that has created a *santri* society which is more modern in character. The same holds true in the wider society in Jombang since the Muslim population is readily influenced by the inevitable change occurring in society at large. These changes in the *pesantren* and in Muslim society in Jombang have impacted on the leadership of the *kiai* in general. There emerges a process of profanisation of charisma. By profanisation I mean that the *kiai's* charisma, which gives them a respected social position in their society, has become less influential. The *santri* demonstration that occurred in *Pesantren Darul Ulum* is an obvious example. A similar event also occurred in *Pesantren Tebuireng*. Such demonstrations would have previously been unthinkable in the world of *pesantren*. It needs to be underlined, however, that this change in regard to *kiai* leadership, as a result of changes in society, has been gradual, since the change in the society itself has been partial, in the sense that it has happened mainly among the younger Muslims, such as the students of the *Universitas Darul Ulum*.

The change in the *kiai* political leadership began when NU launched its 'back to khittah' policy. This change in the *kiai's* politics gave rise to the change in the position of Islamic politics. The *kiai* who introduced the religious obligation on Muslims in regard to politics cancelled this injunction when they freed politics from any religious involvement. Thus despite the external factors which contributed to the decline in political Islam in Jombang, such as the introduction of 'Azas Tunggal' by the government, by which Islam was no longer an ideology for any political party, the change in the *kiai's* politics was actually a decisive factor. The political attitude of the few *kiai* who became affiliated with Golkar gave rise to various political affiliations among devout Muslims in Jombang. As the *kiai* through NU's 'back to khittah' freed themselves and Muslims in general from affiliation with a particular political party, their politics has given rise not only to the emergence of various political orientations among devout Muslims but has also resulted in a redirection decline in Islamic politics and in the *kiai's* political influence as well. It is not surprising that in almost all cases, the politics of individual *kiai'* were not followed by all their followers. While some followers of the *kiai* who have supported Golkar since 1987 copied their lead, others continued to support PPP. In the same way, although a large number of followers of individual *kiai* who supported PPP have continued to support this party, a few of them have deviated from their *kiai* by joining Golkar. These facts indicate that an individual *kiai's* political lead is not necessarily followed by all his followers. To put it differently, in present day Jombang, following the *kiai's* political example is not an absolute obligation for all Muslims. Not only is there no longer a convergence between Muslim ideas of politics and that of the *kiai*, there is also no longer a moral obligation in regard to politics.

Looking at this change in regard to *kiai* political leadership in Jombang, we can assume that a similar pattern has occurred in other regions of Indonesia. As the embeddedness of Islam in the life of Muslims and their politics is not a characteristic solely applicable to Jombang, the change in political Islam brought about by either the introduction of 'Azas Tunggal' or by the change in *kiai* politics has generally affected Muslim politics in other regions. The pattern of local conflict which has occurred in Jombang may also have occurred in other regions. A pattern of *kiai* leadership similar to that in Jombang is also found in other regions. One can therefore infer that a change in the pattern of political leadership is also occurring in other regions, especially in East Java.

It is interesting to note that although the change in Islamic politics in general actually marks an apparent decline in Indonesian Muslim politics, the conflict of NU members with those of other components in PPP has enabled NU leaders and the *kiai* in general to rethink the principle of the 'struggle for Islam'. The 'back to khittah', which essentially pushes *kiai* and NU leaders to focus on developing NU society's religiosity, has encouraged NU *kiai* not just to be politically oriented. They focus now on expanding their *da'wa* activities and developing their Islamic educational programs. This means that their efforts can be directed to the benefit of Islamic society in general. This tendency has had an impact on improving the relationship of NU members with members of other Islamic groups. The ideological line which demarcated various Muslim groups became blurred after NU's involvement in politics was altered.

The efforts not to be politically oriented has benefited the NU society at the grassroots, because *kiai* can now focus their attention more on developing society, and has consolidated the *kiai's* position in their society. The conflict in PPP highlighted the *kiai's* changing political position, as expressed by the decrease of NU influence in this party. NU's return to being a socio-religious organisation can thus be seen as an effort to retain a position for *kiai* in the society. This means that although the *kiai's* position in the formal electoral process is less influential since they have offered Muslims an open political orientation and affiliation, through 'back to khittah' the *kiai* have consolidated and restrengthened their moral position. Furthermore, this restrengthening of their moral position means also restrengthening their political position in a wider context, since by retaining their moral position the *kiai* retain their position as the leading figures in Javanese Muslim society.

The efforts of not being politically oriented received support especially from a large part of NU's younger generation. Nevertheless, a number of NU *kiai* in Jombang and Java in general tried to revive the old paradigm which encouraged NU to be involved in politics after almost a decade of NU's 'back to khittah' policy. The enthusiasm of these *kiai* in politics was expressed by their eagerness to seize the position of President in the PPP national leadership. They held a meeting in a *pesantren* in Rembang, East Java, preceding the PPP congress in the second half of the 1994s. This indicated not only their inclination to be politically oriented as shown by their being continuously active in PPP but also their efforts to bring NU's flag into PPP. Thus despite the formal NU decision not to be politically oriented, the old perspective of a close relationship between Islam and politics or, in a more precise words, of using politics as a means of struggling for Islam remains strong among *kiai*.

Having two distinct political orientations among its members, one can speculate that for the near future the NU's *kiai* will remain important figures. They will play an important role socially and politically. This is because Muslims' willingness to regard the *kiai* as the guardians of the morality of society will continue their dependence on *kiai* legitimation. It is not surprising that the government, for example, will also continue to seek the *kiai's* legitimation for the acceptance of sensitive and crucial policy. Thus the success of *kiai* efforts in introducing an open political orientation, which led to the decrease in their political influence as shown by the changing pattern of electoral behaviour, does not necessarily mean a loss of *kiai* influence in society. Instead, it gave a chance for the *kiai* to consolidate and strengthen their position in society. As 'back to khittah' has enabled NU members to be affiliated with any political party, it means also that the *kiai's* influence is not confined to members of the former Islamic party but also includes those in Golkar and PDI.

Bibliography

Abdullah, Taufik ed. 1983 *Agama dan perubahan Social*. Jakarta : Rajawali Press.

Abdullah, Taufik ed. 1988 *Laporan Pandangan Hidup Ulama Indonesia*. Jakarta : IPSK LIPI.

Ahmed, A.S. 1976 *Millenium and Charisma Among Pathans: A Critical Essay in Social Anthropology*. London, Boston : Routledge & Kegan Paul.

Alfian 1989 *Muhammadiyah: The Political Behavior of a Muslim Modernist Organisation Under Dutch Colonialism*. Yogyakarta : Gadjah Mada University Press.

Ali, Fachry 1994a *How State Comes to the People?: the Acehnese and the New Order State*. A Paper presented at the Indonesian Study group, Research School of Pacific and Asian Studies, ANU, Canberra, 8 June 1994.

Ali, Fachry 1994b *Keharusan Demokratisasi dalam Islam di Indonesia*. A paper presented at a seminar held in LIPI by Majelis Sinergi Kalam, ICMI, Jakarta.

Almond, G. 1978 *Kelompok Kepentingan dan Partai Politik*. In Masud, Mochtar and Mc Andrew, Collin *Perbandingan System Politik*. Yogyakarta : Gadjahmada University Press.

Anderson, B. and Kahin, Andrey 1982 *Interpreting Indonesian Politics: Thirteen Contribution to the Debate*. Ithaca : Cornell Modern Indonesian Project.

Anonymous 1983 *Pedoman Pokok-Pokok Ajaran Wahidiyah*. Kediri : Penyiar Sholawat Wahidiyah Pusar.

Anonymous 1992 *Buku Informasi Pondok Pesantren Al-Lathifiyyah, BU Tambakberas, Jombang*. Jombang : Pondok Pesantren Al-Lathifiyyah.

Arifin, Imron 1993 *Kepemimpinan Kyai: Kasus Pondok Pesantren Tebuireng*. Malang : Kalimasahada Press.

As'ad, M.Z. Widjaja 1991 *Elit Agama dan Massa Pemilih dalam Perspektif Budaya Politik*. Unpublished MA thesis, Gadjahmada University, Yogyakarta.

Barness, Douglas F. 1978 "Charisma and Religious Leadership: An Historical Analysis", *Journal of the Scientific Study of Religion*, 17(1): 1–18.

Barton, Greg and Fealy, Greg ed. (1996, forthcoming) *Nahdlatul Ulama, Traditional Islam and Modernity in Indonesia*. Centre of Southeast Asian Studies, Monash University.

Berger, Peter L. 1963 "Charisma and Religious Innovation: The Social Location of Israelite Prophecy", *American Sociological Review*, 28(6): 940–950.

Berger, Peter L. 1985 *Sosiology Ditafsirkan Kembali*. Jakarta : LP3ES.

Binder, Leonard 1959 "Islamic Tradition and Politics: The Kyai and the Alim", *Comparative Study in Society and History*, (2): 250–256.

Bruinessen, Martin van 1994 *NU: Tradisi, Relasi-Relasi Kuasa, Pencarian Wacana baru*. Yogyakarta : Lkis.

Bruinessen, Martin van 1992 *Tarekat Naqsyabandiyah di Indonesia*. Bandung : Mizan.

Bruinessen, Martin van 1995 *Kitab Kuning, Pesantren dan tarekat: Tradisi-Tradisi Islam di Indonesia*. Bandung : Mizan.

Collins, Randall 1985 *Three Sociological Traditions*. New York : Oxford University Press.

Crouch, Harold 1980 "The new Order: The Prospect for Political Stability in Indonesia". In Fox, J.J. ed., *Indonesia: Australian Perspectives*. Canberra : Research School of Pacific Studies.

Dhofier, Zamakhsyari 1980 *The Pesantren Tradition: A Study of the Role of the Kyai in the Maintenance of the Traditional Ideology of Islam in Java*. Ph.D. Thesis, ANU, Canberra .

Dhofier, Zamakhsyari 1982 *Tradisi Pesantren: Studi tentang Pandangan Hidup Kyai*. Jakarta : LP3ES.

Echols, J.M. and Shadily, Hassan 1975 *An English Indonesian Dictionary*. Ithaca, London : Cornell University Press.

Eickelman, Dale F 1976 *Morrocan Islam: Tradition and Society in a Pilgrimage Center*. Austin and London : University of Texas Press.

Eickelman, Dale F and Piscatori, J. 1990 "Social Theory in the Study of Muslim Societies". In Eickelman, Dale F and Piscatori, James ed., *Muslim Travelers: Pilgrimage, Migration, and the Religious Imagination*. London : Routledge.

Emerson, D.K. 1978 *"The Bureaucracy in Political Context: Weakness in Strength"*. In Jackson, Karl D and Pye, Lucian ed., *Political Power and Communication in Indonesia*. Los Angeles : University California Press.

Fathoni, Khoerul and Zen, Muhammad 1992 *NU Pasca Khittah: Prospek Ukhuwwah dengan Muhammadiyah*. Yogyakarta : Media Widya Mandala.

Fealy, Greg (1996, forthcoming) *Entrenching Traditional Islam: A Political History of Nahdlatul Ulama,* – . In Barton, Greg and Greg, Fealy ed. *Nahdlatul Ulama, Traditional Islam and Modernity in Indonesia*. Centre of Southeast Asian Studies, Monash University.

Feith, H. 1970 *"Introduction"*. In Feith and Castle, Lance ed. *Indonesian Political Thinking, 1945–1965*. Ithaca : Cornell University Press.

Fisher, Michael M.J. 1980 *Iran: From Religious Dispute to Revolution.* Cambridge : Harvard University Press.

Fox, James J. 1991 *"Ziarah Visits to the Tombs of the Wali, the Founders of Islam on Java".* In Ricklefs, M.C. *Islam in the Indonesian Context.* Clayton, Victoria : Centre for Southeast Asian Studies, Monash University.

Fox, James J. and Dirjosanjoto, P. 1989 *"The Memories of Village Santri from Jombang in East Java".* In May, R.J. and O'Mallay, William J. ed. *Observing Change in Asia.* Bathurst : Crawford House Press.

Friedrich, Carl J. 1961 "Political Leadership and the Problem of the Charismatic Power", *The Journal of Politics*, No. 1 February: 3–24.

Gaffar, Afan 1992 *Javanese Voters: A Case Study of Election under a Hegemonic Party System.* Yogyakarta : Gadjahmada University Press.

Geertz, Clifford 1960 *The Religion of Java.* Glencoe : The Free Press.

Geertz, Clifford 1959a "The Javanese Kyai: The Changing Role of a Cultural Broker", *Comparative Studies in Society and History*, (2): 250–256.

Geertz, Clifford 1959b *"The Javanese Village".* In Skinner,G. William ed. *Local, Ethnic and National Loyalties in Village Indonesia: A Symposium. Yale University Cultural Report Series*, Southeast Asian Studies.

Geertz, Clifford 1973 *"Religion as a Cultural System".* In *The Interpretation of Culture.* New York : Basic Book.

Geertz, Clifford 1965 *The Social History of an Indonesian Town.* Cambridge, Massachusets : MIT Press.

Gellner, Ernest 1969 *Saints of the Atlas.* London : Weidenfeld and Nicolson.

Gilsenen, Michael 1973 *Saint and Sufi in Modern Egypt: An Essay in the Sociology of Religion. Oxford Monograph on Social Anthropology.*

Guinness, Patrick 1986 *Harmony and Hierarchy in a Javanese Kampung.* Singapore : Oxford University Press.

Haidar, M Ali 1994 *Nahdatul Ulama dan Islam di Indonesia: Pendekatan Fikih dalam Politik.* Jakarta : Gramedia Pustaka Utama.

Hammond, J.L. 1979 *The Politics of Benevolence: Revival Religion and American Voting Behaviour.* Norwood : Ablex Publishing Corporation.

Heijer, Johannes den 1992 *A Guide to Arabic Transliteration: Comparative Transliteration Tables and a List of Selected Arabic Terms Related to Islamic Studies.* Jakarta : INIS.

Hefner, Robert W. 1987 "Islamizing Java?: Religion and Politics in Rural East Java", *The Journal of Asian Studies*, 46(3): 533–553.

Hill, Michael 1973 *A Sociology of Religion.* Hampshire : Avebury.

Hindess, Barry 1989 *Political Choice and Social Structure: An Analysis of Actors, Interests and Rationality*. England : Edward Elgard.

Hisyam, Muhamad 1989 *Perubahan Aspirasi Kemasyarakatan dalam Komunitas Muslim Pedesaan: Kasus Desa Segaralangu Cilacap*. Unpublished MA thesis, Indonesian University, Jakarta.

Hodgson, Marshal G.S. 1974 *The Venture of Islam: Conscience and History in a World Civilization*. Vol. 1 and 2 Chicago : University of Chicago Press.

Horikoshi, H. 1976 *A Traditional Leader in a Time of Change: The Kyai and Ulama in West Java*. Thesis for Degree of Doctor of Philosophy, University of Illinois, Urbana.

Indonesia 1988: An Official Handbook. Jakarta : Ministry of Information.

Informasi Pondok Pesantren Al-Lathifiyyah, Bahrul Ulum, Tambak Beras. Jombang : Pondok Pesantren Al-Lathifiyah.

Jackson, K.D. 1973 *Traditional Authority, Islam and Rebellion*. Berkeley : University of California Press.

Jam'iyah Ahli Thoriqoh Qadiriyah dan Naqsyabandiyah 1992 *Kitab Pembina Moral dalam Rangka Membentuk Manusia Seutuhnya*. Pasuruan : Pesantren At-Taqwa, Cabean Kraton.

Jay, Robert 1963 "Religion and Politics in Rural Java". *Cultural Report Series No. 12*, Southeast Asia Studies, Yale University

Jenkins, D. 1984 *Suharto and His General: Indonesian Military Politics 1975–1983*. Cornell Modern Indonesian Project.

Kantor Statistik Kabupaten Jombang 1992 "Kabupaten Jombang dalam Angkan, 1991".

Kartodirdjo, Sartono 1973 *Protest Movement in Rural Java: A Study of Agrarian Unrest in the Nineteenth and Early Twentieth Century*, Kuala Lumpur : Oxford University Press.

Kartodirdjo, Sartono 1984 *Ratu Adil*. Jakarta : Sinar Harapan.

Lewins, Frank 1977 "Continuity and Change in a Religious Organization: Some Aspects of the Australian Catholic Church", *Journal for the Scientific Study of Religion*, 16(4): 371–382.

Lewins, Frank 1990 *Writing a Thesis: A Guide to its Nature and Organisation*. Canberra : The Faculty of Arts, ANU.

Lewins, Frank 1992 *Social Science Methodology: A Brief But Critical Introduction*. Melbourne : Macmillan Education Australia.

Liddle, W.R. 1978 *Participation and the Political Parties*. In Jackson, Karl D and Pye, Lucian ed. *Political Power and Communication in Indonesia.* Berkeley : University of California Press.

Liddle, W.R. 1978 *Pemilihan Umum 1977: Suatu Tinjauan Umum.* trans. Yogyakarta : Kelompok Study Batas Kota.

Lockwood, David 1956 "Some Remarks on the Social System", *British Journal of Sociology*, 7: 134–146.

Machbub, Badawi *Silsilah dan Riwayat Hidup Al-Maghfurlah/Alm. K.H. Mohammad Adlan Aly, Cukir, Jombang.* Jombang : Tunas Jaya.

Mansurnoor, I. Arifin 1990 *Islam in an Indonesian World: Ulama of Madura.* Yogyakarta : Gadjah Mada University Press.

McVey 1971 "The Post Revolutionary Transformation of the Indonesian Army". *Indonesia*, 11 April: 131–177.

Mochtar, Hilmy 1989 *Dinamika Nahdlatul Ulama: Suatu Study tentang Elite Kekuatan Politik Islam di Jombang Jawa Timur.* Unpublished MA thesis, Gadjahmada University, Yogyakarta .

Mu'thi, Muchtar M. 1992 *Informasi tentang Thoriqoh Shiddiqiyyah.* Jombang : Yayasan Pendidikan Shiddiqiyyah.

Nakamura, Mitsuo 1979 *The Cresent Arises over the Banyan Tree.* Yogyakarta : Gajah Mada Press.

Netton, Ian Richard 1992 *A Popular Dictionary of Islam.* London : Curzon Press.

Oepen, Manfred and Karcher, W. ed. 1988 *The Impact of Pesantren on Education and Community Development in Indonesia.* Proceedings from an International Seminar, Fredrich-Naumann Stiftung, Indonesian Society for Pesantren and Community Development, and Technical University Berlin.

Panitia Pemilihan Daerah Tingkat II Jombang 1987 *Catatan Penghitungan Suara daerah Tingkat II dalam Pemilu 1987.*

Panitia Pemilihan Daerah Tingkat II Jombang 1992 *Catatan Penghitungan Suara Daerah Tingkat II dalam Pemilu 1987.*

Panitia Pemilihan Daerah Tingkat II Jombang 1977 *Daftar Hasil Penghitungan Suara di Kabupaten Jombang.* Jombang .

Partai Persatuan Pembangunan (Pimpinan Cabang Jombang) 1982 *Hasil Penghitungan Suara Pemilu 1982 di Kabupaten Jombang Tanggal 10 Mei 1982.*

Partai Persatuan Pembangunan (Pimpinan Cabang Jombang) 1982a *Daftar Perbandingan Hasil Pemilu 1971, 1977 dan Pemilu 1982.*

Ulama, PB Nahdlatul 1986 *Hasil Mu'tamar Nahdlatul Ulama ke 27 Situbondo: NU Kembali ke Khittah 1926.* Semarang : Sumber Barokah.

Ulama, PB Nahdlatul 1985 *Anggaran Dasar dan Anggaran Rumah Tangga NU.* Jakarta : Lajnah Ta'lif Wan Nasyar, PB NU.

Pengurus Pondok Pesantren Bahrul Ulum 1994 *Laporan Tahunan.* Jombang : Pondok Pesantren Bahrul Ulum.

Pimpinan Pesantren Attaqwa Cabean (Pasuruan) *Fath Ar-Rabbani Wa Al-Faidlu Ar-Rahmani Li At-Thoriqoti Al-Qadiriyah Wa An-Naqsyabandiyah.* Pasuruan : Pesantren At-Taqwa.

Pimpian Pondok Pesantren Darul Ulum 1983 *Sejarah Pondok Pesantren Darul Ulum.* Jombang : Pondok Pesantren Darul Ulum.

Rodwell, J.M. (trans.) 1992 *The Koran.* London : JM. Dent & Sons Ltd.

Pranowo, Bambang 1991 *Creating the Tradition of Islam in Java.* Ph.D. Thesis, Monash University, Victoria .

Ricklefs, M.C. 1979 *Six Centuries of Islamization in Java.* In Levtzian, N. ed. *Conversion to Islam.* New York : Holmes and Meir.

Robertson, Rolland and Chirico, J.A. 1985 "Humanity, Globalization and Worldwide Religious Resurgence: A Theoretical Exploration", *Sociological Analysis*, 46(3): 219–242.

Rokkan, Stein 1968 "Electoral System", *International Encyclopaedia of Social Science.* New York : McMillan .

Saliba, John A. 1974 "The New Ethnography and the Study of Religion", *Journal of the Scientific Study of Religion*, Vol. 13: 145–159.

Samson, Allan A. 1978 *Conception of Politics, Power, and Ideology in Contemporary Indonesian Islam.* In Jackson, Karl D and Pye,Lucian ed. *Political Power and Communication in Indonesia.* Berkeley : University of California Press.

Sanusi, M. Ruhan 1993 "Sejarah Singkat Lahirnya Sholawat Wahidiyah", *Bulletin Kembali*, Edisi Khusus: 2–9.

Scott, James 1977 *Patronage or Exploitation?* . In Gelner, Ernest and Waterbury, John ed. *Patron and Client in Mediterranean Societies.* Duckworth in Association with the Center for Mediterranean Studies of the American Universities Field Staff.

Smith, D.E. 1971 *Religion, Politics, and Social Change in the Third World.* New York : Free Press.

Steenbrink, Karel A. 1974 *Pesantren, Madrasah, Sekolah.* Jakarta : LP3ES.

Steingass, Francis Joseph *A Learner's Arabic-English Dictionary*. Beirut : Librairie du Liban.

Suhardjo, Achmad 1991 *Kemerosotan Perolehan Suara PPP Pada Pemilu 1987, Studi Kasus di Kabupaten Jombang*. Unpublished MA Thesis, Gadjahmada University, Yogyakarta.

Sukamto 1992 *Kepemimpinan Kiai dan Kelembagaan Pondok Pesantren*. Unpublished MA Thesis, Gadjahmada University, Yogyakarta.

Sundhaussen 1978 "The Military: Structure, Procedures and Effects on Indonesian Society". In Jackson, Karl D. and Pye, Lucian ed., *Political Power and Communication in Indonesia*. Berkeley : University of California Press.

Tamney, J.B. 1980 "Functional Religiosity and Modernisation", *Sociological Analysis*, 41(1): 55–65.

Tim Tujuh Untuk Pemulihan Khittah NU 1926 1994 *Pokok-Pokok Pikiran tentang Pemulihan Khittah Nahdlatul Ulama 1926*. Jakarta : LAKPESDAM, NU.

Thoyib, Anshari and Zuhdi, M. Nadim 1979 *Musim Heboh Islam Jama'ah*. Surabaya : Bina Ilmu.

Turmudi, Endang 1990 "Peran Sosial Agama dan Sikap Keberagamaan Masyarakat Modern dalam Perspektif Sosiologis", *Masyarakat Indonesia* (Tahun XVII), No.2: 175–194.

Turmudi, Endang 1991 "Masih Adakah Hubungan Kausal Agama-Politik?", *Pelita*, 15 Nopember, p.4.

Turmudi, Endang 1994 "Kecenderungan Meningkatnya Sikap Beragama di Kalangan Orang Modern", *Masyarakat Indonesia* (Tahun XXI), No.1, pp.67–82.

Turmudi, Endang 1995 *Ulama dan Politik: Suatu Telaah atas Perubahan Politik Masyarakat Pedesaan*. Paper presented in a seminar organised by the Indonesian Student Association and the Indonesian Embassy, Canberra 20 May 1995.

Turmudi, Endang 1995 "Religion and Politics: A Study on Political Attitudes of Devout Muslims and the Role of the Kiai in Contemporary Java", *Southeast Asian Journal of Social Science*, Vol. 23, No. 2: 18–41.

Usman, Sunyoto 1991 *The Structural Interaction of Elite Groups in Development*. Paper presented at the 4th Forum of Asean Muslim Social Scientist: Bandung.

Viorina, Morris F. 1978 *Restrospective Voting in American National Election*. Edward Brother Inc.

Ward, K.E. 1974 *The 1971 Election in Indonesia: An East Java Case Study*. Monash Paper on Southeast Asia No. 2. Melbourne : Centre of Southeast Asian Studies, Monash University.

Weber, Max 1973 *The Routinization of Charisma*. In Havely, Eva Etzioni and Etzioni, A. ed. *Social Change*. New York : Basic Book.

Weber, Max 1968 *On Charisma and Institution Building*. Chicago : University of Chicago Press.

Weber, Max 1976 *The Protestant Ethic and the Spirit of Capitalism*. London : Allen & Unwin.

Wilson, Bryan 1983 *Religion in Sociological Perspective*. New York : Oxford University Press.

Woodward, M.R. 1989 *Islam in Java: Normative Piety and Mysticism in the Sultanate of Yogyakarta*. Tuscon : The University of Arizona Press.

Zubaida, Sami 1995 "Is there a Muslim society? Ernest Gellner's Sociology of Islam". *Economy and Society*. vol.24, no.2, (May): 151–88.

Newspapers and Magazines

Forum Keadilan, 2 Maret 1995

AULA, August 1991.

Media Indonesia Minggu, 2 July 1995

Panji Masyarakat, 21 January 1995.

Tempo, 15 February 1986.

www.ingramcontent.com/pod-product-compliance
Lightning Source LLC
Chambersburg PA
CBHW060929170426
43192CB00031B/2879